Ancient Glass
in National Museums Scotland

C. S. Lightfoot

Published by
NMSE Publishing
a division of NMS Enterprises Limited
National Museums Scotland
Chambers Street
Edinburgh EH1 1JF

British Library Cataloguing in Publication Data
A catalogue record for this book is available from the
British Library.

10 digit ISBN: 1 901663 28 0
13 digit ISBN: 978 1 901663 28 0

Photographs by Ken Smith.
Cover design by Mark Blackadder.
Cover photograph by NMS Photography.
Illustrations by Marion O' Neil.

Printed and bound in the United Kingdom by Cambridge Printing.

This book is published with the support of
National Museums Scotland.

www.nms.ac.uk

Contents

Acknowledgements
by Dr C. S. Lightfoot

It gives me great pleasure to thank all those colleagues and friends who have provided me with encouragement, advice and assistance during the preparation of this catalogue. First and foremost, I must mention Dr Elizabeth Goring, whose idea it was to compile such a study of the ancient glass collection in National Museums Scotland. I also received much practical help from her assistant, Lesley-Ann Liddiard, during my several visits to the museum to study the material, for which I am extremely grateful. Likewise, Helen Kemp and Lesley Taylor, the former and present Directors of Publishing at NMS Enterprises Limited, remained calm and collected, even though I sorely tried their patience on numerous occasions.

The work of several glass experts has inspired and enlightened me over the years and, although the errors and failings of the present work do them little justice, I wish to acknowledge my scholarly debt to Dr Stuart Fleming, Dr David Grose, Dr Jennifer Price, Dr Marianne Stern and to Dr David Whitehouse. My interest in ancient glass, however, was first nurtured and encouraged by two former colleagues at the British Museum, Dr Veronica Tatton-Brown and Mr Kenneth Painter. It was with their help that I was introduced to Dr Donald Harden, a renowned scholar and pioneer of glass studies. His guidance and wisdom were invaluable, and I feel greatly privileged to have been one of his students.

Finally, I wish to dedicate this volume to all my Turkish friends, colleagues and acquaintances, who during my stay in their country between 1986 and 1999 befriended and looked after me with a warmth and generosity that typifies the kindness and hospitality of the Turkish people.

New York, 2007

Foreword
by Dr Elizabeth Goring
Principal Curator, Mediterranean Archaeology
NATIONAL MUSEUMS SCOTLAND

This publication fulfils a long-standing aim to bring the significant ancient glass collection of National Museums Scotland to wider attention. The majority of the collection is published here for the first time: fewer than 20 pieces have been published before. While some specialists may be aware of the collection, this catalogue presents an opportunity for them (and others) to become better acquainted with its range and quality. It forms part of a programme of work relating to the Ancient Mediterranean collections, within which experts in the relevant disciplines have been invited to undertake scholarly publication as a first step towards wider accessibility. I have every expectation that Dr Lightfoot's presentation of the ancient glass will lead to greater opportunities for access and exhibition.

Like other major museums, NMS can only display a small part of its collections at one time, and constantly seeks alternative ways of making its important stored material more accessible. Except for a few examples currently included in the Ancient Egypt Gallery, the ancient glass collection was last on permanent display in the early 1980s. The development of new galleries includes long-term plans to enable part of this collection to be exhibited again.

This catalogue covers only the ancient, pre-Islamic glass in the Department of World Cultures. There is further ancient glass – almost entirely fragmentary and mostly from Scotland – in the collections of the Department of Archaeology; and glass from later periods and a wide range of areas in the Departments of World Cultures and of Scotland & Europe.

I would like to thank Chris Lightfoot for his careful work, conducted with perseverance and patience over a number of years; Ken Smith for his expert glass photography; Marion O'Neil for her meticulous drawings; Helen Kemp and Lesley Taylor for their long-standing commitment to the project; and especially Lesley-Ann Liddiard without whose hard work and cheerful dedication this project could not have been completed.

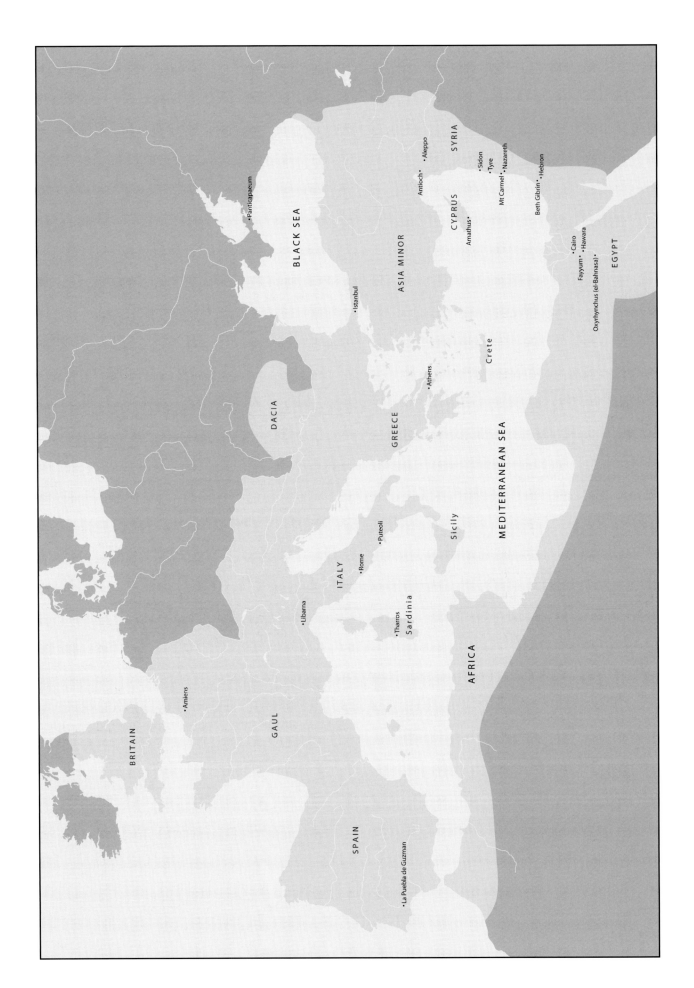

BLACK SEA

•Panticapaeum

•Istanbul

DACIA

ASIA MINOR

SYRIA

Antioch• •Aleppo

CYPRUS

•Sidon
•Tyre
Mt Carmel• •Nazareth
Beth Gibrin• •Hebron

Amathus•

•Cairo
Fayyum• •Hawara
Oxyrhynchus (el-Bahnasa)•

EGYPT

Crete

GREECE

•Athens

MEDITERRANEAN SEA

ITALY

•Puteoli

•Rome

Sicily

•Libarna

•Tharros
Sardinia

AFRICA

•Amiens

GAUL

BRITAIN

SPAIN

•La Puebla de Guzman

Introduction

Donald Harden's *Roman Glass from Karanis*, published in 1936, is generally regarded as the first serious study of ancient glass in the English language.[1] Likewise, many years later, he pioneered the publication of the extensive collections of the British Museum. The first volume in a series planned to cover the glass in the Department of Greek and Roman Antiquities appeared in 1981, followed soon after by a volume covering the much smaller holdings in the Department of Western Asiatic Antiquities. Since then the number of published studies of ancient glass has grown enormously. In particular, the ancient glass finds from archaeological sites are now much more carefully recorded, but there has also been a marked increase in the number of catalogues that have been published. Sadly, however, no further volumes in the British Museum series have appeared, and we must turn to America and Europe to find full-scale catalogues of public and private collections. The present volume, therefore, was intended to fill a gap by presenting a comprehensive study of an entire collection of ancient glass vessels, objects and fragments in a major British collection.

The Collection

The ancient glass collection in the museum formerly known as the Royal Museum, part of National Museums Scotland, has been assembled in the course of the past 150 years. There are in total 379 intact or nearly complete vessels, together with numerous objects and a large group of fragments, of which 38 objects (including ten beads) and 86 fragments have been described individually.[2] As in the case of most museums, the formation of the collection occurred haphazardly as material was either donated or purchased, but the core of the collection is founded upon three main groups of acquisitions.

The first comprises a large number of pieces, mainly fragments, that were acquired from the Northesk Collection in 1879. These were obtained principally in Rome, where in the mid-nineteenth century it appears there was a brisk trade in ancient polychrome glass fragments.[3] Several other museums now house similar collections of early Roman cast glass fragments; outside Italy itself these include the British Museum, the Victoria and Albert Museum, the Toledo Museum of Art, the Metropolitan Museum of Art and the Kunsthistorisches Museum in Vienna.[4] Although it remains unknown where the local traders in Rome obtained such an abundant supply of material, it seems unlikely that the fragments represent chance finds made at construction sites around the city. It is tempting to suggest that a large ancient dump was the principal source since, of course, broken polychrome or brightly coloured glass would not have been suitable for recycling.[5]

The second group was acquired in 1880 from the Piot Collection and consists largely of glass vessels from the Near East. Eugène Piot (1812-90) was a highly respected French scholar and antiquarian.[6] Although the details of how, where and when he acquired such a large collection of glass are unclear, it would seem that most of the pieces were obtained during his travels around the 'Orient' in 1868, although he also returned to Greece and Turkey in 1872 and 1874.[7] The third group, which was purchased in 1921, is made up primarily of glass from Cyprus.[8] In the same year other Cypriot objects, registered A1921.1395-1405, were acquired; they came from excavations conducted on the island in 1882 for the South Kensington Museum (known later as the Victoria & Albert Museum) in London by George Gordon Hake on behalf of Lt. Kitchener RE (later Lord Kitchener of Khartoum).[9] In addition, some Cypriot vessels had already been obtained as a result of work at Amathus conducted on behalf of the British Museum in 1893-94.[10] The emphasis of the collection is, therefore, on the glassware of the eastern Mediterranean and, apart from the polychrome fragments, there are relatively few examples of Roman glass from the West. Sadly, however, it should also be recorded that 95 items were de-accessioned in 1963, and the present whereabouts of these objects is unknown.[11]

Few details are known about the precise circumstances and provenances of the finds. Only one tomb groups is recorded as such (see no. 456), but the rest of the intact vessels must also have been recovered from tombs. Some of the glass, notably the finer wares, may be regarded as grave gifts, representing family possessions that were placed in the tomb to accompany the deceased on their journey to the underworld and intended to be of service to them there in the afterlife. The majority of glass vessels found in tombs, however, were used simply as containers either for offerings to the dead or for anointing the corpse. Many of the plain and poorly made unguentaria were probably used for the sprinkling of perfume or incense during the funerary rite.[12] Monumental or rock-cut tombs often acted as family burial vaults, where several generations were buried over the course of time. In these circumstances a large number of vessels could (and frequently did) accumulate within a tomb. In a few cases the ashes of the deceased were even placed within large glass urns (see nos 247-53) whose pierced lids, when inverted, served as excellent funnels for pouring offerings of wine or perfume onto the remains of the dearly departed.

Roman Glass in Scotland

In addition to the glass described in the present catalogue, NMS also houses ancient glass finds from sites in Scotland itself. These comprise a small number of intact glass vessels, together with a sizeable collection of fragments and objects. Some were already listed in a late nineteenth-century handbook of the collections.[13] Included there is an intact glass cup found in a cist grave at Airlie in Angus in 1885.[14] Another remarkable early find is a jug decorated with diagonal ribbing that was discovered at Brackenbraes near Turriff, Aberdeenshire in about 1857.[15] However, most of the glass finds in NMS come from excavations carried out during the twentieth century, principally at Newsteads, which was the largest auxiliary fort in Scotland during the Flavian conquest and became a major base in the second century AD.[16] The importance of the finds from such sites, which have clearly defined periods of occupation, is that they provide valuable evidence for the close dating of the glassware.[17] Yet not all discoveries of Roman glass are restricted to Roman military sites. Finds such as one group that has recently been reported from the Iron Age site at Mine Howe on Orkney, well beyond the area of Roman penetration and control, may be seen as items of trade or diplomacy that were exchanged with the native population.[18]

It is not appropriate to discuss this material in detail here in a catalogue devoted to the ancient glass that was found and acquired outside Britain. However, these local finds remind us that Scotland was, if only for a relatively brief period, part of the Roman Empire and so came into contact with a much larger world of glass production and supply. The Roman blown, colourless, and cut-glass fragments attest to techniques that were not to be found in Scotland again for many centuries.[19] Although the present catalogue does not include any examples of window glass, its use was ubiquitous in the Roman world.[20] When the Romans left Scotland, such signs of comfort and sophistication disappeared. Indeed, the discovery of small fragments of Roman glass in contexts such as Traprain Law may suggest that the local population came to value these vestiges of Roman rule more highly than the Romans themselves ever did.[21]

The Catalogue

The catalogue has been arranged so as to follow the major technical developments in the manufacture of glass in the ancient world. The entries are placed, wherever possible, in chronological order, but at the same time the catalogue has been divided up into sections that attempt to put the objects in their proper socio-economic groupings, so that it may be possible to understand better the uses to which the various types of objects were put. Some of these divisions may appear arbitrary, but in antiquity there must have existed a clear distinction between luxury glass, used only for display or for special occasions, and vessels that were part of normal daily life.

Each entry is organised in the following way:

1. Catalogue number, accession number and short title
2. Colour
3. Date, find-place, previous collection(s) and probable area of manufacture
4. Dimensions
5. Description
6. Condition
7. Comment
8. References

Dimensions

All measurements are in centimetres. The following abbreviations are used:

D (diameter)	H (height)	L (length)
Th (thickness)	W (width)	

Description

For vessels, the description proceeds from the top to the bottom. Objects are treated, wherever possible, in a similar way; so, for example, the visible surface of a glass inlay is regarded as being the top.

The colour ranges are arbitrarily described as pale, light, dark or deep tones of the stated colour. 'Colourless' is used to denote glass that is assumed to have been intentionally decolourised. All glass is translucent unless otherwise stated.

Museum abbreviations

Other museum collections that are frequently referred to in this catalogue have been abbreviated as follows:

BM	The British Museum, London
CMG	Corning Museum of Glass, Corning, New York
MMA	The Metropolitan Museum of Art, New York
UPM	University of Pennsylvania Museum, Philadelphia
V&A	Victoria and Albert Museum, London

Techniques of glassworking

The technical details of the various methods by which it is thought that ancient glass vessels were made and decorated have been set out on many occasions.[22] It is not my intention, therefore, to describe them again here. Modern glassworkers have also carried out experiments to replicate ancient glass forms and processes,[23] giving us useful insights into the ancient technologies of glass making and working. Nevertheless, there remain uncertainties about some of the techniques that were actually used.[24] The fact that a modern expert can make an ancient-looking glass in a particular way does not automatically mean that this was how an ancient craftsman actually worked. It might justifiably be argued that the easiest, simplest, and (to us) most obvious solution to a problem would not necessarily have occurred to a person living in classical times. Likewise, although a number of ancient glass furnaces have been excavated, little is known about how they were kept at the right constant temperature for the batch of molten glass.

Similarly, in recent years much research has been carried out on the chemical composition of ancient glass.[25] These results, however, only tell us the nature of the basic ingredients and the various elements that were added to colour or decolourise the raw glass. Modern scientific analysis gives no hint of how ancient craftsmen, presumably working in less than ideal conditions, came to get the right mix of ingredients for what they wanted; yet they clearly did, time and time again. While ancient glassmakers were able to master the complex and crucial problems of temperature and chemistry, glassworkers also developed the ability to manipulate the raw glass for a wide range of different applications. These skills were not easily learnt; apprenticeships must have been long and arduous.

It may prove impossible to answer all the questions that we have about the ancient glass industry, but perhaps it is as well that it retains some of its mystique since this adds to the charm and appeal of its surviving products. The delicate shapes, colours and decorative designs of ancient glass continue to fill us with awe and delight, made all the more emphatic by the fact that so many of these fragile objects have survived intact the vagaries of time and fortune.

Brief glossary

alabastron
vase in the shape of an elongated cylindrical container, originally carved in soft Egyptian alabaster but later also made in metal and pottery as well as glass

amphoriskos
two-handled flask, a small version of the terracotta amphora that was used in antiquity for the bulk transport and storage of liquid goods such as wine and oil

ampulla
a small jar, often with two small loop handles for suspension, usually lentoid in shape but generally similar to an aryballos

aryballos
two-handled jar, also made in metal and pottery and often used for carrying oil

batch
the molten glass in a furnace formed from the raw ingredients, cullet, or recycled fragments

cage cup
type of late Roman glass vessel made from a thick cast or blown blank whose exterior was then carved into intricate openwork designs

cameo
glass made in two or more layers of different colours that have subsequently been carved away to create a design

cantharus
two-handled drinking cup with a pedestal base

carinated
description of the profile of a vessel that has a sharp angle on the side or shoulder

cast
glass vessels made by using a former, a one-piece open mould, or a multipart mould

core-formed
vessels made by applying molten glass to a core of other material that could later be removed to leave the inside of the vessel hollow

cullet
raw glass in a cold state from which objects and vessels could be made when heated in a furnace

diachroism
an effect caused by tiny particles of metal in the glass causing it to appear different colours in transmitted and reflected light

diatretarius
worker of cold glass, specifically a glass-cutter

faience
   vitreous material with a porous, crystalline fabric and a glassy outer surface that was cast in moulds to form objects and small vessels

gold-band
   mosaic glass in which sections of gold-glass are combined with bands of brightly-coloured opaque and translucent glass

gold-glass
   glass used for plaques or vessels in which gold leaf has been fused between two layers of transparent and often colourless glass

guttus
   spouted vessel used for pouring liquids

iridescence
   the visible effect of weathering, usually in the form of thin, flaking layers in rainbow-like colours, which distort the original colour and transparency of the glass

krateriskos
   characteristic shape of early Egyptian glass vessels, later adopted by Greek potters to make large vases known as kraters and used for mixing wine

kylix
   stemmed drinking bowl

lentoid
   vessel with flattened sides, resembling the disk shape of a lentil

mastos
   conical bowl, cast over a former mould shaped like a woman's breast

modiolus
   name applied to drinking cups that had the same shape as a modius, a Roman measure of volume, usually for grain

mosaic
   decoration comprising sections of preformed mono-chrome or polychrome glass fused together

mould-blown
   vessels made by inflating a gob of glass on the end of a blowpipe into a reusable mould

network
   also known as reticella, in which threads of opaque white or yellow glass are wound spirally around a cane or rod of translucent, usually colourless, glass

nipt
   pinched protrusions made by using pincers to shape the surface of the glass while hot to form a decorative feature

oinochoe
   one-handled jug, originally used for pouring wine

and so a very popular shape for metal and pottery vases

patella
   Latin name often applied to a small carinated cup, although the term was used generically by ancient authors in reference to any small plate or dish

phiale mesomphalos
   shallow serving or libation dish with a circular pushed-in boss at its centre

polycandela
   multiple hanging lamps

pre-moulded
   vessels made by inflating first in a mould to create a pattern on the glass and then free blown to the full size and shape

pyxis
   cosmetic jar, usually with a lid, also made in silver, bronze and bone

ribbon
   pattern in which strips of differently-coloured mosaic glass, often including bands of network glass, are laid in parallel lengths

scyphus
   drinking cup with two ring handles below the rim, and often with a deeper profile and lower base ring than a cantharus

sprinkler
   flask of distinctive type with constriction in neck to restrict flow of contents to drops when pouring

terra sigillata
   the modern name given to Roman pottery, also known as samian ware, which typically had a shiny red surface slip

trulla
   one-handled pan, similar to a patera but with a deeper body

unguentarium
   perfume bottle, often with a tall, narrow neck that would restrict the flow of the contents during pouring and allow the vessel to be easily sealed

vicennalia
   celebrations to mark the twentieth anniversary of an emperor's accession

weathering
   the decomposition of the surface of a glass vessel or object, caused by long exposure to moisture and/or chemical reaction to the soil in which it was buried

A Brief History of Ancient Glassmaking

Among the many things that I have never been able to understand, one in particular stands out. That is the question of who was the first person who stood by a pile of sand and said, 'You know, I bet if we took some of this and mixed it with a little potash and heated it, we could make a material that would be solid and yet transparent. We could call it glass.' Call me obtuse, but you could stand me on a beach till the end of time and never would it occur to me to try to make it into windows.

[Bill Bryson, *Notes from a Small Island* (Doubleday)]*

*Note

Quotation from *Notes on a Small Island* by Bill Bryson, published by Doubleday. Reprinted by permission of The Random House Group Ltd. For the United States, reprinted by permission of Broadway Books, Random House Inc, New York.

The Bronze Age

The invention of glassmaking is one of those great human achievements whose circumstances are lost in the mists of time. Experiments in the use of fire and in the smelting of various raw materials, mainly metal ores, probably stimulated man's first attempts to manufacture glass. How, where and when the first batch of raw glass was produced can only be guessed at, but it would seem very likely that this occurred somewhere in the Near East, probably at the beginning of the Early Bronze Age. Man was, of course, already familiar with the properties of glass as a shiny and sharp-edged material, for naturally occurring glass in the form of obsidian had been exploited since the Palaeolithic Age. Obsidian is a volcanic product and so occurs over a wide area of the Near East and Mediterranean basin. Evidence for its value to early prehistoric societies is found in the fact that it is known to have been traded widely and over long distances. It was used to manufacture cutting blades and projectile heads (microliths), as well as items of personal adornment. A number of precious ritual vessels were also carved out of blocks of obsidian, while in later times it was also used in large-scale composite sculptures.[26]

Obsidian, however, has one great disadvantage. It is monochrome and is usually so dark that it appears as opaque black. The early attraction of glass was that it was bright and colourful. This is clear from the fact that glassmaking developed out of early experiments at making an assortment of vitreous materials, whereby objects could be decorated with a brightly coloured glaze. So, for example, small faience objects were being produced by the middle of the fifth millennium BC, and the first real glass objects appeared in the late third millennium BC. Glass beads and other items of personal adornment such as amulets are among the earliest examples of ancient glass, although cylinder seals, rods and inlays were also made.

In addition to the link between glassmaking and metalworking (and, more specifically, copper production), there also existed a close relationship with stone carving, for the first objects were often finished using cold-working lapidary techniques. These ties between craftsmen working in glass and those working in metal and stone persisted throughout antiquity. Indeed, it may be argued that glassmaking was largely imitative, borrowing not only the techniques and skills but also the designs and shapes used in other trades. But, on the other hand, it is clear that glassmakers built on the expertise they gained from other crafts in order to master the difficulties and challenges that their medium offered. Combined with this was a clear willingness to experiment. Ancient glassmakers, especially in the Roman period, were innovative in the extreme, and it should perhaps be remembered that only examples of successful experiments and designs have survived.[27] The end result was that glass, despite its intrinsic inferiority to precious metals and stones, came to be used more widely and for a much more varied number of purposes. By the Roman period glass was so ubiquitous that it was taken for granted, much as it is today.

It was, however, a long and tortuous road to this culmination to the history of ancient glassmaking. Some 1500 years after the invention of glass, in about the middle of the sixteenth century BC, the first glass vessels were made.[28] This major leap forward probably took place in northern Mesopotamia in the Hurrian kingdom of the Mitanni, although the technique was soon evident in Egypt too. However, it remains uncertain if this was a separate development or whether the Egyptians learnt about it through their contacts with the Levant and the Fertile Crescent. The latter may be inherently more likely, although the Egyptian glass industry soon established its own distinctive and independent tradition.[29] The fashioning of glass vessels involved a significant augmentation to the glassmaker's skills, for he

was now required much more than before to manipulate the glass in its molten state, both in the formation of the basic body shape and in the application of handles and decorative elements. This required a considerable refinement of the furnace design, ensuring that it kept a more consistent temperature and allowed ease of access to the batch of molten glass. At the same time a greater range of colours began to be produced, indicating that there was now a better understanding and mastery of the use of the various metal oxides that create the colours (they include those of copper, cobalt, manganese, antimony and lead). The great majority of the vessels take the form of small multi-coloured bottles, beakers and goblets, made on a removable core of clay and dung in a manner recalling the lost-wax casting technique used in metalworking.[30]

These developments indicate that in the Late Bronze Age the glass industry was already quite sophisticated. In addition, from the evidence provided by the Uluburun shipwreck, it can be shown that raw glass was already being made for export to workshops scattered across the eastern Mediterranean, while local craftsmen catered for demand by producing a range of glass vessels and objects. On the other hand, glass in the Late Bronze Age was highly prized, and manufacture of the finished goods was probably restricted largely to palace workshops. Certainly the finds of glass vessels are mostly associated with palaces, temples and the graves of the wealthy.[31] As such glassmakers worked within a closed environment and probably suffered from the conservative or, at least, limited tastes of their patrons. Glass production was not only a state monopoly and served to furnish rulers principally with ritual and ceremonial artefacts, but it was also shrouded with secrecy and imbued with an air of mystery. It is difficult to appreciate and understand this aspect of early glassmaking, especially in the modern world where we are surrounded by a wide range of man-made, artificial materials. However, it should be remembered that in antiquity glass was one of a small number of compounds that man could produce, and it was undoubtedly the most spectacular metamorphosis that he could achieve. This mastery of nature enhanced the prestige of glass. Man surely took pride in his ability to create for himself glass imitations of natural objects.

The Iron Age

Given the circumstances under which glass was made in the second millennium BC, it is perhaps surprising that, when the Late Bronze Age civilizations of the Near East collapsed, knowledge of glassworking was not entirely lost.[32] Production probably continued in the Early Iron Age, but it was on a much reduced scale as a result of the fall both in the supply of raw material and in the demand from wealthy patrons. Nevertheless, glass technology survived the Dark Age and re-emerged, if in a slightly different form, at some point in the seventh or sixth century BC. One of the most important changes which occurred at that time was an alteration to the composition of glass. Earlier most glass had been made from a mixture of plant ash and crushed quartz, the collection and preparation of which was labour-intensive and time-consuming. Now deposits of sand and natron (a naturally occurring mineral soda) started to be exploited for the preparation of raw glass. These materials required little processing and existed in certain areas in an almost inexhaustible supply. As a result it was possible to produce glass cullet in larger quantities and so provide the industry with enough raw material to allow it to expand and develop in the Hellenistic and Roman periods. An additional advantage was that natron is a relatively pure form of soda, whereas plant ash contains many impurities, most particularly substantial amounts of potash, lime and magnesia.[33] The major source of natron was in the Wadi Natrun in Egypt, while according to Pliny the Elder (*Natural History* 36,190) some of the best glass sand was obtained from near the mouth of the Belus River (near Haifa in Israel). Together with this came the ability to control more precisely the colour of the glass. After about the seventh century BC small amounts of antimony were added to counteract the green or blue colouration caused by iron oxides, and from the second century BC onwards manganese was used for the same purpose.

The Iron Age saw another important development, for when vessel-making revived in the eighth century BC, in addition to core-formed bottles and jars in opaque or semi-translucent glass, a new technique made its appearance – casting. This innovation was probably inspired by the production of cast-glass inlays, used for decorating ivory and wooden furniture. The centre of this industry lay in Phoenicia, and it would seem likely that it was Phoenician craftsmen who developed the casting technique for vessels, while their skill in carving semi-precious stone was also transferred to the working and decorating of glass. Cast vessels were made in a monochrome translucent glass and were often decorated with cold-cut, engraved decoration. Furthermore, the casting technique allowed glassmakers to expand their repertoire so that, as well as small closed vessels such as bottles, they could produce open forms such as bowls and dishes. Glass thus came to serve a different function in society, for it not only provided attractive and suitably expensive receptacles for perfumes, cosmetics and medicinal ointments, but it now also offered the opportunity for display and presentation. Glass vessels took their place alongside silver and pottery on the dining table at parties, receptions and symposia.

Glass, however, remained an object for the élite, although its place had moved away from a ritual use in the palace, temple or funeral, to a more domestic and everyday setting. With the growth of more egalitarian and democratic societies in the classical Greek world, it is not surprising that glass manufacture there was rather limited and small-scale. The major advances took place further east. The largest and most important group of cast vessels comes from the Assyrian palaces at Nimrud. The so-called Sargon Vase provides a *terminus ante quem* of 705 BC for the beginning of these cast and cut luxury glass vessels, although most of the Nimrud fragments were found in the debris of the 612 BC destruction. In addition to the plain bowls, some pieces have superb wheel-cut decoration, and two fragments of another bowl reveal inlaid and painted decoration.[34] These stand as examples of the consummate skill of the glassmakers of the time, combining the use of lost-wax casting, cutting, painting and mosaic-glass inlaying.

One of the earliest surviving complete cast vessels was found in tumulus P at Gordion, the capital of the Phrygian kingdom in central Anatolia. It is a delicate colourless bowl (phiale mesomphalos), dating to the late eighth century BC, decorated with a cut pattern of 32 radial petals.[35] In shape and decoration it mirrors exactly the metal bowls found in contemporary Assyrian and Phoenician contexts. It should, therefore, be regarded as an import, probably sent as a gift to a Phrygian prince from the Assyrian royal court.

The Classical Period

In the fifth century BC the Persians, with all the wealth and resources of their vast Empire, brought glass vessel production to new heights of excellence.[36] Under their patronage a range of finely made luxury tablewares, whose shapes and cut decoration were modelled on those of metal vessels, was produced.[37] This glassware was formed using the lost-wax technique and employed a high-quality glass that was intentionally de-colourised in direct imitation of rock-crystal.[38] The largest known assemblage of Persian glassware has been recovered from the treasury at Persepolis, the royal palace destroyed in 331 BC

during Alexander the Great's conquest of the Achaemenid Empire, but other examples have been found in disparate and far-flung locations.[39] It has, therefore, been difficult to determine whether the industry was based in the Persian heartland, or in one of the western satrapies, or even in a Greek city on the periphery of the Empire. However, the close correlation between the glass vessels and Persian silverware, combined with the evidence from Persepolis, shows clearly that the industry, wherever it was located, depended heavily on the patronage of the Achaemenid court.

The Hellenistic Period

In the Hellenistic world there were two main centres of glassmaking, the Syrian coast (i.e. Phoenicia) and Alexandria, the capital of the Ptolemaic kingdom of Egypt. In Syria production of the traditional core-formed unguent bottles was sustained until it was superseded by glassblowing in the late first century BC. In addition, a prolific series of cast bowls was produced. The vessels were often decorated with cut lines or grooves and, on later types, with a row of knobs or short ribs around the exterior of the body. At Alexandria, on the other hand, glasses of a more elaborate and technically sophisticated character were made. These cast and cut vessels come in a greater variety of shapes and display a highly artistic quality. The glassmakers at Alexandria also developed the skill of making mosaic and sandwich gold-glass. All of these are represented in the so-called Canosa Group of glass tableware, which may be dated to the second half of the third century BC.[40] They attest to the first concerted effort by ancient glassmakers to manufacture complete dinner services from glass. Like Achaemenid glass, these tablewares were much influenced by the prevailing styles of pottery and metal vessels. It is clear, however, that glass was gaining greater recognition as an attractive and colourful alternative, especially to silver serving and drinking vessels.

Cast glass, however, had two distinct disadvantages: (a) only open forms could be produced with any ease, so items such as jugs, bottles and flasks were not normally made; and (b) the process was costly and laborious. Consequently, glassware remained a relatively scarce and expensive item, and the industry still depended heavily on the patronage of the wealthy, whether leading citizens of Greek cities or members of Hellenistic royal families.

The Roman Period

The Romans were slow to appreciate the qualities of glass, for there is very little evidence for the use of glass in Republican Rome. Despite their familiarity with the Hellenistic world and particularly the Greek cities of southern Italy and Sicily, where glassware was used and clearly much prized, the Romans took little interest in the material until the latter part of the first century BC. Admittedly most of Hellenistic glass was luxury ware, and there was a powerful resistance to adopting the materialistic culture of the Greek world among the conservative Roman élite. In addition, wealthy Romans could afford luxury metal vessels, and they evidently showed a preference for either silver (and silver-gilt) plate or the highly wrought bronze wares from famous workshops in places such as Corinth.[41] It would seem that only after the annexation of Syria in 63 BC did craftsmen from the East move to Rome and take the first steps towards setting up a glass industry in Italy. This coincided with the invention of glassblowing, which after the discovery of glass itself was the most important event in the history of glassmaking. It enabled craftsmen to produce vessels more cheaply and quickly than before. It also meant that they could now cater for a whole new market, and the Romans were quick to adapt to using tablewares and utilitarian vessels made in glass.

The invention of glassblowing was not easily or quickly achieved, for it depended on a number of factors. Evidence from Jerusalem shows that some attempt to blow glass was made there in the early first century BC.[42] It may, however, be doubted if this was the only place where such experiments were conducted or even if this should be regarded as the earliest case, for it is merely an accident of archaeology that this example has survived and been found. However, the appearance of this new glassmaking technique required a further discovery to be made before its full potential could be realised. It required the awareness that a suitable instrument was needed for inflating the hot glass, and it was only some decades later, perhaps c.50-40 BC, that the blow-pipe was invented.[43] The pax Romana established by Augustus after 27 BC was also a major factor in the growth and spread of glassblowing. The restoration of peace and prosperity gave a great impetus to both trade and travel within the Roman world. Augustus likewise encouraged the development of crafts in Italy by bringing skilled workers from the East. Glass was one area where there was a sudden explosion of interest and demand.[44] At first, however, most blown vessels were small and utilitarian, mainly small perfume bottles.[45] One reason for this may have been the use of a ceramic blow-pipe on which only a limited amount of glass could be carried and so inflated.[46] There were, nevertheless, a few startling exceptions, notably the Portland Vase, which show that the glass industry in Rome was already highly sophisticated by the late first century BC.[47]

Although the Roman glass industry was founded on the inspiration and expertise provided by glassmakers from the Hellenistic world, it rapidly developed into an independent and innovative enterprise, which further spread the art of making glass vessels beyond the Mediterranean basin to western Europe and elsewhere. As it grew, it furnished the ancient consumer for the first time with inexpensive, mass-produced glassware. The advantages of glass over other materials was not lost on the practical-minded Romans. They were the first people to appreciate fully the functional uses of glass, not just as a clear and hygienic receptacle, but as a covering for windows and, when backed with a metal (gold or silver) foil, as a reflective material.[48] The use of glass for window panes and mirrors is so much a part of the modern world that, as a result, it is difficult for us to appreciate the magnitude of these innovations.[49] They also tend to be overshadowed by the appearance of vessels that display a high degree of artistic skill. Yet glass mosaics, panelling and windows were probably as ubiquitous and indispensable in the Roman world as the simple free-blown glass bottle was to become.[50]

A further development occurred in around AD 35 when glassmakers started using moulds to form the blown vessels. The inspiration may have come from the use of similar moulds in the mass-production of Arretine pottery, but mould-blowing required a quite different technique from that used by potters.[51] The latter, naturally, applied the clay to a mould in a cold state, whereas glassmakers had to work with a hot, molten material in a way much more akin to metal casting. In fact, the technique of blowing into a mould required a familiarity with not only free-blowing but also of casting glass.

The benefits of using a mould were considerable.[52] It allowed vessels to be produced more quickly and with relatively less skill than in the case of free-blown glass. Mould-blowing was, on the whole, restricted to the production of containers, for which it was ideally suited since the products could be made to a fixed standard and size.[53] Likewise, square mould-blown bottles or jars could be more easily packed for long-distance travel. Examples of wooden crates, especially from Egypt, have survived; these are often divided into a number of compartments into which the vessels can be placed and so held firm.[54] One extraordinary example of a large cylindrical glass bottle is displayed in the British Museum. This was placed in antiquity inside the hollowed-out trunk of a palm tree, which subsequently shrank as it dried out, trapping the vessel for ever inside.[55]

Luxury Roman Glass

Despite their early appreciation of the utilitarian qualities of glass, Roman craftsmen continued to produce a range of objects to cater for all tastes. They strove to compete at both ends of the market, and so, as in earlier times, glass retained its label as a luxury item in the Roman world. Glassmakers did this by enhancing the attractiveness and so the value of their products. The most obvious way of doing this was to decorate their glasses with gold. Luxury gold-glass had been produced in the Hellenistic period, and some Roman examples can be seen as a continuation of this tradition. Such is the case with the application of a layer of gold foil between two layers of (usually colourless) glass.[56] However, the Romans used this technique not only to make vessels but also to decorate their finest buildings with gold-glass mosaics and revetment panels.[57] A more direct and simple technique was the use of gold foil on the surface of the glass, often in combination with coloured decoration.[58] This form of ornamentation probably derives from the use of gold leaf on Greek pottery in the Hellenistic period. It was used in Roman times to decorate vessels – see no. 50 – continuing until the third and fourth centuries AD, although surviving examples are rare.[59] By contrast, Roman glassmakers also showed considerable ingenuity in their use of gold, for they discovered that by mixing particles of gold and silver to the batch, they could create an effect known as dichroism.[60] Examples of this use of gold are extremely rare.[61]

A number of other techniques were also developed by Roman craftsmen to produce luxury items. Cameo glass, for example, undoubtedly falls into this category – see no. 42. Despite the fact that cameo glass aimed to imitate semi-precious stones such as agate and sardonyx, the vessels, inlays and plaques that were made using this complex technique were clearly intended for a clientele coming from the very highest strata of Roman society. Indeed, it has been argued that such pieces as the Portland Vase were made for the imperial family itself.[62] Similarly, in the late Roman period a number of highly ornate and intricately carved vessels, known as 'cage-cups' or *vasa diatreta*, were only produced for the very affluent and influential.[63] One of these, the (now destroyed) Strasbourg cage-cup, bore the name of the tetrarch Maximian (AD 287-305).

One further group may be considered as part of the luxury glass trade. These were vessels made in colourless glass, imitating rock-crystal.[64] Glass, however, is softer than the natural mineral, and so it was possible for craftsmen (called diatretarii) to engrave the vessels with highly accomplished designs.[65] One example may suffice to demonstrate that such pieces were luxury items, equivalent to the finest silverware. It is a fragment of a large dish, found in the Forum Romanorum at Rome, which is carved with a scene celebrating the vicennalia of an emperor, possibly that of Constantine the Great in AD 326.[66]

Roman Tableware

At a slightly lower level stands a second class of vessels: the finely made and often elaborately decorated tablewares. Many of the signed mould-blown vessels can be assigned to this group. In order to achieve these complex and decorative forms, multi-part moulds were required, and here again there is some similarity to metalworking techniques. The shapes and designs, too, bear a close resemblance to contemporary silverware. Among free-blown vessels, cut-glass was very popular as tableware. Their designs, too, relied heavily on silver and pottery prototypes. Free-blowing, however, also enabled glassmakers to experiment with new forms and types of decoration. Some of

these were so elaborate as to render the vessel virtually unusable. Such impractical creations must, therefore, have been intended for show. Likewise, it has been suggested that many of the gold-glass plates, dishes and cups were made as wedding-gifts, wedding anniversary gifts or New Year gifts.[67] Ancient houses contained few items of furniture and so there was little opportunity for displaying glassware as ornaments in the living or dining rooms, but it would be surprising if, for instance, well-to-do Roman matrons did not wish to add a little colour and brightness to their homes with glass vases, especially if they contained a bunch of flowers or an assortment of fruit.

Similarly, in the Roman period we find glass vessels depicted on funerary monuments. Some of the most striking representations are the death masks painted on Egyptian coffins where the deceased is shown holding a glass cup decorated with coloured trails.[68] Such glasses may be seen as symbols indicating the status and relative wealth of the dead, and they are clearly not meant to be taken merely as functional objects. The same argument could be used for many of the glass vessels that were placed in tombs as grave gifts. There was no need to include the more ornate and decorative pieces, so they should probably be regarded as the cherished possessions of the deceased.

Among well-to-do Romans the liking for glass was not restricted only to vessels and receptacles, but extended also to the use of glass for interior decoration in mosaics, panelling and revetments.[69]

Utilitarian Wares

Below the tablewares come the more mundane but still attractive containers – the jugs, flasks and bottles that could be used for both serving and storage; and finally, one has the mass of utilitarian vessels, typified by the plain, cheaply produced perfume bottle. According to the Augustan writer Strabo (*Geography* XVI.2.25), this type of glass 'could be purchased for a copper coin', and it is certainly true that glass more or less supplanted various types of cheap Roman pottery. Indeed, during the Roman period glass came to be regarded as such an inexpensive material that it could even be considered as a disposable item – hence the Roman proverbial use of the term 'broken glass,' *vitrea fracta* for 'rubbish' (Petronius, *Satyricon* 10). Their acceptance of glass as a common (and so almost indispensable) household item may be reflected in the relatively scarce references to it in contemporary literature.[70]

Despite the fact that some effort was clearly devoted to collecting up broken glass for recycling (Martial, *Epigrams* I, 41), the large amounts of glass fragments that are found by archaeologists during excavations suggests that there was considerable wastage.[71] Bottle banks, of course, did not exist, but it is nevertheless surprising how much broken glass seems to have been left lying around on ancient sites. Clearly little care was taken about clearing away glass fragments, despite the obvious health and safety hazards of leaving them lying around. This, too, suggests that the intrinsic value of glass was minimal and that a glass vessel, when accidentally broken, was discarded in much the same way as a piece of pottery, whereas metal containers and utensils were by and large repaired or traded in for recycling.[72]

The specific uses to which Roman glassware were put are also largely unclear. Most surviving ancient glass vessels have, of course, been found in tombs. Their presence there as grave gifts or containers for offerings such as oils and fragrances is, however, in the majority of cases only evidence for their secondary use. Some vessels have been found in tombs still sealed and with their contents intact, while other large containers saw secondary use as cinerary urns.[73] Wall-paintings from Pompeii and Herculaneum include still-life scenes that include depictions of glass vessels, serving as fruit bowls.[74] Unlike in the modern world, very few ancient glass vessels were made as decorative objects. The great majority were functional and utilitarian. Indeed, as in the case of their re-use as grave goods, many vessels may have found a variety of uses in daily life, for glass was eminently suitable for storing a wide range of substances. A simple analogy would be the way coffee jars today are kept and re-used as kitchen storage jars and the like.[75]

It is, however, evident that some glassware was made specifically for certain goods or purposes. Some free-blown perfume bottles, for example, were fire-sealed after filling so that the contents did not spoil or leak. When required, the end was snapped off the top of the neck in order to release the liquid stored inside.[76] Some mould-blown containers would also appear to have been made for specific purposes or customers. They bear stamps indicating the origin of either the vessel itself or its contents.[77] Whether these stamps acted as trademarks in the same way as (say) those found on modern milk, beer or cola bottles remains debatable. There does not appear to have been much awareness in the ancient world of the value of commercial advertising. It seems inherently more likely that these marks relate to the glass manufacturer than the producer of the goods that they were destined to contain.[78] Some mechanism, however, must have existed for the regular supply of such containers to the place where they were filled with oil, wine, perfume or whatever. If full bottles were indeed sold in this way, one wonders if the cost of the bottle was included in the price of the goods. Even today, in countries such as Turkey it is possible to see a system operating that may have a bearing on ancient practices. Vendors of liquids such as cologne or scent keep their goods in larger containers and dispense them to purchasers who bring their own bottles. Again it is likely that other liquids such as oil and wine were bought in bulk and stored in the house in large pottery amphorae, from which glass bottles could be filled when required. So, it would seem likely that the average Roman household would have possessed a number of glass vessels that could serve a number of purposes in the storage, presentation and consumption of both dry goods and liquids.

Manufacture and Trade

Glass was ubiquitous in the Roman Empire, and evidence for its use has been found at archaeological sites right across Europe, North Africa and the Near East. But our understanding of the Roman glass industry is still relatively poor. Too little is yet known about the ancient sources of the chemical and mineral ingredients used to make raw glass, and about the scale and organisation of the recycling of glass waste, for us to say precisely how the Roman glass industry operated. It is frustrating that two well-known shipwrecks off the south-west coast of Turkey, which provide insights into the functioning of a pre-industrial glass industry, belong at opposite ends of the timescale.[79] The Ulu Burun shipwreck dates to the Late Bronze Age; its cargo included more than 150 diskoid glass ingots, which had clearly been produced at a centre for the manufacture of raw glass (probably from somewhere along the Syro-Palestinian coast) and were being traded around the eastern Mediterranean.[80] The second shipwreck was found in Serçe Limanı, a small natural harbour. A number of Hellenistic and Roman ships floundered in this deceptively safe anchorage, but the wreck for which it is best known is that of a mediaeval merchant ship. Objects found during excavation indicate that the boat sank in c.1025. The cargo included three tons of glass, of which one ton comprised broken glass, largely waste from an unidentified Islamic glassworks.[81]

It remains difficult to provide explanations of how the spread of glassworking (especially blowing) came about, what mechanisms for the manufacture (and recycling) of glass existed, and on what scale finished glassware was traded over long distances. A small number of production centres have long been recognised, and these, it would seem, spread from east to west. The industry originated in the Near East, where two principal areas of manufacture are known – Syria and Egypt. Craftsmen were drawn westwards to work in Italy after Rome had eclipsed the Hellenistic kingdoms of the East, seeking fresh markets and patrons among the new masters of the ancient world. From there glassmaking spread to the Rhineland, which remained a major centre of production until the collapse of the Roman frontier in the fourth century. Glass, however, is also found in other parts of the Roman Empire, and so it may be assumed that local industries existed in most provinces. Even in Britain there is evidence for a limited amount of glass production in the third century.[82]

On the other hand, it is clear that much of the glass found in Roman Britain was imported from glassmaking centres in Gaul, the Rhineland or Italy itself.[83] There is, therefore, some evidence for a considerable amount of trade in Roman glass. Indeed, finds beyond the imperial frontiers put this in no doubt; Roman glassware is recorded at sites as far away as Scandinavia, the Sudan, the Persian Gulf, the Indian sub-continent, and even the Far East.[84] Yet it cannot have been easy or attractive to transport glassware, especially in large quantities. Vessels are bulky but fragile, requiring special packaging and careful handling. Some examples of the way this was achieved have been preserved – most notably and dramatically in the discovery of a packing case full of glass vessels, including cast, mould-blown and free-blown pieces, in a shop at Herculaneum.[85] But in general it must have been easier for craftsmen to move with the markets and for merchants to concentrate on supplying them with the necessary material to make the finished products locally.[86]

A small number of Roman shops have been excavated that clearly sold glass vessels, along with other household items such as fineware pottery and terracotta lamps. One example was found at

Colchester in 1927; another has recently come to light at the Lycian city of Arykanda in south-west Turkey.[87] The only real evidence we have for glass prices in Roman times comes from Diocletian's Price Edict, issued in AD 301.[88]

Apart from trade, some glassware must, of course, have been carried in people's personal effects as they moved from one part of the Empire to another.[89] In this respect the army played a major role. Legions and auxiliary units often travelled long distances on campaign or were reassigned to a different province. Individual soldiers, too, could be transferred from one unit to another or made long journeys either on official business or to visit distant relatives. Glass is one group of material where the role of the military as one of the principal agents of dispersion can be seen quite clearly. Vessels of the same type, made using the same techniques and serving the same functions, have been found at opposite ends of the Empire.[90] Despite the fact that it has been argued that there was limited acculturation in the Roman world, many everyday objects, including ones made in glass, would have been familiar right across the Empire.[91]

Detailed studies of some glass corpora, such as those from Cyprus, Karanis and Dura-Europos, have allowed us to identify certain regional traits and to make tentative attributions to workshops in specific areas. However, the majority of Roman glass vessels belong to the same basic group of forms that are found throughout the Empire. The consistency of shape, technique and decorative elements employed by glassmakers must be taken to reflect the high degree of interaction and movement among producers in the Roman period. Likewise, since the raw glass probably came from a number of different sources, including primary producing centres and recycled glass, attempts to isolate regional groups by means of chemical analysis have proved inconclusive.[92]

Most of the utilitarian glass vessels were undoubtedly made locally, possibly by itinerant craftsmen using temporary facilities. The ephemeral nature of their activities may help to explain why so few glass workshops have been identified at archaeological sites.[93] Likewise, because of their limited distribution, the common domestic wares display a great variety of form. Despite their simple and often careless manufacture, they are extremely difficult to classify, both geographically and chronologically. So at the lowest level the popularity of glass led to the fragmentation of the glass industry. By contrast, it is apparent that luxury glass was made in a small number of highly specialised workshops. Scholars have devoted a considerable amount of energy to demonstrating the fact that such items as cameo vessels and cage-cups were produced centrally and then distributed by means of trade or gift-exchange to members of the Roman élite living scattered across the Empire.[94]

Just as the means by which the glass industry spread across the ancient world are complex and difficult to unravel, so it should be recognised that the manufacturing process operated as a series of interdependent but distinct stages, whose exact relationship to each other is still improperly understood. Glass manufacture involved a number of different skills, so that it is likely that no single craftsman could, working in isolation, fashion a glass vessel or object. First, the glass has to be produced from the raw materials by heating the chemical and mineral components together in a furnace. Certainly by the Roman period this was being done on a large scale at specific places where the raw materials were abundant. Evidence for mass-production of raw glass or cullet in antiquity comes principally from the discovery of 17 large furnace tanks at Bet Eli'ezer in Israel where solid blocks of glass weighing 8-10 tons were made.[95]

Another important aspect in the production of raw glass was the availability of fuel, namely wood, to fire up the furnaces. Much higher temperatures were required to frit the raw ingredients and make a batch than to reheat the glass cullet in order to work it into individual objects. So glassmaking, as opposed to glassworking, demanded a large supply of wood to bring the furnace up to the right temperature. In northern Mesopotamia and Lebanon, where forests were plentiful in antiquity, this would not have been a great problem; but further south in Palestine and, more especially, in Egypt, the lack of adequate supplies of wood may seriously have affected the scale of local glassmaking.

A second stage in the process was the manipulation of molten glass to create vessels and objects. In Roman times this essentially meant glassblowing; craftsmen engaged in such activity are known from both ancient depictions and inscriptions.[96]

A third element in making glass could be the working of glass in its cold state by carving and cutting. The craftsmen involved in this work were probably different from those who fashioned the glass in its molten state, and the level of expertise involved could vary from making a few simple wheel-cut lines to carving intricate figural scenes in relief. Likewise, those who added other forms of decoration such as paint or gold leaf are clearly distinct from the glassworkers. With mould-blown glass there is an additional process: that of making the mould itself. Ennion, whose name appears on mould-blown tableware, is assumed to be a master glassmaker, and the implication is that he made his own moulds, but it remains unproven.

Conclusion

A dominant theme running through this brief survey of the history of ancient glass has been the importance of the role played by wealthy patrons. Glass was often produced in workshops under direct royal patronage, or was designed to cater for the needs of rich private clients. Yet from the earliest times, man has used glass as a cheaper alternative to precious stone and metal artefacts. Until the Roman period practically all glass manufacture was geared to producing imitations of stone, metalwork and pottery.[97] The fascination of

glass is, therefore, something of an enigma. Unlike natural semi-precious stones, it was not durable, although it had the same qualities of translucency, smoothness and cleanliness. Similarly, whereas gold, silver and bronze vessels could be melted down and converted into 'cash', glass was a material of transient value. Once broken, it was discarded as virtually worthless.

On the other hand, glass had qualities that made it outshine other materials. It imparts no taste or smell; it is thus an ideal container and, when sealed, can preserve contents for a considerable time. It is relatively light in weight and can be transported in a number of different forms – as the basic raw materials, glass cullet, finished products, or even as broken glass. In the Roman period the invention of glassblowing brought this highly versatile material within the reach of 'the ordinary man in the street'. No longer was it a luxury item, but one that could be used for countless different purposes and in every imaginable form. The ubiquity of glass on Roman archaeological sites is testimony to its ability to span the gap between the disparate geographical and social elements of the Roman Empire. Finally, although glass production declined both in quality and quantity with the so-called 'fall of the Roman Empire' between the fifth and seventh centuries AD, it provided a lasting legacy for succeeding ages. The result is that it would be impossible to imagine the modern world without glass.

Notes

1   Doubts, however, have been expressed about the dating of the Karanis material, including the glass. It would now seem that occupation of the site continued into the sixth and seventh centuries and did not cease, as Harden supposed, in the fifth century AD; see most recently Whitehouse 1999.

2   In addition to the cast fragments recorded on pages 51-66, there are four blown vessel fragments: A1879.34.23.24 (body fragment of colourless glass, decorated with a blue trail formed into the shape of a chain of hollow circles, not dissimilar to 'spectacle pattern' threads; see Auth 1976, 148-9 nos 191-3), A1887.384-384A (two base fragments) and

A1914.105 (neck fragment; found in Cyprus). Most of the beads in NMS collection (922 separate items), have not been included in the detailed catalogue.

3   For an account of the trade at Rome in the 1870s and 1880s when Charles Caryl Coleman acquired the fragments that are now in Toledo, see Grose 1989, 22-3, 243-4 and fig. 115.

4   Grose was apparently unaware of the existence of the material in Edinburgh. Its acquisition in 1849 shows that the trade in such fragments continued for several decades. For other groups of similar fragments, see Kunina 1997, 267-8 nos 91-2; *Sangiorgi* 1999, 91-5 nos 239-45.

5   On recycling of glass in ancient Rome, see Stern 1999a, 450-1; Saguì 1998, 40, fig. 55.

6   For more detailed biography, see Perrot 1894, x-xviii.

7   As well as glass, Piot also collected Tanagra terracotta figurines, which he bought in Athens, and brought back to Paris some of the first examples of Cypriot art. There is no reference to glass in the account of his travels and collecting activities; see Perrot 1894, xvi.

8   The glass formed part of the collection of Julius Robertson van Millingen; see Goring 1988, 33-4. Other Cypriot objects registered as A1921.1395-1405 came from excavations conducted on the island in 1882 by George Gordon Hake on behalf of Lt. Kitchener (later Lord Kitchener of Khartoum).

9   See Bailey 1965, 5-10 and Souyoudzoglou-Haywood 2004, 1-3. For a brief account of the complicated history of these antiquities, see Goring 1988, 21.

10 See Goring 1988, 27-8 and Souyoudzoglou-Haywood 2004, 3. Note also a group of nine Roman blown glass vessels from Cyprus that was acquired by the Hunterian Museum in Glasgow during the mid to late 19th century; Başak, Knapp, and Webb 2005, 31-2 nos 41-49, pls III, XIII.

11 Amazingly, the entire group was given to a London dealer in exchange for a single lead-glazed terracotta drinking cup (A1963.64). This largely explains the gaps that appear in the numbering sequence in the concordance.

12 On the use of perfume bottles at Roman funerals, see Ferrari 1998, 173.

13 Catalogue 1892, 221 nos FR200-7, FR211. This handbook also records material from other parts of Roman Britain; op. cit., 222 nos FS44-5 (from Colchester), 223 nos F84-6, F172-8 (both groups from Bath).

14 Op. cit., 190 no. EQ150; see also Davidson 1885-6, 136-7, fig. 1; Curle 1931-2, 291, 387-7, fig. 3; Price and Cottam 1998, 100.

15 Dunbar 1929-30; Curle 1931-2, 291, 389, fig. 67; Thorpe 1933-4; Clarke, Breeze, and Mackay 1980, 44 no. 36, pl. 5; Breeze 1996, 112, fig. 93; Price and Cottam 1998, 154.

16 The excavations at Newsteads between 1905 and 1910 were published in exemplary fashion by James Curle; see Keppie 1986, 104-5. For the glass finds, including window glass and beads, see Curle 1911,

271-3, fig. 36, 336-7, pl. XCI. For a fragmentary pane of window glass from Rough Castle fort on the Antonine Wall, see Clarke, Breeze, and Mackay 1980, 31 no. 20 (with refs.). Other examples of window glass, deposited during the abandonment of the Antonine Wall fort at Bar Hill in *c.* AD 161, are displayed in the Hunterian Museum, Glasgow.

17 For the glass finds from the legionary fortress at Inchtuthil, see Price 1985b.

18 Hunter 2006, 27; see also Breeze 1996, 112.

19 For a list of cut glass finds from Scotland, including Traprain Law, see Price and Cottam 1998, 81-2, 90, 95, 98, 121.

20 Above footnote 16, and Whitehouse 2001b, esp. 31-2. For an example in the Afyonkarahisar Museum, Turkey, see Lightfoot 1989, 28-9 no. 17, pl. 2/3 (with refs.). Many fragments of window panes have also been found at the Roman and Byzantine city of Amorium, not far from Afyonkarahisar; Gill 2002, 101-3 nos 584-611, 225-8 nos 812-42.

21 Breeze 1996, 112-14.

22 For glossaries, see Goldstein 1979, 12-14; Grose 1989, 29-36; Tait 1991, 242-7; Stern 1995, 19-32; Grossmann 2002, 4-5 (with entries on the different techniques used to make and decorate glass vessels, pp. 7-21). For useful, illustrated descriptions of shapes and parts of vessels, see Israeli 2003, 14-17.

23 See, for example, Tait 1991, 213-42, figs 1-214; Stern 1995, 36-44, figs 18-39; Wight 2000, 71-9, figs 13-22; Hill and Taylor 2003.

24 Some techniques, notably the forming and cutting of cast bowls, remain the subject of hotly-contested scholarly disputes; see, for example, *Wolf* 1994, esp. 68-79; Lierke 2002; Pilosi and Wypyski 2002.

25 The bibliography is extensive; see recently Thirion-Merle 2005.

26 For example, a spouted bowl, dated *c.*3500-3100 BC, from Tepe Gawra in Iraq, in the University of Pennsylvania Museum (no. 35-10-287 excavated in 1934-5). See also Harden 1987, 28 no. 6 (this object is wrongly described as 'glass'; later analysis proved it to be made of obsidian). Pliny the Elder refers to the use of obsidian in Roman composite statuary (*Nat. Hist.* 36.197); see Forbes 1957, 163-4.

27 One may note the story told by Trimalchio (Petronius, *Satyricon* 51) of a glassmaker who made a glass bowl that would not break but could be hammered back into shape if it got dented. He presented his invention to the emperor Tiberius but was rewarded for his efforts with the death penalty since, as Trimalchio explains, the emperor feared that, if the secret formula for unbreakable glass became known, the price of gold would plummet. The story also appears in Pliny the Elder (*Nat. Hist.* 36.195), Dio Cassius (57.21.7) and Isidore (*Orig.* 16.6.6).

28 The earliest datable example comes from the site of Atchana (ancient Alalakh) on the plain of Antioch near the modern Turkish border with Syria; see Barag 1985, 36 and 42 no. 7. For examples of

Mesopotamian glass in the Istanbul Archaeological Museums, see Atık 1998.

29 For an account of the Egyptian glass industry, see Tait 1991, 26-38.

30 National Museums Scotland contains only a few examples of Egyptian glassware; see below pp. 186-9.

31 *The Oxford Encyclopedia of Archaeology in the Near East*, sv. 'Vitreous Materials' (Oxford 1997), vol. 5, 312 [E. Peltenberg].

32 Literary evidence for glassmaking has been found in both Middle Babylonian cuneiform texts and Neo-Assyrian tablets from Nineveh; cf. Oppenheim 1970, 9-101.

33 *The Oxford Encyclopedia of Archaeology in the Near East*, vol. 5 (Oxford 1997), 306-9 sv. 'Vitreous Materials' [I. C. Freestone].

34 Oppenheim 1970, 219-21 nos 22, 25-8, figs 20-4; Barag 1985, 65-6 nos 38-40A, fig. 3 and pl. 4.

35 Von Saldern 1959, 23 and 25-7, figs 1-2. The vessel is now displayed in the Museum of Anatolian Civilizations, Ankara.

36 The earliest dated example of this Achaemenid glass tableware belongs to the third quarter of the fifth century BC; Vickers 1972. Slightly later, a famous reference to luxurious glass vessels being used at the Achaemenid court in Persepolis appears in Aristophanes' play the *Acharnians* (lines 73-5), staged in 425 BC. See also von Saldern 2004, 106-15; Curtis and Tallis 2005, 108, 119 nos 113-14.

37 Grose 1989, 80, especially note 44.

38 Vickers 1996a.

39 Oliver 1970.

40 Grose 1989, 185-9.

41 This may explain the inclusion of glass among 'the cheap, showy goods (from Egypt)' invoiced by Rabirius in 55 BC; Cicero, *Pro Rab. Post.* 40 (cf. also 14.50); Forbes 1957, 153.

42 Israeli 1991; see also Israeli 2005, 55-6, fig. 3.

43 See *Wolf* 1994, 81-5.

44 For the spread of the glassblowing industry in the early imperial period, see Stern 1999a, 442-4 (with refs).

45 Grose 1977; see also Tait 1991, 62-5.

46 Stern has recently proposed that the invention of the iron blow-pipe and other important improvements in glass technology took place under Roman influence during the first century AD; see Stern 1999a, 444-50.

47 See Painter 1991; Walker 2004, esp. 32, 36-7, fig. 14.

48 For window glass, see Forbes 1957, 181-4. According to Forbes (op. cit., 183), 'Window panes as known in Italy from the first century AD onwards are either unknown or extremely rare in the East'; so also Barag 1987, 116. In fact, window glass is common at most Roman sites in Asia Minor and is found in considerable quantities during excavations. For a published example, see Lightfoot 1989, 28-9 no. 17 (with discussion). These views on the extensive use of window glass in the East find support in a recent article; see Stern 1999a, 464 (with refs). For mirrors, see Kisa 1908, 357-61; Trowbridge 1930, 184-6;

Forbes 1957, 184 (cf. refs in note 252); for e.g. from Cyprus, see Vessberg 1956, 112 fig. 33:3. The only literary reference to glass mirrors occurs in the work of Alexander of Aphrodisias, dated around AD 220 (*Prob.* 1.132). For a late Roman or early Byzantine example in the Leiden Museum, see Braat 1966, 62-3, together with *Benzian* 1994, 19 lot 12.

49 For a general discussion of the important role that glass played in the daily life of ancient Rome, see Winfield Smith 1949, 49-51.

50 See, e.g., Goldstein 1979, 244-66; Grose 1989, 356-8.

51 Fleming 1996b, 26.

52 Few ancient moulds have survived. The majority were made of stone and sheet copper, although clay moulds were also popular, and others were made of wood.

53 Charlesworth 1966. For 'Frontinus' bottles, see Sennequier 1985, 169.

54 E.g., a square wooden box divided into four compartments, containing three small one-handled glass bottles and one jar, from Akhmim in Egypt and dated to the first century AD (British Museum, EA20774).

55 British Museum, OA1923.10-17.1. For other vessels that have retained their packing or protective cover, see Whitehouse 1997, 43 no. 240 and 183-4 no. 323.

56 It has been argued, however, that gold-glass was not made for the imperial court or for aristocratic patrons; cf. Cameron 1996, 299.

57 Another technique used principally in the Hellenistic and early Roman periods was the addition of strips of gold foil to mosaic glass.

58 Whitehouse 1996, figs 2-5.

59 See Whitehouse 2001, 254; von Saldern 2004, 445-7, pls 360-1; 452-6, pls 350-2, 357-8 and 362.

60 Whitehouse 1996; Whitehouse 1997, 223.

61 The most famous surviving example is the Lycurgus Cup in the British Museum (MLA 1958.12-2.1); see Harden 1987, 245-9 no. 139. For recent discoveries of Byzantine dichroic glass, see Gill and Lightfoot 2002.

62 Painter 1991, 40-1.

63 Harden 1987, 238-44 nos 134-8.

64 Vickers 1996b, 4 and figs 1-2.

65 Harden 1987, 180-5. For specific examples, see especially Harden 1987, 190 no. 100 (with a reference in Martial's *Epigrams* XI, 11 to *calices tepidique toreumata Nili*), 196 no. 106 and 220-1 no. 122.

66 Harden 1987, 223-4 no. 124. For another example, see Oliver 1975.

67 Cameron 1996, 298.

68 Walker 1997, 156-9 nos 175-8 (all from Deir el-Bahri). For examples of plainer, utilitarian glass vessels depicted on mummy portraits, see Walker 1997, 87-8 no. 77, 102 no. 95 and 118 no. 114.

69 Scranton 1967.

70 Grose 1989, 242. It is, however, interesting to note a late reference to the use of glass storage bottles. According to Procopius (*Wars* III.13.23-24), during Belisarius' expedition to Africa in 533 the army was ferried across from Greece to Sicily by ship. The

fresh drinking water on Belisarius' ship was stored in the hold in glass jars buried in sand.

71 For further references to the trade in broken glass, see Forbes 1957, 179. Stern has recently suggested that glass recycling was also an important Roman discovery, made during the Flavian period; see Stern 1999a, 450-1.

72 For evidence for the cheapness of glass at the time of Diocletian's Great Persecution, see Forbes 1957, 157 and no. 151. A reference in the Talmud (Tosephta, Peah 4:11 '... if he formerly used bronze vessels, he must sell them and use glass vessels'), dating from the third century AD, also indicates that glassware was regarded as generally much less valuable than vessels made of base and precious metals.

73 For example, a glass jug filled with an oily substance found in a Roman-period tumulus tomb; Ayabakan 1991, 51 no. 3, fig. 7. For cinerary urns, see Harden 1987, 96 no. 38 (found in Kent in 1801 and still containing many fragmentary cremated bones) and 97 no. 39 (from Flamersheim, Germany).

74 Naumann 1991.

75 Fleming 1996b, 17 and fig. 8.

76 Fleming 1996b, 22 and fig. 19. See also below, p. 143.

77 Compare Höricht 1991 (for vessels stamped with the name of P. Gessi Ampliati, who owned the glass workshop) and Price 1977 (for stamps regarded as belonging to the purveyors of the original contents).

78 For discussion of stamped bottles, see now Stern 1999a, 467-9 (with refs). Most examples are dated to the first/second centuries AD; see, e.g., Jacobson 1992, 38. However, a very interesting group of prismatic bottles that have bases stamped with names in Greek has been excavated at the Lycian city of Arycanda (south-west Turkey) in a destruction layer dated to c. AD 430; Tek 2003, 85-6 nos 3-22, figs 1-5. For other examples from Turkey, see Akat 1984, 54 no. 90, illus 40 and no. 92, illus. 42; 55 no. 96, illus. 45 (Sadberk Hanım Museum); Czurda-Ruth 1989, 139 and figs 7, 87-90 (two examples from Ephesus); Özet 1987, 597 and 605 no. 13 (Ankara Museum); Antalya Museum (inv. no. 14.12.77, unpublished); and Aphrodisias Museum (inv. no. 67-71, unpublished).

79 For Roman shipwrecks containing glass, see refs in Stern 1999a, 468, 472-3; Foy/Nenna 2001, 101-12.

80 Bass 1986; The Oxford Encyclopedia of Archaeology in the Near East, vol. 5 (Oxford 1997), 266-8 sv. 'Uluburun' [C. Pulak and G. F. Bass]; see also recent exhibition catalogue; Yalçın, Pulak and Slotta 2005.

81 Bass 1984; The Oxford Encyclopedia of Archaeology in the Near East, vol. 5 (Oxford 1997), 2-4 sv. 'Serçe Limanı' [G. F. Bass].

82 Harden 1970, 64; Jackson 1998.

83 Price 1978. A cast ribbed bowl, part of a rich cremation burial found at Hertford Heath and dated c.70-10 BC, is the earliest recorded import of glass from the eastern Mediterranean (British Museum, P&RB 1958.7-4.724).

84 Seligman 1939, 556 and pl. 2, figs 1-2; Goepper 1984, 92 no. 82 (see also pp. 85 no. 71 and 87 no. 73); Taniichi 1983; Taniichi 1990; Stern 1991. For a detailed survey of the evidence for trade in glass beyond the Roman frontiers, see Stern 1999a, 476-8; see below, page 89 no. 200.

85 De Franciscis 1963; see also Stern 1999a, 471. For straw-protected bottles depicted on a mosaic from El Djem, Tunisia, see Forbes 1957, 148 no. 109. For other examples of vessels with protective covers, see Harden 1936, 222 and 315, fig. 4, d; Walker 1997, 205-6 no. 290; Whitehouse 1997, 143-4 no. 240 and 183-4 no. 323. For Roman packaging in general, see Stern 1999a, 474.

86 For glass ingots of the Roman period found in shipwrecks, see Stern 1999a, 475 and no. 213. Stern also points out that raw glass could be transported by sea very cheaply because it could double as ballast (loc. cit. with refs in nos 215 and 216).

87 Cool 1996, 57-8 and fig. 9. Information about Arycanda was kindly provided by Prof Dr Cevdet Bayburtluoğlu and Doç Dr Ahmet Tolga Tek, see Bayburtluoğlu 2003; Tek 2003, 83.

88 Erim 1973; Barag 1987; for additional comments, see Jackson 1998, 60-1; Barag 2005. For further discussion, see Stern 1999a, 460-6.

89 Fleming 1996b, 18, quoting the example of a young man stationed at Alexandria in the third century AD who sent some glassware as a present to his father living at Karanis in the Fayoum.

90 See, for example, Lightfoot 1993, 36-7.

91 D. Kennedy (ed.), The Roman Army in the East (Ann Arbor 1996), 17.

92 The Oxford Encyclopedia of Archaeology in the Near East, vol. 5 (Oxford 1997), 316 sv. 'Vitreous Materials' [M. C. McClellan].

93 A glass workshop was found at Tamassos in Cyprus at the end of the nineteenth century, but it was only partially excavated and imprecisely recorded. Subsequent attempts to locate the installation have been unsuccessful; see Seefried 1986, 148.

94 The major study of this aspect of the 'universality' of Roman glass is the catalogue that accompanied an exhibition entitled 'Glass of the Caesars' that was held at various venues in Europe and America in 1987-8; see Harden 1987.

95 Gorin-Rosen 1995, 42-3; Stern 1999a, 482. The installations are dated to the early seventh century AD. A huge slab of raw glass, probably made in a similar tank, was found at Bet She'arim, also in northern Palestine; see Brill 1967 and Freestone 1999 (where, however, the slab is reassigned to the Islamic period and tentatively dated to the early ninth century AD); see also Gorin-Rosen 2000, 52-6; Tal, Jackson-Tal and Freestone 2004, 56-7, fig. 6. Similar large slabs are said to exist in western Asia Minor (pers. comm. Kasim Akbıyıkoğlu, former director of the Uşak Museum).

96 For depictions on terracotta lamps, see Baldoni 1987.

97 Von Saldern 1991, 119-21; Vickers 1996b.

Core-formed Bottles of the Classical and Hellenistic Periods

Between the sixth and first centuries BC the largest share of glass production was devoted to the making of core-formed vessels. They were almost exclusively small bottles intended for holding scented oils, unguents, perfumes and cosmetics, and they show the way that the industry was to develop, for they may at the same time be regarded as both luxury items and utilitarian containers. The bottles and their contents became part of everyday life; they were used in the home, were offered as votive gifts to the gods at sanctuaries, and were used at funerals to anoint the dead. Their shapes consciously imitate those of Greek pottery, which dominated the Mediterranean ceramics market, but they stand out from them because of their brilliant colouring and vivid patterns. Despite their attractive appearance, however, core-formed vessels have one major drawback. They were not very practical or suitable for storing valuable unguents and perfumes in. Apart from their lack of transparency (which meant that it must have been almost impossible to tell how much they contained at any point in time), close inspection of broken examples shows that the insides of these bottles were extremely rough and often clogged with the remains of the core.[1] Such extraneous material might well be thought to have spoilt or contaminated the contents.

Three successive periods of production have been identified, each distinguished by a new repertory of forms, decorative motifs, handle forms and colour combinations.[2] The bottles circulated widely in the lands bordering the Mediterranean, but no factory site has yet been discovered and thus it remains uncertain where precisely they were made. Various locations have been suggested, including Rhodes, Cyprus, southern Italy and the coastal cities of Phoenicia. It is likely, in fact, that there were a number of different centres, each producing its own variants. Since core-formed bottles were produced over a very long period, numerous examples have survived, many of which are still miraculously intact. But the fact that both vessels and fragments have been found at sites throughout the Mediterranean indicates that core-formed glass was both popular and relatively accessible.[3] Their bright colours may be taken as to represent the showy display of the well-to-do citizen rather than a sign of real wealth.

The invention of glassblowing gave rise to the mass production of small, simple containers such as perfume bottles, and this led to the abandonment of core-forming in the early first century AD.[4]

1   A1880.18.50   Alabastron

Slightly translucent white with opaque deep purple trail
Middle of sixth to end of fifth century BC; formerly Piot Collection
H 9.55, D (rim) 3.6-3.4, D (body) 2.75

- Broad, flat, applied rim; jagged edge to top of
  mouth above rim; short, concave neck; uneven
  sides to body, expanding downwards; small, round
  bottom; two white ring handles applied to sides,
  ending in projecting knobs below.
- Purple trail wound round outer edge of rim; another applied to top of body and wound round in
  a spiral downwards for seven turns, then tooled
  into zigzag pattern for four to five turns.
- Intact, except for chip in rim trail and small hole
  in neck. Little weathering; black impurities in top
  of rim; pitting of surface bubbles.

Mediterranean Group I, Form I:2

Compare Harden 1981, 62-3 nos 85-9 (esp. no. 85 from a grave
at Camiros, Rhodes, dated 500-475 BC); Canav 1985: 29 no. 6;
Grose 1989, 133-4 no. 66; *Wolf* 1994, 204-7 nos 44-5

2   A1880.18.48   Alabastron

Translucent cobalt blue with opaque yellow and turquoise trails
Late sixth to mid-fifth century BC; formerly Piot Collection
H 11.3, D (rim) 2.8, D (body) 3.3, W (across handles) 3.15-3.0

- Everted, cup-shaped rim, tooled out from neck,
  with rounded upward outer lip; short, cylindrical
  neck; small shoulder; straight sides, expanding
  downwards; round bottom, tooled flat at centre;
  two blue ring handles applied at different heights
  to sides, with trailed knob below.
- Turquoise trail around rim; unmarvered yellow
  trail at top of body; unmarvered turquoise trail
  under handles; pair of single yellow and turquoise
  trails below.
- Broken and mended around body and bottom.
  Slight dulling and some surface pitting; many
  bubbles.

Mediterranean Group I, Form I:2

Compare MMA 17.194.756; Harden 1981, 66 no. 113 (from a tomb
at Camiros, Rhodes, dated 450-25 BC); see also Grose 1989, 137
no. 77

3   A1880.18.49   Alabastron

Translucent white with opaque pale purple trails
Late sixth to fifth century BC; formerly Piot Collection
H 8.75, D (rim) 2.9, D (body) 2.45, W (across handles) 3.4

- Thick, everted rim, tooled out from neck; cylindrical neck; short, sloping shoulder; straight sides to tall body; round bottom; two white ring handles applied to sides, ending in projecting knobs below.
- Purple trail around rim; another applied at top of body and wound round in a spiral downwards for five turns, then tooled into zigzag pattern from left to right (anti-clockwise); another thin trail below, wound round from right to left (clockwise) in two turns.
- Intact. Thick, creamy weathering and pitting on one side; bubbles on other.

Mediterranean Group I, Form 1:3A

Compare Harden 1981, 63 nos 93-5; Grose 1989, 133-4 nos 66 and 68; *Wolf* 1994, 204-7 nos 44-5

4   A1880.18.47   Alabastron

Cobalt blue with opaque white and yellow trails
Late sixth to fifth century BC; formerly Piot Collection
H 12.0, D (rim) 3.05, D (body) 3.55, W (across handles) 3.5

- Applied, uneven rim disk; jagged upper lip to mouth; short, funnel-shaped neck, with tooling marks at bottom; tall body with bulbous sides; small, round bottom; on opposite side of body near top, two ring handles, one in blue, the other in blue and white, with downward long trails ending in projecting knobs.
- White trail applied to neck and wound round in a spiral downward across body under the handles; overlaid at the bottom with a single, thick yellow trail, running from left to right (clockwise), then continuing as a band of yellow and white zigzag trails; below, another spiral trail in white in five turns.
- Intact. Dulling, pitting and iridescent weathering; many pinprick bubbles.

Mediterranean Group I, Form I:4

Compare Harden 1981, 68 no. 122; Grose 1989, 137-8 no. 78; *Wolf* 1994, 204-7 nos 44-5

5   A1950.39   Alabastron

Translucent cobalt blue with opaque yellow and white trails
Late sixth to early fifth century BC
H 8.55, D (rim) 2.35, D (body) 2.7, W (across handles) 3.15

- Flaring rim, drawn out from neck, with tooling impressions on underside; funnel-shaped neck; short, sloping shoulder; convex sides; round bottom; two blue ring handles, prominent on sides, with pressed in trails ending in knobs below.
- Yellow trail around rim; white trail running around neck and entire length of body in a tooled festoon pattern with some deep indents at the top.
- Intact. Very little weathering; some pitting of surface bubbles.

Mediterranean Group I, Form I:6
Compare Harden 1981, 72 nos 141-6 (esp. no. 143); Grose 1989, 142 no. 93; Kunina 1997, 247 no. 5

6   A1950.42   Amphoriskos

Slightly translucent cobalt blue with opaque yellow and turquoise blue
Late sixth to fifth century BC
H 9.9, D (rim) 3.0, D (body) 5.5-5.3, D (base) 1.6

- Everted, uneven rim; cylindrical neck, expanding at bottom and joining sloping shoulder; elongated, ovoid body, tapering downwards to point; round base knob; two rod handles applied to shoulder, drawn up vertically and trailed down onto neck below rim. Uneven tooled surface around neck and rim.
- Yellow trail would round edge of rim; another yellow trail wound around shoulder (anti-clockwise) in several turns, then tooled into feathery zigzag; turquoise trail applied over yellow trail around outer edge of shoulder, and another trail in a zigzag pattern; below, trail around body 5-6 times with varying thickness.
- Broken and repaired around neck and rim; large chip in side. Pitting of surface bubbles; faint iridescence.

Mediterranean Group I, Form I:1
Compare Harden 1981, 78-81 nos 163-75; Grose 1989, 146-7 no. 106; Kunina 1997, 251 no. 29

7

7 A1880.18.41 Amphoriskos

Slightly translucent white with bluish tinge, with opaque purple
Fifth century BC; formerly Piot Collection
H 7.9, D (rim) 2.6-2.5, D (body) 4.8, D (base) 1.1

- Everted, tooled out rim; cylindrical neck; rounded,
  sloping shoulder; pointed, ovoid body; applied,
  circular base knob; two rod handles applied to
  shoulder, drawn up and turned in onto neck
  below rim.
- Purple trail wound round outer edge of rim; another
  trail trailed on around shoulder (anti-clockwise)
  in several turns, then tooled into zigzag around
  upper body; single horizontal trail below; turquoise trail applied from right to left (clockwise) over
  yellow trail in a zigzag pattern in five turns; single
  trail below, trailed off upwards across pattern;
  irregular turquoise trail applied to knob base.
- Intact, except for slight internal cracks. Faint
  dulling; pitting of surface bubbles.

Mediterranean Group I, Form I:2

8 A1880.18.53 Amphoriskos

Dark turquoise blue and opaque yellow
First half of fifth century BC; formerly Piot Collection
H 8.6, D (rim) 3.3-3.2, D (body) 5.45, D (base) 1.5

- Everted rim, uneven and sloping inwards to short,
  funnel-shaped neck; jagged lip to mouth, rising
  above inner edge of applied rim; rounded, sloping
  shoulder; pointed, ovoid body; circular base knob
  with rounded outer edge. Two rod handles, applied
  to shoulder, drawn up and curved in slightly, then
  pressed on to underside of rim.
- Yellow trail around outer edge of rim; another
  yellow trail applied before addition of the handles
  on to shoulder, wound spirally to right (anti-clockwise) twice before becoming zigzag of four turns,
  some thick, some thin; another trail wound round
  from right (clockwise) on undercurve nearly three
  times; slight vertical ribbing around upper part of
  body, caused by tooling of trails.
- Intact. Thick, creamy weathering covering most of
  surface.

Mediterranean Group I, Form I:3
Compare Grose 1989, no. 108; Kunina 1997, 251-3 nos 28, 30-5

9   A1880.18.44   Amphoriskos

Translucent dark blue with opaque yellow and turquoise blue
First half of fifth century BC; formerly Piot Collection
H 8.3, D (rim) 2.5-2.4, D (body) 5.55, D (base) 1.6-1.4

• Everted rim, sloping inwards below; slightly
  concave, cylindrical neck; jagged lip to mouth,
  rising above inner edge of applied rim; rounded,
  sloping shoulder; pointed, ovoid body, with shallow, vertical ribs formed by tooling of trails into
  zigzag; oval base knob with rounded outer edge;
  two turquoise rod handles applied with small
  claws to shoulder drawn up and in at an angle,
  pressed onto neck below rim.
• Turquoise trail would round edge of rim; yellow
  trail trailed on around shoulder (anti-clockwise)
  in several turns, then tooled into zigzag around
  upper body; single horizontal trail below; turquoise trail applied from right to left (clockwise)
  over yellow trail in a zigzag pattern in five turns;
  single trail below, trailed off upwards across pattern; irregular turquoise trail applied to knob base.
• Intact. Faint dulling; pitting of surface bubbles.

Mediterranean Group I, Form I:3
Similar to no. 8; compare Grose 1989, no. 108

10   A1880.18.39   Aryballos

Translucent cobalt blue with opaque yellow and turquoise blue
Late sixth to fifth century BC; formerly Piot Collection
H 5.85, D (rim) 2.5, D (body) 4.6

• Everted rim, tooled out from neck; short, cylindrical neck; spherical body, with slight downward
  taper, with slight vertical ribbing; rounded bottom;
  two blue, ring handles with knobbed trails, pressed
  onto shoulder and looped round below rim and
  attached to neck.
• Turquoise trail applied to outer edge of rim;
  yellow trail of irregular thickness applied to shoulder before handles, wound round in a spiral four
  times to right (anti-clockwise), then in a zigzag
  four times; at bottom, single turquoise trail applied
  over yellow, also in a zigzag pattern; below, one
  yellow and one turquoise trail wound round body
  (yellow twice, turquoise once).
• Broken and repaired around body. Faint iridescent
  weathering and dulling; pitting of surface bubbles.

Mediterranean Group I, Form I:1A

Compare Harden 1981, 91-3 nos 226-41 (esp. no. 226 from Eretria,
Greece); *Wolf* 1994, 214-5 no. 48; Kunina 1997, 251 nos 23-6

11 A1880.18.40 Aryballos

Translucent cobalt blue with opaque yellow and turquoise blue
Late sixth to fifth century BC; formerly Piot Collection
H 6.6, D (rim) 3.25-3.05, D (body) 4.95

- Flaring, uneven, applied rim, with upward outer lip; jagged lip to mouth above level of inner edge of rim; short, funnel-shaped neck; sloping shoulder; globular body, with almost straight side in middle; rounded, almost pointed bottom; two blue, ring handles with knobbed trails to shoulder, looped up and in onto neck below rim.
- Yellow trail wound around neck from left to right (anti-clockwise) and then in a thicker trail around shoulder, continuing on body as a zigzag pattern; turquoise trail applied over yellow at bottom; below, one yellow and one turquoise trail, one on top of the other, twice around body.
- Intact. Many pitted surface bubbles.

Mediterranean Group I, Form I:1A
Similar to no. 10

12 A1880.18.38 Aryballos

Dark cobalt blue with opaque yellow and turquoise blue
Late sixth to fifth century BC; formerly Piot Collection
H 6.15, D (rim) 2.9-2.75, D (body) 5.25

- Everted, applied rim, curving in below to short, cylindrical neck; broad, sloping shoulder; spherical body, tapering slightly downwards, with slight vertical ribbing to sides; rounded, uneven bottom; two turquoise ring handles, ending in knobs, pressed onto shoulder and looped round under rim and onto neck.
- Turquoise trail trailed around outer edge of rim; yellow trail wound twice round upper body and then tooled into a zigzag pattern, overlaid by thicker turquoise trail wound from left to right (anti-clockwise); below, single yellow and turquoise trail around body; one translucent blue blob on zigzag trails.
- Intact. Many pitted surface bubbles.

Mediterranean Group I, Form I:1A
Similar to no. 10

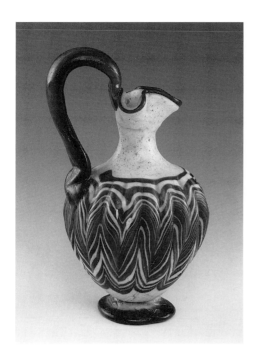 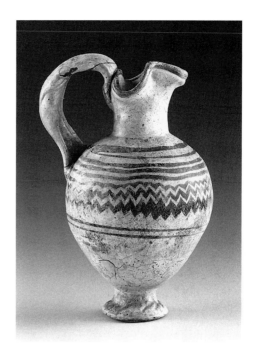

13 A1887.367 Oinochoe

Opaque white with deep blue tinge and cobalt blue trails
Late sixth to early fifth century BC
H (max.) 12.9, L (rim) 3.0, W (rim) 3.75, D (body) 7.3,
D (base) 4.0-3.85

- Applied, tooled, trefoil rim; neck flaring downwards to join broad shoulder; ovoid body, tapering downwards; applied, splayed base-ring, with tooling marks on upper surface; slightly concave and uneven bottom; heavy strap handle applied to outer edge of shoulder, drawn up and out in an elegant loop above rim and then pressed down onto rear of neck.
- Thick trail on rim; another trail applied to shoulder, wound round from left to right (anti-clockwise) and tooled into a close-set feather pattern with deep, vertical indents.
- Broken and mended around body. Base and handle contain some opaque white glass; one jagged blob of white glass attached to side of body. Some soil encrustation in ribs and mouth. Little weathering; many pinprick bubbles.

The colour scheme of this piece is both striking and unusual; for a similar vessel in Boston, said to have been purchased in Greece, see von Saldern 1968, no. 5. For amphoriskoi with similar decoration, see Fossing 1940, 69-70 and fig. 43.

Mediterranean Group I, Form I:I

14 A1880.18.46 Oinochoe

Opaque white with purple trails
First half of fifth century BC; formerly Piot Collection
H (max.) 9.7, L (rim) 2.65, W (rim) 3.4, D (body) 5.65,
D (base) 2.65

- Applied, trefoil rim with rounded edge; cylindrical neck; sloping shoulder; ovoid body, tapering downwards; short pedestal and splayed base-ring, concave on bottom; strap handle applied to outer edge of shoulder, drawn out and up in a loop above rim and then pressed down onto rear of neck.
- Purple trail on top edge of rim; another trail applied to shoulder, wound round eight times in a spiral (before handle applied) from left to right (clockwise) and tooled into a zigzag pattern in the middle of the body; below, another trail wound from right to left twice round lower body; thick trail around outer edge of base.
- Handle broken and mended. Creamy iridescent weathering, dulling and pitting of surface bubbles.

Mediterranean Group I, Form I:I; possibly Rhodian
Compare Harden 1981, 96 no. 245 (from a tomb at Camiros, Rhodes, dated 475-50 BC); Grose 1989, 148 no. 110; *Wolf* 1994, 212-13 no. 47; Kunina 1997, 250 no. 20

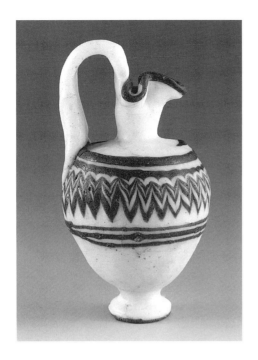

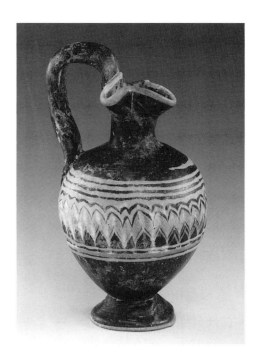

15 A1880.18.42 Oinochoe

Opaque white with purple trails
First half of fifth century BC; formerly Piot Collection
H (max.) 11.2, L (rim) 2.9, W (rim) 3.7, D (body) 6.4-6.3,
D (base) 2.85-2.65

- Tooled trefoil rim; slightly uneven, funnel-shaped neck; almost horizontal shoulder; ovoid body, tapering downwards; short pedestal and everted, oval, saucer-shaped base-ring, concave on bottom; strap handle applied to outer edge of shoulder in thick pad, drawn up in a loop above rim and then pressed down onto rear of neck.
- Thick, purple trail on rim; another trail applied to shoulder, wound round twice in a spiral, then in a fine zigzag pattern from left to right (anti-clockwise) three times; below, another trail wound nearly three times round horizontally; trail around bottom edge of base.
- Cracked around body and repaired. Little weathering; pitting of surface bubbles.

Mediterranean Group I, Form I:2; possibly Rhodian
Compare Harden 1981, 96 no. 246 (from Eretria, Greece); Grose 1989, 148-9 nos 111-12

16 A1880.18.43 Oinochoe

Translucent cobalt blue with opaque yellow and turquoise blue trails
First half of fifth century BC; formerly Piot Collection
H 11.4, L (rim) 3.0, W (rim) 3.3, D (body) 6.3, D (base) 3.9-3.6

- Applied, broad trefoil rim with rounded edge; cylindrical, slanting neck, with jagged lip visible in mouth; rounded, sloping shoulder; ovoid body, tapering downwards; applied, outsplayed base, tooled unevenly onto bottom; broad blue strap handle, applied to shoulder, drawn up, out, curved in, then pressed onto neck and rear edge of rim.
- Turquoise trail on top edge of rim; yellow trail applied to shoulder and wound round in a spiral (before handle applied) five times from left to right (anti-clockwise), becoming a close-set zigzag pattern; overlaid at bottom with a turquoise trail, in a zigzag around the middle; below, two yellow trails above and below a single turquoise trail wound horizontally once around body, with unsightly tooling marks on side where trailed off; turquoise trail around outer edge of base. Ribbing around middle of body from tooling of trails. Opaque yellow stud pressed into base of handle.
- Intact. Slight iridescent weathering, dulling and pitting of surface bubbles.

Mediterranean Group I, Form I:2A; possibly Rhodian
Compare Harden 1981, 98 nos 258-9 (both from Camiros, Rhodes); Canav 1985: 28 no. 4; Grose 1989, 149 no. 114; *Wolf* 1994, 212-13 no. 47

17 AI936.435 Alabastron

Translucent cobalt blue with opaque white, pale yellow and turquoise blue trails
Second half of fourth century BC
H 12.4, D (rim) 4.0, D (body) 4.2, W (across handles) 4.05

- Applied, broad, slightly drooping rim disk; funnel-shaped neck, with tooling indents; small, rounded shoulder; sides expanding unevenly downwards; round bottom; two ring handles, applied at different heights to sides of body, in blue with trailed ends below.
- Yellow trail around outer edge of rim; three trails trailed from right to left over entire body, forming closely packed feather pattern. Several deep, vertical tooling indents.
- Broken around body and across bottom, repaired; parts of trail around rim are missing. Faint iridescent weathering; some surface pitting.

Mediterranean Group II, Form II:1
Compare Harden 1981, 106 no. 274 (from Nola, Italy); Grose 1989, 152-4 nos 122-5; *Wolf* 1994, 216-21 nos 49-51

18 AI906.353 Alabastron

Dark blue, mixed with patches of dull yellow-brown, with opaque white and yellow trails
Second half of fourth century BC
H 8.8, D (rim) 3.4, D (body) 3.0

- Broad, horizontal rim disk; very short, concave neck; straight sides, expanding slightly downwards; round bottom; on opposite side of body near top, two small ring handles (surviving handle in blue and dull yellow-brown).
- Yellow trail would round edge of rim; another yellow trail trailed on around top of body from right to left (clockwise), first in a wavy pattern, then a zigzag, nine times around body; overlaid on final turn with a white trail, which continues down body for nearly six turns; then a yellow trail begins and runs to bottom, ending with two thick turns, tooled into zigzags/chevrons with vertical, irregular tooling indents. Tooling marks also visible on top of rim. Vertical ribbing on body.
- Intact, except for one handle. Dulling; patches of surface pitting; pinprick bubbles.

Mediterranean Group II, Form II:2
Compare *Wolf* 1994, 216-21 nos 49-51; Kunina 1997, 249 no. 14 (from the Panticapaeum necropolis)

19 A1956.516 Alabastron

Dark cobalt blue with opaque white, yellow and turquoise blue trails
Second half of fourth century BC
H 11.5, D (rim) 3.6, D (body) 3.0, W (across handles) 3.45

- Applied, broad, horizontal rim disk; jagged upper lip to mouth; short, funnel-shaped neck, with tooling marks; slightly convex sides to tall, elongated body; round bottom; on opposite side of body near top, two ring handles, with downward trailed ends.
- White trail around top of body from right to left (clockwise) in a downwards spiral; replaced by turquoise trail a third of way down body and then by a yellow trail two-thirds of the way down, dragged up and down to form a feather pattern with swirls at top of tooling with slight raised slit.
- Intact. Some dulling and surface pitting of bubbles.

Mediterranean Group II, similar to Form II:2
Compare Harden 1981, 107 no. 277 (from Cyprus); Grose 1989, 153-4 no. 125; Kunina 1997, 250 no. 17

20 A1965.258 Alabastron

Cobalt blue with opaque yellow trails
Middle of fourth to early third century BC
H 8.75, D (rim) 2.3-2.2, D (body) 2.3, W (across handles) 2.75

- Everted, uneven rim with rounded outer lip; cylindrical, slightly convex neck; tall, off-centre body, irregular in shape, with vertical tooled ribbing, tapering downwards; round bottom; two small lug handles applied to sides, with vertical loop holes in top.
- Yellow trail applied to neck and wound round many times in spiral at top of body, then in a zigzag pattern on lower body and ending in a spiral at the bottom.
- Broken and mended around body. Gold-coloured specks in rim. Some dulling and pitting of surface bubbles.

Mediterranean Group II, Form II:4
Compare Grose 1989, 156 no. 131; *Wolf* 1994, 222-3 no. 52

21 A1880.18.37 Lentoid amphoriskos

Translucent cobalt blue, with opaque yellow and white trails
Mid- to late fourth century BC; formerly Piot Collection
H 9.0, D (rim) 3.2, L (body) 7.4, W (body) 4.1

- Everted, horizontal rim, applied to top of neck,
  with lip inside mouth; cylindrical neck, expanding
  downwards; lentoid body with sloping shoulders
  to either side; rounded bottom with four applied
  stud feet in white; two blue handles applied to
  shoulder, drawn up and pressed onto top of neck;
  applied rod of twisted blue and white spiral trails
  running down sides, with horizontal ring/cylinder
  ornaments at top in blue and decorated with
  yellow trails.
- Relief spiral trail in yellow around neck four
  times; close-set trails in yellow and white, tooled
  into a feather pattern on body, with some vertical
  tooling indents in sides.
- Intact, except for parts of rim; gaps filled with
  fragments from other vessel(s) coloured blue and
  opaque, dullish red-brown. Dulling; surface cracks;
  deep pitting of bubbles.

Mediterranean Group II, variant to Forms II:1 and 2

Compare Goldstein 1979, 38 fig. 11; Canav 1985, 31 no. 9 (found
at Bigadiç in ancient Bithynia, Turkey); Grose 1989, 164-5 nos 153-4;
Lightfoot 2001, 62 fig. 5 (MMA 91.1.1348); Schlick-Nolte 2002a,
70-1 no. V-23

21

22 A1950.41 Oinochoe

Very dark blue, appearing black, with opaque yellow and
turquoise blue trails
Middle of fourth to early third century BC; given by Mrs D Callender
H (max.) 8.65, L (rim) 2.7, W (rim) 2.55, D (body) 5.4, D (base)
2.8-2.6

- Trefoil rim; cylindrical neck; tall, ovoid body; pad
  base; handle applied to shoulder after trail decoration to shoulder and drawn up in a curve and
  pressed onto back of rim.
- Yellow trail around rim, then wound down in fine
  spiral around neck; spiral and zigzag patterns in
  yellow and blue on body; fine yellow trail around
  outer edge of base.
- Intact. Dulled and pitted surfaces, especially on
  handle.

Mediterranean Group II; Form II:3

Compare von Saldern 1974, 54 nos 116-17; von Saldern 1980, 29
nos 7-8; Harden 1981, 117 nos 302-6 (esp. no. 305); *Kofler* 1985,
155 lot 304; *Wolf* 1994, 224-5 no. 53

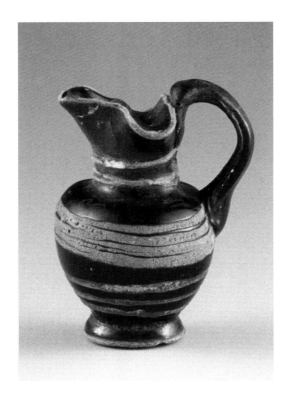

23 A1887.370 Oinochoe

Very dark blue (or green?), appearing black, with opaque yellow and turquoise blue trails

Middle of fourth to early third century BC; given by Sir Hugh Hume-Campbell of Marchmont, Bart

H (max.) 4.3, L (rim) 1.9, W (rim) 2.0, D (body) 2.9, D (base) 1.75-1.65

• Trefoil rim with upturned, flaring mouth; short cylindrical neck; ovoid body; low pad base; handle applied to shoulder after trail decoration and drawn up in a curve and pressed onto back of rim.
• Yellow trail around rim; a second spiral trail around neck, continuing on body in broad, tightly packed bands; another trail around edge of base.
• Intact. Turquoise trail weathered off, leaving reddish-brown grooves in body.

Mediterranean Group II; Form II:8

Compare Auth 1976, 41 no. 30 (reputedly from Beth Shan, Palestine); von Saldern 1980, 36-7 nos 24a-f; Harden 1981, 118 nos 308-9; *Kofler* 1985, 154 lot 302

24 A1965.259 Unguentarium

Translucent blue and opaque white
Third century BC
H 10.7, D (rim) 2.8-2.65, D (body) 3.9, D (base) 1.8

• Horizontal, everted rim, with thick outer lip and tooling marks on upper surface; tall, cylindrical but uneven neck; small, sloping shoulder; ovoid body, tapering downwards; tall, concave, solid stem, with tooling marks around bottom; applied base pad, uneven on bottom.
• Single white trail applied to neck and wound round from right to left (clockwise) twice, then drawn down across shoulder and into a tooled zigzag pattern in two and a half turns around body; two and a half further turns as straight lines and then trailed off in a loop around bottom.
• Intact. Faint dulling and iridescence; surface pitting; many bubbles.

Mediterranean Group III, Form II:2

Compare Goldstein 1979: 38 fig. 11; Canav 1985: 32 no. 10 (citing another example in the Adana Regional Museum, inv. no. 18.5.74); Grose 1989, 166 nos 158-9

25 A1927.90 Unguentarium

Translucent dark blue with opaque yellow and white trails
Third century BC
H 10.9, D (rim) 2.6, D (body) 3.8, D (base) 2.8-2.65

- Everted rim, with slightly concave upper edge; tall, cylindrical; narrow shoulder; ovoid body, tapering downwards; applied, solid stem, with tooled, oval disk base and tooling indent in bottom.
- White trail applied to neck and wound nearly twice, then drawn down across shoulder and into a tooled zigzag pattern around top of body; six further turns as close-set spiral; another yellow trail also applied to neck and wound more than twice, then across shoulder and made into zigzag at top and then straight for three turns on lower body.
- Broken around stem and repaired; parts of trails weathered off, leaving impressions in body of vessel. Thick iridescence weathering, covering almost entire surface; severe surface pitting.

Mediterranean Group III, Form II:2
Similar to no. 24; compare *Wolf* 1994, 230-1 no. 56

26 A1880.18.36 Alabastron

Translucent blackish-blue with opaque white trail
First half of first century BC; Cypriot; formerly Piot Collection
H 11.8, D (rim) 2.65, D (body) 3.35, W (across handles) 2.7

- Everted, saucer-shaped rim, tooled out from neck; uneven and irregularly shaped neck, expanding downwards and joining imperceptibly with body; rounded carination about three-quarters of the way down body; convex, pointed bottom; two horizontal, coiled lug handles in blue, pressed into top of body.
- Single white trail wound round edge of rim and trailed down neck and entire length of body, ending in a spiral at the bottom; trail tooled into a festoon pattern on body.
- Intact. Whitish iridescent weathering covering most of surface; pitting of surface bubbles.

Mediterranean Group III, Form III:4
Compare Harden 1981, 128 no. 343; Canav 1985: 30 no. 8; Grose 1989, 168 no. 165; *Wolf* 1994, 232-3 no. 57

27 A1880.18.35 Alabastron

Translucent blackish-blue with opaque white trail
First half of first century BC; Cypriot; formerly Piot Collection
H 11.95, D (rim) 2.95-2.75, D (body) 3.2, W (across handles) 2.8

- Everted, oval and uneven rim, tooled out from neck, with rounded outer edge; cylindrical neck; tall body, with sides expanding downwards, then tapering in to pointed bottom; two horizontal, lug handles in blue at top of body.
- Thick white trail applied to edge of rim and drawn down from right to left (clockwise) over entire length of body, ending in a spiral at the bottom; trail tooled into an irregular feather pattern on body.
- Intact. Slight weathering, dulling and deep pitting of surface bubbles; iridescence on top of rim.

Mediterranean Group III, Form III:5
Compare Grose 1989, 168-9 nos 166-7

28

28 A1880.18.34 Amphoriskos

Opaque blackish-purple with opaque white trail and
colourless handles
First century BC to early first century AD; formerly Piot Collection
H (as extant) 14.1, D (rim) 2.6, D (body) 5.5, W (across handles) 6.3

- Everted, tooled out rim, concave on top, with
  indent around top of neck below; cylindrical neck
  at top, then expanding downwards and joining
  imperceptibly with shoulder; elongated, bulbous
  body, tapering to point at bottom; two rod handles
  applied to shoulder in tooled pad, drawn up vertically to level of rim and folded over and down,
  then pressed onto neck.
- White trail wound applied to top of neck under
  rim, wound round in a spiral (under handles)
  eleven times to left, then close-set feather pattern
  on body and ending in a thick, spiral trail around
  bottom.
- Base knob broken off and missing. Patches of thick,
  brown weathering on handles, flaking off to leave
  iridescence; on body, creamy weathering, partially
  flaked off, leaving iridescent film; surface dulling
  and pitting; pinprick bubbles.

Mediterranean Group III, Form III:2D
Compare *Wolf* 1994, 234-41 nos 58-61

29 A1965.249 Body fragment

Dark blue, appearing black, with yellow and white trails
Probably second to first century BC
H 4.0, L 5.1, Th 0.4

- On exterior, trails partially tooled into feather
  pattern; on interior, metallic, gritty surface.

Probably part of an amphoriskos of Mediterranean Group III;
compare Grose 1989, 170 no. 170; *Wolf* 1994, 236-9 nos 59-60

Cast Vessels of the Hellenistic Period

Monochrome

30 A1880.18.12 Cosmetic jar (pyxis)

Pale blue-green
Fourth to third century or late second century BC; found in Crete; formerly Piot Collection
H 3.9, D (rim) 8.45-8.35, D (base) 11.6-11.5

- Spool-shaped pyxis with lid; box probably made by tooling on a potter's wheel; lid sagged; both cut and polished.
- Vertical rim with stepped outer lip to receive lid and lid grooved to match; short, thick cylindrical walls, rising vertically from a broad, flanged base; bottom almost flat but slightly concave at centre.
- Cut decoration, comprising a number of wheel-cut grooves; one groove cut into exterior edge of rim; another very broad but shallow groove in upper surface of lip to base-ring; pattern of concentric grooves and raised circles on bottom.
- Intact, except for one chip in edge of base; patches of limy weathering, iridescence and dulling; few pinprick bubbles; rotary polishing marks.

The rim fits inside band on lid (no. 31). Glass pyxides appear to have been produced in a single workshop located in south-west Crete. For discussion of the group, see Weinberg 1959.

Compare Merseyside 1979, 7 no. A12; Goldstein 1979, 133-4 no. 276; *Wolf* 1994, 282-3 no. 78 (with discussion and refs); Kunina 1997, 255 no. 46

31 A1880.18.12A Lid

Pale blue-green
H 3.1, D 11.85

- Rounded horizontal rim; flattish band, 1.6 wide, then cut in on interior and curving up to conical tip; on exterior, flattish band surrounding conical body with round peak at centre.
- Cut decoration on exterior, comprising a groove on top edge of rim; another groove 0.7-0.8 from rim.
- Intact; thick limy weathering on exterior; pitting and dulling; pinprick bubbles.

Found with no. 30

31

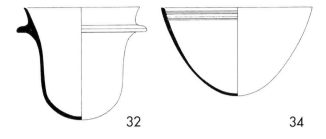

32   34

32 A1880.18.6 Bowl or lamp

Pale green with yellowish tinge
Third century BC; formerly Piot Collection
H 11.9, D (rim) 12.7, D (max.) 14.2

- Slightly everted, rounded rim; below, solid outward collar; vertical sides, slightly concave,
  curving in to round bottom.
- Broken and mended with some plaster fill. Creamy
  white weathering, flaking off to leave iridescence
  and dulling; very few bubbles.

This vessel, which appears to have been cast as a
thick blank and then cut down into the pouch-shaped
bowl with a horizontal collar, is very unusual and no
close parallel has been found. The rounded bottom
and the broad collar suggest that it may have been
used as a lamp, suspended either by a chain attachment under the collar or, more likely, in a solid
metal frame similar to early Byzantine polycandela
(see Fleming 1997a, 33 fig. 19). However, a more
attractive hypothesis is that it served as the inner
lining of a metal bowl.[5]

33 A1880.18.10 Hemispherical bowl

Blue-green
Probably second to first century BC; formerly Piot Collection
H 6.9, D (rim) 11.8-11.7

- Everted, bevelled rim with ground edge or outer
  lip; sides curving round to convex bottom; bottom
  is uneven and off-centre.
- Cut decoration on exterior, comprising six grooves,
  0.25-0.35, 0.5-0.6, 2.2-2.3, 2.5-2.6, 3.15-3.25 and
  3.4-3.5 below rim.
- Intact. Enamel-like weathering in patches, iridescent dulling and pitting elsewhere.

The vessel is somewhat unusual in having a lip to
the rim and cut decoration only on the exterior, both
of which features may suggest that it is a relatively
early example of Hellenistic cast glassware. For other
examples, see *British Rail* 1997, 24-5 lot 9; *Solid
Liquid* 1999, 30 no. 33.

Compare *Verres* 1985, no. 78

34 A1880.18.2 Conical bowl (mastos)

Opaque royal blue
Mid-second to early first century BC; formerly Piot Collection
H 9.05, D (rim) 15.7, Th 0.2-0.35

- Rim rounded on inner edge; sides curving in to
  round bottom.
- Cut decoration on interior, comprising three grooves
  around sides, 0.3-0.4, 0.7-1.0 and 1.1-1.2 below
  rim.
- Broken into two halves; patchy weathering and
  iridescence; dulling and pitting of surface bubbles
  on interior; rotary polishing marks.

The colour may have been intended to imitate the
rare semi-precious stone lapis lazuli. For other
opaque Hellenistic vessels, see Nenna 1993a, 15
(with refs).

For a rare stone example of a conical bowl, see *Wolf* 1994, 288-9
no. 81

35 A1880.18.4 Conical bowl (mastos)

Deep amber brown
Second to first century BC; formerly Piot Collection
H 8.9, D (rim) 15.6

- Rounded, slightly inverted rim; slanting sides;
  rounded bottom.
- Cut decoration on interior, comprising two grooves
  around sides, 0.4-0.5 and 0.7-0.9 below rim.
- Intact, except for one large chip in interior below
  rim and some mending of rim; internal strain cracks;
  small amount of weathering and iridescence; surface pitting on interior; rotary polishing marks on
  interior, fire-polished on exterior.

Similar to no. 34, but also compare von Saldern 1974, 93 no. 244
(with refs); Welker 1987, 14 no. 5; Lightfoot 1993, 24-5 figs 6-10;
Wolf 1994, 284-5 no. 79 (with discussion and refs)

34

35

36

36   A1880.18.5   Small conical bowl (mastos)

Pale yellow-green; second to first century BC; formerly Piot Collection
H 7.2, D (rim) 11.85-11.5

- Ground rim with bevelled outer lip; slanting sides; small rounded bottom.
- Cut decoration on interior, comprising three grooves around sides, 0.35-0.5, 0.6-0.8 and 3.6-3.8 below rim.
- Intact; faint iridescent weathering and dulling; many pinprick bubbles; rotary polishing marks on interior, fire-polished on exterior.

Similar to 34 (A1880.18.2) and 35 (A1880.18.4)

37   A1883.22.4   Hemispherical bowl

Pale yellowish-green
Mid-second to early first century BC; probably Syro-Palestinian
H 7.0, D (rim) 14.7

- Slightly inverted rounded rim; convex sides curving in to round bottom.
- Wheel-cut decoration on exterior, comprising two concentric circles (D 5.8-5.95 and 4.95-5.4) around bottom; on interior, two sets of two grooves (1.0 and 1.4, 5.9 and 6.0 below rim; depth of lower set 8.6 and 8.1).
- One small hole and a larger patch of fill in side; iridescent pitting on interior, thick enamel-like weathering on exterior, flaking to leave dulling and patches of iridescence.

Compare Grose 1989, 206-7 nos 218-22

38   A1879.34.1.4   Rim fragment

Yellow-green
Mid-second to early first century BC; formerly Northesk Collection
L 5.1, H 3.8, Th 0.4-0.2

- Three horizontal cut grooves on interior below rim. Probably part of a hemispherical bowl.
- Dulling; pinprick bubbles.

Compare Grose 1989, 206 no. 218

39   A1921.202   Rim fragment

Brownish-yellow; first century BC; from Cyprus
L 6.5, H 4.0, Th 0.4

- Rounded rim; convex curving side.
- On exterior, decoration of pronounced ribs (five extant), with flattened end at the top of each rib; on interior, two horizontal cut grooves, 3.6 and 6.0 below rim.
- Faint iridescent weathering in patches; dulling elsewhere.

Compare Grose 1989, 207 no. 223

Mosaic

41   40

40   A1883.22.1   Deep bowl

Deep purple, light blue, green, opaque yellow and opaque white in spiral canes, stripes and blocks
Early second century BC
H 7.4, D (rim) 13.3-13.4, D (base) 5.0

- Rounded, slightly inverted rim; hemispherical body; convex sides curving in to small, slightly concave bottom. Composite mosaic pattern formed from polygonal sections of a cane; one millifiori cane in side. Purple network cane wound spirally with a opaque white thread to form added rim band. Fire-polished.
- Broken and mended; some iridescence, pitting and dulling.

Compare Grose 1989, 190-1, 198-9 no. 184

41   A1883.22.2   Shallow dish

Blue, purple, green, opaque white and opaque yellow in spiral canes, stripes and blocks
Second to mid-first century BC
H 3.1, D (rim) 12.75-12.6

- Rounded, slightly everted rim; gently curving sides; shallow convex bottom.
- Composite mosaic pattern formed from polygonal sections of a cane. Added rim band in blue and opaque yellow stripes, closely twisted at one end but widely spaced at the other. Fire-polished.
- Intact; some dulling and surface pitting.

For discussion of this type of shallow dish, see Grose 1989, 191-2 fig. 105.

Compare (for similar colours and pattern) Grose 1989, 201 no. 196; *Ancient Glass* 2001, 88 and 202 no. 119; *JGS* 47 (2005), 215 no. 1

Notes

1   See *Wolf* 1994, 37, 44 and fig. 175. This is also shown on two core-formed vessel fragments in NMS: (a) part of an amphoriskos – cat. no. 29 (A1965.249) – and (b) an unidentified body fragment (A1965.255) in translucent purple with opaque turquoise blue trails; vertical ribbing over broadly spaced horizontal festoon trails; thick encrusted matter on interior.
2   See Grose 1989, 110-31; *Wolf* 1994, 38.
3   See, for example, the finds from Gordion in central Anatolia, indicating that although sea-borne trade

played a significant part in the dispersion of core-formed vessels such objects also reached inland areas; cf. Duncan Jones 1995, *passim*. Three vessels of Mediterranean Group I are also in the Afyon Museum; see Lightfoot 1989, 21-2 nos 1-3.
4   Grose 1989, 122-5.
5   I owe this very helpful suggestion to David Grose. For a late Hellenistic alabastron in silver and glass, see Hill 1972, *passim*.

Roman Luxury Glass

The skill and inventiveness of glassmakers and glassworkers in the Roman world are best illustrated by the top-of-the-range vessels. In colour, shape and decoration these glasses often imitated luxury items in other materials, especially gold, silver and semi-precious stones. But, in addition, Roman craftsmen were able to exploit the special qualities of glass to create masterpieces that find no parallel in any other medium. Many of these pieces, while based on practical forms, are so intricate and delicate that they can never have been used or, indeed, intended for use. Some Roman luxury glass, therefore, must have been only for display, intended as decorative ornaments to please the eye of the owner and to impress his guests; see no. 51 (shown below).[1] As such they should be imagined against the background of a richly decorated, if sparsely furnished, room, adding further colour to the brightly painted wall frescoes and the polychrome marble floors and fittings.

42

42 A1983.1104 Fragment of cameo glass, head of satyr

Opaque white and translucent dark blue; probably blown, cased and carved
Late first century BC to first century AD; probably Italian
H 3.0

- The fragment, probably from a cup or bowl, depicts part of a male figure that appears to be crouching, kneeling or sitting, with the hand of a second figure resting on his head. The figure, which may be identified as a satyr, faces to the right, but his head is turned to the left so that he is looking back over his bare right shoulder towards the figure whose left hand has seized him by his tussled hair.

For general discussion of Roman cameo glass, see Goldstein 1982, 8-19 (with 98-104 nos 1-17); Whitehouse 1997, 41. For similar fragments in the Corning Museum of Glass, see Whitehouse 1997, 58-65 nos 59-75. Few examples of early Roman cameo glass are provenanced, but they appear to have been found mainly in Italy (especially at Rome itself) and Asia Minor; see Whitehouse 1991, 19-25. For the only known example excavated in Roman Britain, see Lightfoot 1988.

Published: *JGS* 26 (1984), 136 no. 1

43 A1987.355 Gold-band carinated bottle

Dark blue, green, opaque yellow and opaque white, turquoise blue, gold and colourless bands; cast and cut
Early to mid-first century AD; probably Italian
H 9.4, D (rim) 2.1, D (max.) 5.4

- Everted rim, flat on top and tapering outer lip; cylindrical neck; sloping narrow shoulder; conical upper body, then inverted conical undercurve; slightly concave bottom.
- Decoration of three fine grooves on body: two at top, 2.8-2.9 and 2.95-3.05 below rim, the third 7.7-7.8 below rim; two concentric grooves on base: 2.6 and 1.9 in diameter.
- Broken and mended, some fill. Slight surface dulling.

The complex process by which such vessels were made is still improperly understood. Strips of gold foil were combined with layers of coloured glass, the opaque white and yellow stripes serving to highlight the broad bands in the darker, translucent colours. These were then fused together during the casting of the vessel. This was the most expensive and luxurious form of ribbon mosaic glassmaking. As a consequence its use was restricted to a number of small vessel forms (see Grose 1984, 31-2 figs 10-11). As well as perfume bottles such as the present example, lidded boxes (small pyxides; see Harden 1987, 42 no. 18) and other small items of tableware were manufactured. For examples of gold-glass vessels and objects, see von Saldern 1974, 102-5 nos 269-77; Goldstein 1979, 203-8 nos 556-87; Milleker 2000, 64, fig. 52.

Isings Form 7
Compare MMA 17.194.259 (Oliver 1967, 23 no. 1); CMG 59.1.87 (Harden 1987, 41 no. 17; Whitehouse 1996, 8 and fig. 1); La Baume 1977, 29 no. 30; *Fitzwilliam* 1978, 25 no. 36; *Luzern* 1981, 68 no. 198; *Kofler* 1985, 94 lot 161; *Verres* 1985, 45 no. 97 (with refs); Maier 1994, 269 and fig. 244 (from a Roman tomb at Nea Paphos, Cyprus); Kunina 1997, 268 no. 96; Sternini 1998, 70 no. VI9 (with refs); Tartari 2005, 109-10 no. 186, fig. 5 (from Dyrrachium); Page 2006, 29 and fig. 6.1

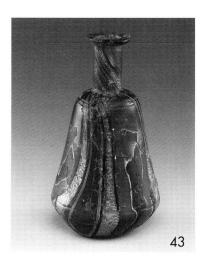

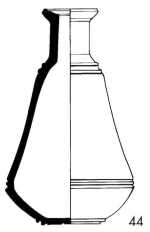

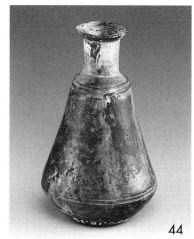

43

44

44

44 A1880.18.16 Carinated bottle

Opaque deep blue; cast and lathe-cut
First century AD; probably Italian; formerly Piot Collection
H 8.15, D (rim) 2.3, D (max.) 5.05, D (base) 2.35

- Flaring rim, tapering to pointed lip; cylindrical neck; conical upper body, then inverted conical undercurve; flat bottom.
- Decoration of cut grooves and raised circles, comprising (a) two concentric grooves on inner edge of mouth, (b) a single concentric groove on outer edge of mouth, (c) two grooves and two raised circles at top of body, (d) two grooves at bottom of conical sides, (e) two raised circles between undercurve and base, and (f) small groove around centre of bottom.
- Intact, except for small chip in rim; some fine enamel-like weathering and iridescence; pitting of surface bubbles; rotary polishing marks.

The method of manufacture for such cast bottles remains uncertain; it may have involved the use of a removable core-mould. Similar vessels were also made by glassblowers either as free-blown or mould-blown bottles; see von Saldern 1968, no. 26 (blown with cut decoration); Platz-Horster 1976, 28 no. 30; Matheson 1980, 22 no. 57 (blown); *Napoli* 1986, 220 no. 20 (blown with linear cut decoration, from Pompeii); *Constable-Maxwell* 1979, 62 lot 91 (mould-blown); Stern 1995, 148-9 no. 49 (mould-blown). The shape was also used for metal and pottery vessels. For example in red-slip pottery found at Amorium in eastern Phrygia (Turkey), see Lightfoot 2003, 342, fig. 1,8.

Similar to no. 43

45 A1880.18.11 Cosmetic jar (pyxis)

Translucent deep green; cast and wheel-ground; fire-polished
First half of first century AD; probably Italian; formerly Piot Collection
H 4.8-4.7, D (rim) 11.5-11.4, D (base) 11.1-11.0

- Thick, horizontal projecting rim; vertical sides; projecting base-ring; flat bottom.
- Cut decoration on bottom, comprising a central raised boss and a raised circle around the edge.
- Intact; pinprick bubbles and impurity streaks; patches of enamel-like weathering and dulling; circular grinding marks on bottom, sides and interior.

Compare Merseyside 1979, no. A12; see also Grose 1989, 255 fig. 139; Grose 1991, 10 pl. III*b*

45

47   46

46 A1966.358 Marbled perfume bottle

Deep amber brown and opaque white; cast and blown
Early to mid-first century AD; probably Italian
H 7.0, D (rim) 2.1-2.0, D (base) 6.4-6.3

- Everted rim with chamfered upper edge; cylindrical, slightly convex neck; squat, bulbous body;
  slightly concave bottom.
- Marbled mosaic pattern formed from canes of
  translucent and opaque glass.
- Intact. No weathering, except for slight surface
  dulling.

Probably Italian, although marbled perfume bottles
are a fairly common type, and it would seem that
they or their makers travelled widely. A similar vessel
was found in a tomb (Grave 1B) in the al-Hajjar
necropolis on the island of Bahrain in the Persian
Gulf; see Lombard 1989, 117 no. 208.

For discussion of cast and blown mosaic bottles,
see Grose 1989, 261-2; Whitehouse 1997, 39. In
decoration these glass vessels resemble early imperial
marbled pottery; see *Napoli* 1986, 194 nos 151-2.
Both were deliberate imitations of vessels carved
from semi-precious stone, especially sardonyx; see
no. 109. For bottles of the same form in gold-glass,
see MMA 30.115.16 (Oliver 1967, 23 no. 3, fig. 17);
Kunina 1997, 268 no. 95. For an unusual millifiori
example, see *Winfield Smith* 1957, 85 no. 141.

Isings Form 6
Compare *Winfield Smith* 1957, 89 no. 149; von Saldern 1974, 132
no. 365; *Fitzwilliam* 1978, 25 no. 38; *Kofler* 1985, 78-84 lots 131,
133-47; Grose 1989, 339-40 no. 609; *Ancient Glass* 2001, 95 and
203 no. 127; Arveiller-Dulong and Nenna 2005, 74-5 nos 94-5
and 97

47 A1880.18.32 Marbled perfume bottle

Deep amber brown and opaque white; cast and blown
Early to mid-first century AD; formerly Piot Collection
H 5.45, D (rim) 1.7, D (base) 5.1

- Everted rim with flat upper edge; cylindrical,
  slightly convex neck; squat, bulbous body; slightly
  concave bottom.
- Marbled mosaic pattern formed from canes of
  translucent and opaque glass.
- Broken and mended around base of neck; small
  chips in rim. No weathering.

Produced by a combination of casting and blowing;
see Grose 1989, 261-2. The marble pattern was made
by fusing together different coloured canes of glass,
which were then blown into the required shape.

Similar to no. 46

48 A1880.18.33 Marbled perfume bottle

Deep brown(?) and opaque white; cast and blown
Early to mid-first century AD; formerly Piot Collection
H 7.0, D (rim) 2.2, D (base) 5.4-5.2

- Everted rim with flat upper edge; cylindrical neck, slightly tooled at top and bottom; piriform body; slightly concave bottom.
- Marbled mosaic pattern formed from canes of translucent and opaque glass.
- Intact. Thick white enamel weathering and iridescence.

Similar to nos 46 and 47; compare also von Saldern 1974, 130 no. 354.[2]

49 A1879.34.19 Disk fragment

Colourless; blown and cut; probably second to third century AD
L 4.3, Th 0.2

- Rounded circular edge; bowed in shape.
- Cut decoration comprises a grooved border around edge surrounding a head (possibly Medusa) on an arched platform, flanked to right by an uncertain creature or object (a sea monster?); below arch, a stick or wand with a knobbed end.

The grooved edge suggests that the piece was originally fixed in a setting, perhaps as a large pendant or as an inlay. However, the fact that the object is not flat but is slightly bowed may indicate that it has been cut down from a vessel.

For mid-imperial vessels with engraved decoration, see discussion in Whitehouse 1997, 222.

50 A1880.18.76 Flask

Colourless; blown and gilded
Third to fourth century AD; formerly Piot Collection
H 11.6, D (rim) 3.9, D (body) 9.0

- Vertical, thickened and rounded rim; funnel neck; spherical body; concave bottom.
- Gold-leaf decoration on neck and body: horizontal line below rim; band with downward saw-like edge at base of neck; on shoulder, lines radiating

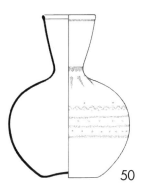

from base of neck; on upper body, wavy line with dots above and below; on body, parallel lines interspersed with dots.
- Intact, but some of decoration is fugitive. Some enamel-like weathering and dulling on exterior; soil encrusted with iridescent weathering on interior; pinprick bubbles.

Described in the NMS register as 'late Byzantine or mediaeval'. No detailed scientific analysis has as yet been carried out to verify that the gilding is ancient, but it is here assumed to be so, despite the fact that some Roman glasses are known to have embellished in modern times with gilding and other forms of decoration; for an example in the MMA (26.82.1), see Pilosi 1998, esp. 25-6.

For discussion of this type of flask or globular jar, see Isings Form 104b; Whitehouse 1997, 161-2 no. 279 (with additional refs). There are relatively few examples of Roman glass vessels decorated with surface gilding; Whitehouse 1989, 97-8. For individual pieces, see *Winfield Smith* 1957, 169-71 nos 346-50; Thomas 1976, 28 no. 113; Matheson 1980, 95-6 no. 257; Follmann-Schulz 1992, 76-81 nos 42-3; *Benzian* 1994, 72-3 lot 133.

51 A1983.61 Large jug, with miniature vessel inside

Pale green, with dark blue trails; blown and trailed
Fourth century AD; probably eastern Mediterranean
H (max.) 33.3, H (to rim) 29.0, D (rim) 9.85, D (body) 13.4, D (base) 9.7-9.3

- Rounded rim; broad, flaring mouth; conical neck, expanding downwards to join imperceptibly with piriform body; deep, pushed-in bottom with pontil scar; thick rod handle, tooled into deep ribs, attached to body at point of greatest diameter, drawn up in a straight line at an angle away from vessel, turned in at an acute angle, trailed onto rim, splayed out into wings to either side and tooled up into a thumb-rest in the middle with backward curl at end.
- On underside of mouth, a single trail applied before handle; around neck, thick band applied as coil and then tooled, with irregular, pinched and slanting ribs; similar tooled coil applied around bottom to form crimpt base-ring. Attached to bottom inside vessel is a small, two-handled flask with trailed decoration; handles in dark blue, pressed onto shoulder and drawn up vertically, then turned in and onto neck; trail applied to rim and wound round in a spiral neck to top of handles.
- Intact, except for internal strain cracks around neck and body; top of thumb-rest to handle broken and mended. Patches of iridescent weathering and dulling; one streak of opaque white glass in handle, with white gritty inclusion; pinprick and larger bubbles.

Other examples of 'flasks within flasks' are known from both the West, notably Cologne, and the East; see Fremersdorf 1959, 60-1; La Baume 1964, 61 no. 49; Abdul Hak 1965, 33 (found in excavations at Homs, Syria); Barag 1970, 74-5 and *8 (English summary); Lang 1978, 147, illus. 42: drawing of a 'glass decanter with smaller vessel inside (Garni, tenth century)'; Harter 1999, 140 and 274 no. 0141 (from a sarcophagus in Mainz, dated to the first half or middle of the fourth century AD); von Saldern 2004, 513-14.

Part of another example was found recently in a late Roman burial at Gloucester; it comprised the base of the outer large colourless vessel and the intact smaller vessel attached to it; Cool 2003, 248. This miniature vessel is in the form of an amphoriskos with blue handles and an opaque yellow trail decorating the body. These colours and design show a close resemblance to so-called snake-thread decoration, which was a distinctive feature of the Cologne workshops; see Harden 1987, 104-8.

Stern has recently pointed out that the production of such complex vessels in different parts of the Roman world means that there must have been direct contact between craftsmen, for only in that way could the necessary skills have been passed on from one workshop to another; see Stern 1999a, 482.

For jugs with the same treatment of the handle and similar decorative elements, compare Yağcı 1990, 34 illus. 35 (Hatay Museum, inv. no. 8559, recorded as purchased by Sir Leonard Wooley in 1933); Kunina 1997, 331-2 nos 394-6, 398 (usually regarded as Syrian, but examples of this type of jug are also found in Asia Minor and the Black Sea region); Whitehouse 2001, 215-16 no. 783 (with opaque white 'feather' decoration).

Published: *Constable-Maxwell* 1979, 142-3 lot 258; *JGS* 26 (1984), 136 no. 2

Notes

1 Even utilitarian forms such as the late Roman kohl bottle – for example, as no. 265 (A1961.953) – could be adapted for such display pieces; see also *Kofler* 1985, 20 lot 22; Harden 1987, 149-50 no. 77.
2 Additionally, there is a fragment (A1879.34.16.4) of another marbled bottle in deep purple and opaque white.

Roman Cast Fragments

The cast fragments, all from the Northesk Collection, constitute a rich and varied assemblage, representing many of the different types of luxury glass that were produced in the first decades of the first century AD. All were obtained in Italy, and probably most of them came from dealers and traders in Rome itself (see above, pp. 7-8). The collection in the Toledo Museum of Art, being the only one to have been fully published, provides most of the parallels for the pieces in the NMS described below. Together they show the extraordinary range of colours that the glassmakers were able to produce and the originality of designs and colour combinations that were then achieved.[1]

52   A1879.34.2.13   Base fragment

Opaque copper red; monochrome glass
L 7.35, W 3.4, H (with base-ring) 0.8, Th 0.2

- Flat bottom; low rounded base-ring. Probably part of a dish.
- Upper surface polished and unweathered; edges and underside covered in verdigris and corrosion from the leeching out of the copper colourising agent.

For similar inlay fragments, see no. 123. Many of the surviving intact vessels are small bowls, but the NMS fragment shows that larger dishes were also made in this copper-rich and thus heavily weighted glass; see von Saldern 1974, 108 no. 286 (contrast a larger bowl; *loc. cit.* no. 287); Auth 1976, 193 nos 292 and 294; Goldstein 1979, 145 no. 299; Grose 1989, 306-7 nos 424-5 and 427; *Wolf* 1994, 328 no. 99 (with refs); Kunina 1997, 259-60 no. 63 (a shallow plate, from the Panticapaeum necropolis). For a miniature sculpture also in opaque red glass, see Whitehouse 1997, 30-1 no. 29.[2]
   Other vessels in copper red glass include two piriform cast and cut bottles, see *Benzian* 1994, 36 lot 50 and *British Rail* 1997, 22-3 lot 8. Four other small bowls are known (one in the MMA [13.198.1], another in Berlin), while two others were formerly in well-known private collections; see Platz-Horster 1976, 29 no. 32 (with discussion and refs); *Constable-Maxwell* 1979, 31 lot 29; *Kofler* 1985, 96 lot 166. For discussion of the chemical composition of this type of opaque red glass, see Brill 1988.

For the vessel shape of the NMS fragment, compare Grose 1989, 310-11 nos 446-8

53   A1879.34.2.33   Base fragment

Opaque pale blue; monochrome glass
L 5.7, W 2.8, H (with base-ring) 0.7, Th 0.4

- Slightly convex side; flat bottom; low rounded base-ring. Probably part of a dish.
- Milky weathering film on exterior, partly flaked off.

Similar to no. 52. For colour, compare Goldstein 1979, 145-6 no. 301; Grose 1989, 307 no. 428

54   A1879.34.7.35   Rim fragment

Network glass.[3]
L 3.2, H 2.5

- Applied coil rim with rounded edge in colourless glass wound spirally with a broad blue and a fine opaque white thread; on body, five horizontal canes of colourless glass, each decorated with two spirally twisted opaque white threads.
- Faint dulling and iridescence.

This type of decoration is also known as reticella. For discussion, see Grose 1989, 253.

Compare Goldstein 1979, 193-5, nos 523-8; Grose 1989, especially 301-2 nos 400-1

55   A1879.34.7.32   Rim fragment

Network glass
L 1.85, H 3.05, Th 0.3-0.15

- Applied coil rim with rounded edge in colourless glass with spiral decoration in dark translucent blue and opaque white threads; straight side to body, tapering slightly at bottom, in vertical, wavy canes of colourless glass with opaque white threads.
- Dulling, slight iridescence and pitting.

Similar to no. 54

56   A1879.34.7.30   Rim fragment

Network glass
L 3.05, H 2.1, Th 0.25-0.1

- Applied coil rim with rounded edge in colourless glass with very fine opaque white spiral thread; straight side to body in colourless glass with single white spiral thread in slanting canes.
- Highly polished exterior surface; iridescent weathering and pitting on interior.

Similar to no. 54

57 A1879.34.7.33 Rim fragment

Network glass
L 2.3, H 2.1, Th 0.2

- Applied coil rim with rounded edge in blue and opaque white spiral threads; on body, side tapering slightly downwards in colourless glass with single white spiral thread in vertical canes.
- Polished exterior surface; slight dulling and pitting on interior.

Similar to no. 54

58 A1879.34.7.34 Rim fragment

Network glass
L 2.25, H 2.5, Th 0.2-0.1

- Applied coil rim with rounded edge in translucent purple with fine opaque white spiral thread; colourless body with single white spiral thread in vertical canes.
- Polished exterior surface; slight dulling and pitting on interior.

59 A1879.34.7.31 Rim fragment

Network glass
L 2.65, H 2.25, Th 0.2-0.1

- Applied coil rim with rounded edge in purple and opaque white spiral threads; on body, colourless horizontal canes with white spiral threads.
- Polished exterior surface; slight dulling and pitting on interior.

60 A1879.34.7.6 Rim fragment

Ribbon glass.[4]
L 3.55, H 3.3, Th 0.25

- Applied coil rim with rounded, vertical edge in colourless glass with opaque yellow thread; on body with almost vertical side (viewed from exterior), slanting from top left to bottom right, a pattern of roughly straight bands in green, opaque yellow sandwiched in colourless glass, yellow thread and colourless, cobalt blue and opaque deep red, flanked by two narrow opaque white stripes. Almost vertical side. Probably from a hemispherical bowl.
- Faint dulling.

For discussion of vessels decorated with ribbon glass, see Grose 1989, 249-52.

Compare Goldstein 1979, 197-202, especially nos 536, 540 and 542; Grose 1989, especially 289 no. 339 and 292 no. 353

61 A1879.34.7.3 Rim fragment

Ribbon glass
L 2.85, H 3.05, Th 0.25-0.15

- Applied coil rim in colourless glass with fine yellow spiral thread; on body, colourless glass with canes in blue, opaque brick red, yellow and white; yellow and blue overlaid to produce green.
- Highly polished exterior; iridescence and dulling on interior.

Compare Grose 1989, 289 no. 339

62 A1879.34.7.2 Rim fragment

Ribbon glass
L 3.2, H 2.05, Th 0.15-0.1

- Applied coil rim in colourless glass with fine yellow spiral thread; on body, canes in slanting stripes of colourless glass with yellow spiral thread, cobalt blue, turquoise, opaque brick red, yellow and white; yellow and turquoise overlaid to produce green.
- Polished exterior; dulling and slight iridescence on interior.

Similar to no. 61

63   A1879.34.7.9   Rim fragment

Ribbon glass
L 2.85, H 2.6, Th 0.25-0.1

- Applied coil rim with rounded outsplayed edge in colourless glass with opaque yellow thread; on body with side tapering downwards, banded decoration in translucent honey brown, cobalt blue with opaque brick red stripe inside, colourless with opaque yellow on interior, colourless flanked on either side by yellow. Side tapering downwards. Possibly from a shallow dish.
- Highly polished exterior surface; dulling and pitting on interior.

Compare Grose 1989, especially 284 no. 318 and 291 no. 350

64   A1879.34.7.10   Rim fragment

Ribbon glass
L 3.35, H 2.5, Th 0.2

- Applied coil rim with rounded vertical edge in blue with pale yellow spiral thread; on body, banded decoration in translucent honey brown with opaque yellow thread on both surfaces, deep turquoise blue-green, another honey brown band, cobalt blue, colourless with opaque yellow sandwich, deep purple, and honey brown with opaque white sandwich. From a deep bowl.
- Dulling on exterior surface; iridescent weathering on interior.

Compare Grose 1989, especially 285-6 no. 324 and 288 no. 333

65   A1879.34.7.1   Rim fragment

Ribbon glass
L 2.6, H 2.65, Th 0.25-0.15

- Applied coil rim with rounded vertical edge, decorated with yellow spiral thread; on body, horizontal bands around curving sides to body in pale blue-green with opaque yellow and cobalt blue.

- Highly polished exterior surface; iridescent weathering and pitting on interior.

The horizontal banding is unusual. Compare Grose 1989, 288-9 no. 337 and 291 no. 348

66   A1879.34.7.19   Rim fragment

Ribbon glass
L 4.4, H 2.2, Th 0.2-0.15

- Applied coil rim with rounded edge in blue with opaque white spiral thread on interior; slanting bands on body, blue with opaque white thread on interior, blue with opaque yellow sandwich appearing green, colourless with single yellow spiral thread.
- Polished exterior surface; dulling, pitting and slight iridescence on interior.

Compare Grose 1989, 286 no. 325

67   A1879.34.7.21   Rim fragment

Ribbon glass; L 2.65, H 1.95, Th 0.3-0.2
- Applied coil rim with rounded edge in colourless glass with yellow spiral thread; mosaic body with sections and lengths/stripes in blue, yellow, brick red and white.
- Broken and repaired. Dulling and slight iridescence.

Compare Grose 1989, 284-5 no. 319

68   A1879.34.7.18   Rim fragment

Ribbon glass; L 3.8, H 1.75, Th 0.2
- Applied coil rim with rounded edge in colourless glass with yellow spiral thread; on body, canes in blue, turquoise and purple, and irregular stripes in opaque yellow and white, with colourless coils decorated with spiral yellow threads.
- Polished exterior; pitting and dulling on interior.

Compare Grose 1989, 286 no. 328

69 A1879.34.7.4 Rim fragment

Ribbon glass
L 4.15, H 2.6, Th 0.25-0.2

- Applied coil rim in blue, opaque white and colourless spiral threads; mosaic body with slanting stripes in blue, opaque white and yellow, brick red and colourless glass, including one spiral band in blue and opaque white. Probably from a hemispherical bowl.
- Highly polished exterior; slight dulling, pitting and iridescence on interior.

Similar to no. 68; compare also Follmann-Schulz 1992, 11 nos 2-3 (the latter from excavations at Neuss, Germany in 1893)

70 A1879.34.7.25 Rim fragment

Ribbon glass
L 1.9, H 2.85, Th 0.15

- Applied coil rim in blue with opaque white stripe thread on interior; on body, wavy horizontal bands on body in translucent blue, opaque white, red and yellow stripes, together with vertical stripes in blue and white.
- Open vessel, clearly intended to be viewed from above showing polychrome decoration on interior. Part of a shallow bowl or possibly from a lens-shaped dish; see Grose 1989, 252.
- Polished exterior; slight dulling and iridescence on interior.

Compare Grose 1989, 293-4 no. 359 (with very similar design)

71 A1879.34.7.12 Rim fragment

Ribbon glass
L 2.9, H 2.05, Th 0.15

- Applied coil rim in blue with opaque white stripe thread on interior; on body, wavy horizontal bands in translucent blue and honey brown, with opaque white, brick red and yellow.

- Highly polished exterior; iridescent weathering on interior.

Similar to no. 70

72 A1879.34.7.16 Rim fragment

Ribbon glass
L. 3.15, H. 2.5, Th. 0.25-0.2

- Applied coil rim in blue and white spiral threads; on body, wavy slanting bands in colourless with yellow spiral thread, cobalt blue, turquoise and opaque white.
- Thick iridescent weathering and dulling.

73 A1879.34.7.5 Rim fragment

Ribbon glass
L. 3.35, H. 3.8, Th. 0.25-0.15

- Applied coil rim in purple and colourless glass with fine white spiral thread; on body, canes in vertical stripes of purple, turquoise, colourless, opaque yellow and white; the turquoise and yellow segments are overlaid to give a green colour. Probably part of a large bowl with offset rim; for shape, see Grose 1989, 287 no. 329.
- Slight dulling and faint iridescence.

For shape, see Grose 1989, 287 no. 329

74 A1879.34.7.15 Rim fragment

Ribbon glass
L 2.3, H 1.8, Th 0.2

- Applied coil rim in colourless glass with fine yellow spiral thread; on body, canes in wavy, horizontal lines in cobalt blue, turquoise, opaque yellow and white, and colourless with yellow spiral thread; yellow and turquoise overlaid to produce green.
- Polished exterior; iridescent weathering on interior.

75   A1879.34.5.4   Rim fragment

Ribbon glass
L. 2.7, H. 1.8; Th. 0.3

- Applied coil rim in colourless glass with blue and opaque white spiral threads; on body, wavy, vertical stripes in blue, yellow, purple and white as sandwich between layers of colourless glass.
- Polished exterior; iridescence and dulling on interior.

Compare Grose 1989, 285-6 no. 324

76   A1879.34.5.8   Rim fragment

Ribbon glass
L. 2.9, H 2.8, Th 0.3-0.2

- Applied coil rim in colourless glass with blue and opaque yellow spiral threads; on body, vertical stripes in turquoise blue and yellow, appearing green, yellow, blue, brick red, in places as sandwich between layers of colourless glass.
- Polished exterior; faint iridescence, dulling and pitting on interior.

Compare Grose 1989, 288 nos 333-4

77   A1879.34.5.1   Rim fragment

Ribbon glass
L. 3.45, H 2.65, Th 0.35-0.3

- Vertical, rounded, coil rim, applied to outer lip, in colourless glass with fine, opaque yellow vertical stripes; convex side, curving in at bottom; on body, wavy bands in blue, yellow and light honey brown as sandwich between layers of colourless glass.
- Polished exterior; brown, creamy weathering and dulling on interior.

78   A1879.34.1.128   Rim fragment

Ribbon glass
L 2.85, H 2.25, Th 0.2-0.1

- Coil rim with white thread on inner edge; straight, slanting side; on body, dark purple with specks of opaque white, yellow, brick red and wavy blue stripes, slanting from top left to bottom right.
- Polished exterior; iridescent weathering on interior.

79   A1879.34.5.12   Rim fragment

Short-strip mosaic glass
L 4.85, H 2.6, Th 0.25-0.15

- Applied coil rim in blue with white stripe on inner edge; on body, canes in blue, brick red, white, yellow (appearing green in places) and colourless glass. Probably part of a hemispherical bowl.
- Polished surfaces.

Compare Grose 1989, 296-8 nos 374-5 and 380

80   A1879.34.5.9   Rim fragment

Short-strip mosaic glass
L 4.6, H 2.75, Th 0.3-0.2

- Applied coil rim in cobalt blue with fine white spiral thread; on body, slabs and sections in colour-less, cobalt blue, yellow (appearing green in places), brick red and white.
- Polished exterior; iridescent weathering on interior.

Similar to no. 79

81 A1879.34.5.14 Rim fragment

Short-strip mosaic glass
L 2.75, H 2.5, Th 0.2

- Applied coil rim in colourless glass with vertical, opaque white stripes; on body, sections in yellow, brick red, white, blue, and yellow with blue appearing green, as sandwich between layers of colourless glass.
- Polished exterior; iridescence and dulling on interior.

Similar to no. 79

82 A1879.34.6.27 Base fragment

Mosaic glass; L 6.5, H 3.3, Th 0.45-0.3

- Rounded edge; outsplayed base-ring. Swirling pattern in deep (almost opaque) purple, opaque white and colourless glass, with unusually large areas of transparency. Part of a large vase or bowl; see Grose 1989, 248.
- Polished exterior; iridescent weathering and dulling on interior.

Compare Grose 1989, 277 nos 283-4 and 336 nos 589-91; *Wolf* 1994, 316 no. 93

83 A1879.34.6.18 Rim fragment
of carinated bowl

Mosaic glass
L 8.55, H 4.1, Th 0.25-0.1

- Everted, rounded rim; side in two convex curves. Polygonal sections of circular floral patterns in opaque blue, white and yellow; blue and yellow overlaid to produce green.
- Dulling; slight weathering, especially on breaks; deep pitting of surface bubbles.

For discussion of mosaic carinated bowls, see Grose 1989, 256-8.

Compare Grose 1989, 319 no. 500; *Wolf* 1994, 330-1 nos 100-1

84 A1879.34.6.22 Rim fragment
of carinated bowl

Mosaic glass
L 8.55, H 4.1, Th 0.25-0.1

- Everted, horizontal rim; double convex side to body, decorated with polygonal sections of circular floral patterns in deep purple and opaque white.
- Highly polished exterior; dulling, iridescence and pitting on interior.

Similar to no. 83
For the pattern, compare Grose 1989, 319 no. 498

85 A1879.34.6.1 Rim fragment

Mosaic glass
L 5.0, H 2.7, Th 0.4-0.2

- Thick, rounded, everted rim; sides curving in downwards, decorated with a pattern in deep (almost opaque) purple, blue and opaque white. Part of a large vessel, possibly a carinated dish; see Grose 1989, 257-8.
- Iridescent weathering and dulling on exterior; highly polished surface on interior.

Compare Grose 1989, 308 no. 431

86 A1879.34.6.33 Rim fragment

Mosaic glass
L 3.5, H 1.4, Th 0.25

- Everted, rounded, horizontal rim; double convex side to body, decorated with polygonal sections, edged in opaque white, of circular patterns of colourless, pale purple, opaque yellow, white and red; red dot at centre surrounded by a white circle and yellow dots. Part of a large vessel, probably a carinated dish.
- Polished exterior; dulling and iridescent weathering on interior.

Similar to no. 85

87 A1879.34.6.12 Rim fragment
of carinated bowl

Mosaic glass; L 2.7, H 2.35, Th 0.3

- Everted, rounded, horizontal rim; double convex side to body, decorated with a pattern in opaque white radiating veins around central yellow dots circled in red on a slightly translucent turquoise blue ground.
- Polished exterior; dulling and iridescence on interior.

Compare Grose 1989, 319 no. 497 (slightly different pattern)

88 A1879.34.6.19 Rim fragment
of carinated bowl

Mosaic glass; L 2.3, H 2.3, Th 0.25-0.15

- Everted, rounded, horizontal rim; double convex side to body in greyish-turquoise blue-green ground with a pattern of circular designs comprising a white centre, encircled in red, with black band and yellow dots.
- Polished exterior; dulling, pitting and iridescent weathering on interior.

Compare Grose 1989, 316 no. 483 and 317 no. 487

89 A1879.34.6.2 Rim fragment
of carinated bowl

Mosaic glass
L 3.1, H 2.75, Th 0.25

- Everted, rounded, horizontal rim; double convex side to body in translucent purple polygonal sections, outlined in opaque white, with two different central designs: (a) white dot within a red circle, surrounded by yellow spots and (b) green floral pattern with yellow spokes.
- Dulling, iridescence and deep pitting on exterior; polished interior.

Compare Grose 1989, 331 no. 562 (very similar pattern)

90 A1879.34.6.4 Rim fragment

Mosaic glass
L 2.8, H 1.6, Th 0.3-0.1

- Applied coil rim with rounded vertical edge in translucent dark purple with white thread on inner edge; slightly convex side to body in purple, cobalt blue, opaque red, white, yellow and colourless glass, with yellow and blue mixed in places, appearing as green. Probably part of a hemispherical bowl.
- Polished exterior; dulling on interior.

Compare Grose 1989, 303 no. 411

91 A1879.34.7.24 Rim fragment

Mosaic glass
L 2.55, H 2.05, Th 0.25-0.15

- Applied coil rim in blue with fine white threads on inner edge; on body, sections in purple, opaque yellow and white. Probably part of a deep bowl.
- Iridescent weathering, dulling and pitting.

Compare *Wolf* 1994, no. 77

92   A1879.34.6.31   Rim fragment

Mosaic glass
L 6.5, H 3.3, Th 0.45-0.3

- Rounded, everted rim; straight sides, tapering downwards. Floral pattern in cobalt blue with irregular sections in opaque yellow, brick red and white.
- Polished exterior; iridescent weathering on interior.

Compare Grose 1989, 333-4 nos 578-9

93   A1879.34.6.3   Rim fragment

Mosaic glass
L 3.05, H 2.1, Th 0.2

- Rounded applied coil rim in cobalt blue; sections in cobalt blue and turquoise with opaque yellow and white, overlaid to appear as green, and purple in stripes and circles.
- Polished exterior; iridescence and pitting on interior.

For the applied rim, see Grose 1989, 253-4.

Compare Grose 1989, 277, 279 no. 287 (ribbed bowl fragment)

94   A1879.34.2.65   Rim fragment of large dish or bowl

Mosaic glass
L 3.25, H 3.35, Th 0.3

- Rounded edge to broad, horizontal rim in translucent turquoise blue with hollow circles of opaque yellow, making glass appear green.
- Polished exterior; iridescence, pitting and dulling on interior; burst surface bubbles.

Compare Grose 1989, 325-6 no. 530 (where the glass is simply described as green with opaque yellow circles)

95   A1879.34.2.76   Rim fragment of bowl

Mosaic glass; L 2.4, H 1.7, Th 0.4

- Plain angular rim with sloping side to body in translucent turquoise blue with hollow circles of opaque yellow, making glass appear green.
- Fine cut groove, 0.25 below rim, on exterior.
- Dulling and faint iridescence.

Similar pattern to no. 94. For cut decoration on mosaic vessels, see Grose 1989, 260

96   A1879.34.2.68   Rim fragment

Mosaic glass; L 4.2, H 2.1, Th 0.2-0.15

- Rounded coil rim in cobalt blue and opaque white; acute sloping side in translucent turquoise blue with hollow circles of opaque yellow, making glass appear green.
- Polished exterior; iridescence and pitting on interior.

An unusual example with an applied rim.

Similar pattern to no. 94

97   A1879.34.6.8   Rim fragment

Mosaic glass
L 2.5, H 2.65, Th 0.25-0.15

- Coil rim in cobalt blue with white thread on interior; sides tapering downwards and curving in at bottom. Sections in blue, white, yellow and colourless glass; blue and yellow overlaid to appear green.
- Polished exterior; iridescent weathering and pitting on interior.

An unusual, irregular pattern, similar to that on short-strip and meandering-strip mosaic vessels; see Grose 1989, 252-3.

Compare Grose 1989, 300 no. 393

98 A1879.34.5.17 Rim fragment

Mosaic glass
L 2.9, H 2.1, Th 0.25-0.15

- Uneven, rounded rim, slightly inverted; convex side. Marble pattern in translucent blue with opaque white and yellow stripes.
- Polished exterior; iridescence and dulling on interior; pitting of surface bubbles.

99 A1879.34.6.9 Rim fragment

Mosaic glass
L 2.8, H 1.6, Th 0.3-0.1

- Rounded, outsplayed rim; convex curving side in dark purple decorated with two different patterns: (a) an opaque white circle surrounding a central opaque yellow spiral, and (b) translucent blue rosettes outlined in opaque white or yellow.
- Polished exterior; dulling on interior.

Compare Grose 1989, 309 no. 439 (slightly different pattern)

100 A1879.34.6.6 Rim fragment

Mosaic glass
L 2.65, H 2.5, Th 0.2

- Applied coil rim in dark purple with white thread on inner edge; slightly convex curving side decorated with canes in purple, cobalt blue and opaque white in patterns of circles and splashes.
- Polished exterior; dulling on interior.

Compare Grose 1989, 303 no. 407 (slightly different pattern)

101 A1879.34.6.7 Rim fragment

Mosaic glass
L 2.7, H 2.4, Th 0.3-0.2

- Applied coil rim with rounded edge in cobalt blue with opaque white diagonal thread on outer lip; flaring mouth; concave side to body decorated with canes in translucent dark purple, cobalt blue and opaque white, in patterns of circles, blocks and stripes. Probably part of a concave-sided bowl similar in shape to the CMG example (72.1.11); see Goldstein 1979, 199 no. 540.
- Iridescent weathering and pitting on exterior; polished interior.

Similar colours and design to no. 100

102 A1879.34.6.17 Rim fragment of vase or bowl

Mosaic glass
L. 3.3, H. 2.4, Th. 0.4-0.2

- Rounded rim; broad, flaring mouth, tapering slightly downwards.
- Translucent cobalt blue and deep purple with opaque white in a marbled pattern.
- Uneven, tooled surface on exterior; polished interior. Slight iridescent weathering and dulling.

Compare Grose 1989, 272 no. 259 (a ribbed bowl with a not dissimilar pattern)

103 A1879.34.6.28 Rim fragment

Mosaic glass
L 3.3, H 2.4, Th 0.4-0.2

- Rounded rim; sides curving in downwards. Opaque purple ground with opaque white and yellow swirls; yellow overlaid on translucent turquoise blue to appear as green.
- Polished exterior; iridescent weathering on interior.

Compare Grose 1989, 330 no. 559

104 A1879.34.5.16 Body fragment of ribbed bowl

Mosaic glass; H 3.95, W 2.1, Th 0.5-0.1

- Two tooled, vertical ribs. Translucent turquoise, with opaque yellow, red and white stripes, appearing green in places. Probably from a deep bowl, possibly with a base-ring.
- Polished exterior; iridescent weathering and dulling on interior.

For mosaic ribbed bowls, see Grose 1989, 247-9

105 A1879.34.1.80 Rim fragment of ribbed bowl

Mosaic glass; L 5.9, H 4.75, Th 0.45-0.2

- Rounded, flaring rim; tooled ribs on exterior; ribbon mosaic pattern in brown, blue and white.
- Polished exterior; dulling, faint iridescent weathering and pitting of surface bubbles.

Compare Grose 1989, 283 no. 310

106 A1879.34.1.110 Rim fragment

Mosaic glass
L 2.55, H 3.4, Th 0.35-0.15

- Vertical, ground rim; convex curving side in marbled mosaic pattern in purple with numerous small opaque white splashes.
- Polished surface; faint iridescence.

Compare Grose 1989, 274 no. 274 and 327 no. 539

107 A1879.34.1.94 Rim fragment

Mosaic glass
L 3.0, H 2.05, Th 0.25-0.15

- Vertical, ground rim; convex curving side in marbled mosaic pattern in purple and opaque yellow.

Compare Grose 1989, 279 no. 289

108 A1879.34.1.129 Rim fragment

Mosaic glass
L 2.8, H 2.9, Th 0.2

- Vertical, applied coil rim in horizontal bands; convex curving side in marbled mosaic pattern in blue, purple, yellow, turquoise (appearing as green) and colourless glass.

The pattern and colour combination were clearly meant to give the impression that the vessel was made from some exotic semi-precious stone.

109 A1879.34.1.137 Rim fragment

Mosaic glass
L 2.5, H 1.8, Th 0.3

- Rounded vertical rim and convex curving side in brown, opaque yellow and white. Cut groove on exterior below rim.

The colours and pattern imitate vessels carved out of sardonyx. Compare, for example, the Romanos Chalice, the original carving of which is dated, like mosaic glass, to the first century BC or early first century AD; see Buckton 1984, 129-35 no. 10.

Compare Follmann-Schulz 1992, 12 nos 4-5 (from Xanten, Germany)

110 A1879.34.1.105 Rim fragment

Mosaic glass
L 3.15, H 2.5, Th 0.25-0.1

- Rounded vertical rim and convex curving side in a swirling marbled pattern combining purple and yellow brown, appearing in places as green, and opaque white.

The colour combination may be compared with that of luxury fluorspar cups such as the cantharus in the BM (GR1974.4-19.1); see Harden 1949b.

111 A1879.34.1.115 Rim fragment

Mosaic glass; L 3.35, H 2.95, Th 0.25-0.15

- Rounded vertical rim and convex curving side in dark purple, appearing black, decorated with a marbled pattern of opaque white canes.

112 A1879.34.4.11 Rim fragment of shallow ribbed bowl

Mosaic glass; L 6.6, H 4.35, Th 0.35-0.1, Th (max. at rib) 0.75

- Slightly inverted, rounded rim; curving side in translucent cobalt blue and opaque white. Tooled ribs on exterior, rounded at top and tapering downwards. Irregular indents on inside of body from tooling of ribs.
- Polished exterior; iridescent weathering and dulling on interior.

For an almost intact example, found at Radnage, England, see Harden 1987, 51 no. 27.

Compare Grose 1989, 279 no. 291

113 A1879.34.4.12 Rim fragment of ribbed bowl

Mosaic glass; L 6.05, H 5.95, Th 0.35-0.1

Probably from same vessel as no. 112, but not a conjoining piece.

114 A1879.34.4.2 Rim fragment of deep ribbed bowl

Mosaic glass[5]; L 4.8, H 3.0, Th 0.4

- Outsplayed rim with rounded edge; curving side in blue, white and honey brown.
- Polished exterior; faint iridescence and dulling on interior.

Compare Grose 1989, 281 no. 300 but in blue and opaque white only

115 A1879.34.4.8 Rim fragment of deep bowl

Mosaic glass; L 2.8, H 2.6, Th 0.35

- Rounded, vertical rim; straight side to body, tapering downwards in blue ground with opaque white wavy streaks.
- Polished exterior; iridescent weathering on interior.

The pattern is slightly different to that commonly found on blue and white mosaic bowls.

116 A1879.34.4.16 Rim fragment of bowl

Mosaic glass; L 2.6, H 2.3, Th 0.4

- Rim with upper edge ground flat, straight side to body, tapering downwards in blue decorated with numerous opaque white streaked rods.
- Polished exterior; rotary grinding marks and dulling on interior.

Similar to no. 115, but compare also Grose 1989, 328 no. 546 and 329 no. 549

117 A1879.34.4.10 Rim fragment of bowl

Blue and white; mosaic glass; L 3.4, H 2.5, Th 0.35-0.25

- Outsplayed rim with ground edge; convex curving side with fine opaque white threads in wavy, horizontal stripes on blue ground, forming a ribbon mosaic pattern.
- One large pitted bubble in side; enamel-like weathering and iridescence.

Compare Grose 1989, 269 no. 250

118 A1879.34.1.1 Rim fragment of ribbed bowl

Mosaic glass[6]; L 9.0, H 5.6, Th 0.45-0.25

- Outsplayed, almost horizontal rim with rounded edge; vertical sides to body in honey-brown and opaque white with patches of yellow-brown; two widely spaced ribs, set vertically on exterior. Probably part of a deep bowl with base-ring.

- Dulling and iridescent weathering, especially on white.

Compare Grose 1989, 270 no. 255

119 A1879.34.1.58 Fragment of small bowl

Mosaic glass; L 6.05, H 3.4, Th 0.4-0.35

- Complete profile, with rounded rim; straight, slanting side to body and flat bottom in dark brown with opaque white and yellow threads.
- Polished surfaces; no weathering.

Compare Grose 334 no. 582 (regarded as possibly part of a base-ring)

120 A1879.34.1.70-79, 81-93, 95-104, 106-109, 111-114, 116-127, 130-136 and 138

Mosaic glass

1 One rim fragment (A1879.34.1.133) of a ribbed bowl in purple and opaque white.

2 Body fragments of ribbed bowls:
- Two in purple and opaque white, one in purple with opaque white and blue, six in brown and white, five in light yellowish-brown, blue and white (including A1879.34.1.77, L. 5.7, H. 4.6, Th. 0.5-0.15, with highly polished exterior), one (A1879.34.1.120) in dark purple, white and yellow-brown, one (A1879.34.1.136), in dark opaque brown, appearing black, and white, and one (A1879.34.1.111) in dark brown, pale yellow-brown, white and pale blue.[7]

3 Miscellaneous body fragments with plain convex sides:
- Nine in marbled brown, white and blue, including one (A1879.34.1.104) in dark purple, white, blue and yellow.

4 Inlay or architectural revetment fragments:
- Nine in opaque white and deep purple, appearing black, three in marbled purple and white, eight in marbled purple and yellow, two in cobalt blue and yellow, appearing green, and one edge fragment (A1879.34.1.103) in opaque purple, brick red and turquoise dots.[8]

121 A1879.34.2.1-11 Inlay or architectural revetment plaques

Monochrome glass

- Eleven fragments, in different shades of green and of varying thickness, including one (A1879.34.2.4, L. 6.6, W. 3.1, Th. 0.35, with burst bubbles on upper surface) in opaque pale 'celadon' green, one (A1879.34.2.5, L. 4.45, W. 4.4, Th. 0.3-0.25) in opaque dull green, and one (A1879.34.2.10, L. 3.2, W. 2.9, Th. 0.4, with considerable pitting of surface bubbles) in opaque green with marvered blobs of blue and bluish-green, perhaps part of a design intended to represent foliage.

122 A1879.34.2.28-32, 34-39 Inlay or architectural revetment plaques

Monochrome glass

- Seven fragments, in different shades of opaque blue, together with one (A1879.34.2.29, L. 5.7, W. 2.8, Th. 0.4) in a deeper shade of opaque 'celadon' green, one (A1879.34.2.34, L. 5.4, W. 2.85, Th. 0.3, with burst bubbles on upper surface) in opaque white, and another (A1879.34.2.38, L. 3.7, W. 2.6, Th. 0.4, edge fragment; pitting of numerous surface bubbles on upper surface; iridescent weathering on underside) in a pattern of blue and yellow, appearing as pale green.

For several other examples in blue, see *Sangiorgi* 1999, 94 no. 243
For opaque white vessels, see Goldstein 1979, 144 nos 297-8 and 149 no. 315

123 A1879.34.2.12, 14-17 Inlay or architectural revetment plaques

Monochrome glass.[9]

- Five fragments in opaque red, including four pieces in brick red (A1879.34.2.12, L. 6.7, W. 5.2, Th. 0.25, plus A1879.34.2.14, 16, 17) and one fragment in copper red (A1879.34.2.15).

Compare Goldstein 1979, 244 no. 707; Grose 1989, 369 no. 666

124 A1879.34.2.26 Inlay

Monochrome glass.[10]
L 4.0, W 1.65, Th 0.4

- Flat, with polished upper surface, edges trimmed to form the shape of an eye in pale yellow.
- Intact. Many bubbles.

It is uncertain whether the shape is ancient but, if so, it would have been fashioned as part of the polychrome decoration on a piece of furniture or an architectural revetment panel.

For comparison, see the mosaic panel with yellow birds in the CMG (66.1.215), see Harden 1987, 32-3 no. 10; Whitehouse 1997, 36-8 no. 33

125 A1879.34.6.29 Inlay or architectural revetment plaque

Mosaic glass
L 5.5, L (extant edge) 2.3, W 5.3, Th 0.4

- Edge fragment, rounded in section on underside. Blurred pattern of floral canes in opaque red, yellow, turquoise and yellow, in field of deep purple and opaque white; turquoise and yellow overlaid to produce green.
- Dulling; slight weathering, especially on breaks; deep pitting of surface bubbles.

For discussion of the possible uses to which such inlays were put, see Grose 1989, 356-7.

Compare Grose 1989, 325 no. 526 (vessel fragment with similar pattern)

126 A1879.34.6.21 Inlay or architectural revetment plaque

Mosaic glass; L 3.95, W 2.7, Th 0.5
- Fragment decorated with floral pattern in circular segments or red with yellow and green petals on opaque purple and white ground.

- Dulling and pitting of surface bubbles; iridescence on underside.

Similar pattern to no. 125

127 A1879.34.6.36 Inlay fragment

Mosaic glass
L 4.0, W 3.55, Th 0.25-0.2

- Floral pattern in opaque white with red petals on an opaque, dull turquoise ground.
- Polished surface. Pitting of surface bubbles; iridescence and dulling on underside.

An unusual colour combination, for which few parallels are known; compare Grose 1989, 312 no. 455 and 313 no. 463 (both vessel fragments).

128 A1879.34.6.26 Inlay fragment

Mosaic glass
L 2.9, L (of extant edge) 2.7, W 2.5, Th 0.25-0.2

- Blurred floral pattern in turquoise blue with green and red dots as flowers; green made by overlay of yellow with turquoise.
- Polished surface. Iridescent weathering and dulling on underside.

Compare Grose 1989, 318 no. 492 (bowl fragment with similar pattern)

129 A1879.34.6.13 Inlay fragment

Mosaic glass
L 4.6, W 2.7, Th 0.25-0.2

- Irregular floral pattern of rosettes in brick red and yellow on a ground of purple with opaque white dots and splashes.
- Polished surface. Iridescent weathering and dulling on underside.

Cf. Grose 1989, 313 no. 461 (bowl fragment with similar pattern)

130 A1879.34.6.24 Inlay fragment

Mosaic glass; L 3.4, W 2.0, Th 0.35

- Deep purple (appearing black) with pattern of white concentric circles.
- Polished surface. Iridescent weathering and dulling on underside.

131 A1879.34.5.11 Inlay

Mosaic glass; L 3.6, W 4.1, Th 0.6-0.35

- Oval fragment with ground, bevelled edge. Deep turquoise blue (appearing opaque) with vegetal or butterfly pattern in yellow, appearing green at edges.
- Polished upper surface; uneven, tooled underside. Some pitting of surface bubbles; patches of iridescence and dulling on underside.

132 A1879.34.5.6 Inlay fragment

Mosaic glass.[11]
L 2.3, W 1.85, Th 0.4

- Brick red, white, yellow and purple marbling.
- Polished surface. Iridescent weathering and dulling on underside.

133 A1879.34.2.58 Revetment plaque fragment

Mosaic glass.[12]
L 6.25, W 4.6, Th 0.4-0.3

- Flat and then angled down on one side. Dark turquoise blue-green with multiple circular rods in opaque yellow, making ground appear dark green.
- One large pitted bubble on upper surface; dulling and weathering on underside.

For vessels with the same pattern, see no. 94.

Compare Goldstein 1979, 249-50 nos 729-30 and 734a; Grose 1989, 369 no. 664

134 A1879.34.2.40 Revetment plaque fragment

Mosaic glass.[13]
L 9.15, W 4.9, Th 0.65-0.5

- Smooth, flat, polished upper surface; uneven underside. Dark green ground with multiple irregularly shaped rods in pale opaque green.
- Surface pinprick bubbles; iridescent pitting on underside.

Made in imitation of antico verde marble. Fragments of glass revetment imitating coloured marble have been found in very large quantities at the imperial villa of Lucius Verus (AD 161-9) just outside Rome; see Saguì 1998, 27, fig. 30.

Compare Grose 1989, 369 no. 665

135 A1879.34.3.3 Revetment plaque fragment

Mosaic glass.[14]
L 6.9, W 4.0, Th 0.25

- Smooth, flat, polished upper surface; uneven underside. Dark reddish-brown ground with many small rods in opaque white.
- Broken and mended.

Made in imitation of porphyry.

Compare Goldstein 1979, 251 no. 742

136 A1879.34.2.19 Inlay fragment

Mosaic glass.[15]
L 3.95, W 3.9, Th 0.25

- Flat, with polished upper surface; trimmed on one side to form a circular edge with an orange marbled pattern made from mixing opaque red and yellow.
- Many pitted bubbles on upper surface.

Compare *Sangiorgi* 1999, 94 no. 243 (a very similar circular disk)

Notes

1 For another small group of 22 fragments of unknown provenance in Frankfurt, see Welker 1987, 16 no. 9. A further 34 pieces once formed part of the Constable-Maxwell Collection, while a large group of mosaic, ribbon and network fragments were once in the Kofler-Truniger Collection; see *Constable-Maxwell* 1979, 114-15 lots 194-5; *Kofler* 1985, 111-13 lots 208-19.

2 None of the descriptions state clearly that these are copper red pieces, but the references to 'green weathering' imply that this is the case. Several more vessel fragments are among the unpublished material in the British Museum.

3 There is also a body fragment in network glass (unrecorded).

4 There are also two body fragments in similar ribbon glass: A1879.34.7.13 (L. 3.1, W. 2.5) and A1879.34.7.28 (L. 22.5, W. 1.55).

5 There is one ribbed body fragment in blue, white and yellow (A1879.34.4.3), and four in blue and white (A1879.34.4.1, 4, 6, 13). In addition, there are seven other curved fragments in blue and white mosaic glass that probably belonging to vessels (A1879.34.4.5, 7, 14, 15, 20, 23, 28), while one fragment (A1879.34.4.29) with an everted, bevelled rim and tapering side appears to belong to a blown, not a cast bowl. Finally, there are nine inlay or revetment plaque fragments in similar blue and white patterns (A1879.34.4.9, 17, 18, 22, 23, 24, 25, 26 and 21); all with a flat upper surface, apart from the last example, which is angled at one end.

6 Taken as a sample from a group of 68 fragments (A1879.34.1.1-69, excluding A1879.34.1.4) with similar mosaic patterns in opaque yellow and white threads on a translucent brown or dark purple ground. Other examples include six rim (A1879.34.1.38, 52, 54, 65 and 68-69) and 14 body fragments (A1879.34.1.3, 10, 17, 18, 21, 25, 41, 42, 47, 50, 51, 57, 60, 67), all belonging to ribbed bowls. Four more rim fragments (A1879.34.1.39, 43, 44 and 55), together with part of a base-ring (A1879.34.1.59), are decorated with additional blue threads; compare Grose 1989, 269-70 nos 252-3, 273 no. 266, 275-7 nos 282-3. The group also includes 20 inlay fragments, of which one (A1879.34.1.49), in a very dark brown or purple appearing black decorated with opaque white threads, has a rounded edge (L. of edge as extant 4.45, W. 2.4, Th. 0.4-0.3), while the other (A1879.34.1.46) is a corner fragment with rounded edges and polished upper surface in reddish-brown with opaque white threads (L. 4.0, W. 3.7, Th. 0.4).

7 For A1879.34.1.77, compare Goldstein 1979, 190 no. 508.

8 For the marbled purple and yellow examples, compare *Sangiorgi* 1999, 92-4 nos 241-2 and 245.

9 Another sizeable group of fragments (A1879.34.20.3-99), largely pieces of inlay or revetment plaques, was left unrecorded. But they also included two glass canes (A1879.34.20.91 and A1879.34.20.40, the latter bearing marks of the pincers or tongs used to draw out the cane) similar to ones found at Amarna and other Egyptian glassworking sites; compare *Wolf* 1994, figs 172 and 174 respectively, and see also Grose 1989, 52-3 and figs 26-7.

10 There are four other flat inlay or revetment plaque fragments in yellow glass (A1879.34.2.18, 21, 23 and 25); compare Goldstein 1979, 244 no. 710. Another fragment (A1879.34.2.22) is in a yellow and opaque white pattern. Additionally, there are two other rectangular slabs (A1879.34.13.1-2) in dark blue-green with an opaque yellow border; they have sharp, squared-off edges, with a flat polished upper surface and uneven, iridescent underside.

11 Another similar fragment is A1879.34.2.20 (L. 3.6, W. 3.35, Th. 0.3-0.15); broken and mended; tooling indents on the underside.

12 One of 20 fragments (A1879.34.2.51-60, 63-4, 66-7, 69-75), all with similar patterns. Five pieces are curved (A1879.34.2.63, 67, 73-75) and may belong to vessels; the rest are flat.

13 One of 13 fragments (A1879.34.2.40-50 and 61-2), all with similar mottled patterns. One piece (A1879.34.2.48) is curved at one end; the rest are all flat.

14 One of 15 fragments (A1879.34.3.1-15 – 14 in total, 1879.34.3.5 missing), all flat but varying in thickness in the range 0.6-0.2; some are in dark shades of chocolate brown, while others have a bright brick red ground (compare, for example, A1879.34.3.8, 2 and 6). One piece preserves part of the original edge (A1879.34.3.3). Two small fragments (A1879.34.11.1-2) of other polychrome mosaic revetment plaques have not been recorded.

15 There are two other flat inlay or revetment plaque fragments in orange glass (A1879.34.2.24 and 27); compare Goldstein 1979, 251 no. 740; Grose 1989, 368 no. 661.

Roman Tablewares

The cast bowl was one of the most common forms of late Hellenistic glass. It was adopted by the Romans and remained popular until the latter part of the first century AD. In the East natural colours (mainly shades of amber brown and green) predominated, but the Romans preferred bolder colours, either as vivid monochromes or in mosaic and marbled combinations. Cast ribbed bowls, in both monochrome and mosaic glass, were produced in large quantities in Italy during the first half of the first century AD.[1] Such vessels enjoyed a wide distribution both within the Roman Empire and beyond; examples have been found from Britain to China.[2]

Early Imperial Cast Tableware

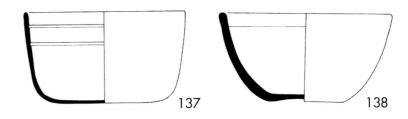

137

138

137 A1880.18.13 Deep bowl

Manganese purple
Late first century BC to early first century AD; formerly Piot Collection
H 6.1, D (rim) 11.1-11.0

- Rounded vertical rim; vertical sides, curving in gently to flat bottom.
- Cut decoration on interior, comprising two broad grooves (each 2 mm wide) running around sides 0.9-1.1 and 2.1-2.3 below rim.
- Intact; iridescent weathering; deep pitting (especially on interior) and dulling.

Compare Kunina 1997, 257 no. 51 (with refs)

138 A1880.18.8 Deep bowl

Pale amber-brown
Late first century BC to early first century AD; formerly Piot Collection
H 6.0-6.2, D (rim) 12.3-12.4

- Thick rounded rim; hemispherical body with convex sides curving in to bottom; concave, uneven bottom, making vessel stand aslant.
- Single wheel-cut groove on interior, 0.8-0.95 below rim.
- Intact; enamel-like weathering and iridescence, partially flaked off leaving dulling and fine pitting.

Compare Grose 1989, 268-9 nos 247-8

139 A1880.18.7 Deep bowl

Pale amber-yellow
Late first century BC to early first century AD; formerly Piot Collection
H 5.4, D (rim) 11.6-11.7

- Slightly everted, rounded rim; vertical sides, tapering to bottom; slightly convex, flattish bottom.
- Wheel-cut decoration on interior, comprising two horizontal grooves cut in sides 0.4-0.6 and 1.8-2.0 below rim.
- Broken and repaired; thick enamel-like weathering on interior; flaked-off weathering on exterior, leaving pitting and dulling; many pinprick bubbles.

Compare Grose 1989, 269 no. 249

140 A1921.150 Shallow bowl

Pale blue-green with large purple streak
Late first century BC to first half of first century AD
H 3.95, D (rim) 12.1

- Rounded vertical rim; sides tapering downwards with shallow undercurve; slightly rounded, convex bottom.
- Wheel-cut decoration on interior, comprising three horizontal grooves, 0.6-0.75, 2.3 and 2.5 below rim.
- Intact; some enamel-like weathering, pitting and dulling; strain cracks around line of grooves; a few bubbles and gritty inclusions.

For discussion of this type of vessel, see Grose 1979
Compare Grose 1989, 267-8 nos 244-6

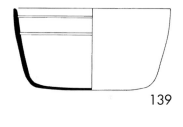

139

140

141

142

141   **A1966.64**   Small bowl

Deep blue-green
Late first century BC to first half of first century AD
Bequeathed by Mrs A. W. Acworth; formerly in the Acworth Collection
H 2.6, D (rim) 4.0, D (base) 2.2

- Bevelled rim with lip below; slightly convex sides to body, tapering to low flaring base-ring; flat bottom.
- Intact, except for internal strain cracks in sides and bottom. Dulling and faint iridescent weathering; grinding and polishing marks around interior.

142   **A1979.127**   Small carinated bowl ('patella' type)

Opaque deep blue-green
First half of first century AD; probably Italian
H 3.6-3.5, D (rim) 7.1, D (base) 3.25-3.15

- Everted rim, flattened on top edge; double convex sides; flaring base-ring; slightly convex bottom.
- Broken and mended, some in-fill; dulling and faint iridescence; surface pitting.

Isings Form 2; bowls of this type are also found in silver and terra sigillata (pottery)
Compare von Saldern 1974, 105 nos 278-84; Goldstein 1979, 144-6 nos 297-302; Harden 1987, 44 no. 20; Grose 1989, 305-6 nos 419-22; *Ancient Glass* 2001, 70 and 198 nos 78-81; *La fragilitat* 2005, 69 nos 60-1
Published *Constable-Maxwell* 1979, 30 no. 25

143   **A1880.18.73**   Bowl with short, close-set ribs

Blue-green
Late first century BC to mid-first century AD; formerly Piot Collection
H 4.3, D (rim) 12.4, D (max.) 12.55, Th (rim) 0.3

- Vertical, fire-rounded rim; straight-sided collar above slight ridge, then curving sharply to small, concave bottom.
- On interior, two wheel-cut grooves around outer edge of bottom and a single cut circle, 2.0 in diameter, at centre; band of short, close-packed, tooled ribs around exterior, 87 in total. Top of sides ground smooth, with rotary scratch marks around collar.
- Intact. On interior, weathering and deep pitting; on exterior, patches of creamy weathering, flaked off in places leaving iridescence and dulling; pinprick bubbles.

Isings Form 3c
For discussion, see Grose 1989, 245-7
Compare Grose 1989, 265-6 nos 235-7; Lightfoot 1992, 34 no. 3 (with refs); *Shining Vessels* 1991, 18 no. 24; Lubsen-Admiraal 2004, 333 no. 710 (from Cyprus, 'mould-blown' [*sic*])

144

145

144 A1921.164 Shallow ribbed bowl

Blue-green; early first century AD.
Marked on bottom: '3/-' (purchased for 3 shillings = 15 pence)
H 3.8, D (rim) 14.9, Th (rim) 0.4-0.35

- Everted, rounded rim; sides curving in, with tooled collar around top; concave bottom. On interior, two wheel-cut concentric grooves around junction of sides and bottom; on exterior, 24 ribs of varying length around sides, some with rounded, fire-polished end at top, others tooled flat, extending onto bottom and slanting from right to left.
- Broken and mended. On interior, very slight weathering; on exterior, iridescent weathering and dulling; few bubbles; one large gritty inclusion in side.

Compare Fleming 1996b, 20 and fig. 12 (UPM no. 86-35-45); Grose 1989, 263 no. 229

145 A1955.12 Shallow ribbed bowl

Blue-green
Early first century AD
H 4.2, D (rim) 13.3-13.0, D (max.) 13.65, Th (rim) 0.3

- Vertical rim with fire-rounded edge; straight-sided collar below; sides curving in sharply to flat bottom.
- On interior, two concentric grooves at junction of side and bottom and a single circle at centre; on exterior, 23 long, pronounced ribs around sides, tapering downwards and extending onto bottom; ribs curve gently from upper right to lower left and slant to right; irregularly spaced. Tooling groove runs horizontally around collar; tops of ribs are

flattened, with small, horizontal tooling indents; slight ridge at top of side between ribs below collar.
- Intact. Patches of deep pitting on surface; faint iridescence and dulling; pinprick bubbles.

Similar to no. 144, but also compare Grose 1989, 264 no. 232

146 A1889.497 Deep ribbed bowl

Blue-green
First century AD
H 5.7, D (rim) 11.4-11.5

- Rounded vertical rim; flat band below rim; tapering sides; flattish bottom but with a bump at centre, making vessel unstable.
- Ribs tooled into sides below band, tapering from top to bottom, slanting from left to right; fire-polished on exterior.
- Intact; some larger and pinprick bubbles; a few gritty inclusions; dulling on interior; tooling indent in side between two of the ribs.

Isings Form 2b
Compare Grose 1989, 266-7 nos 239-42; Kunina 1997, 257-8 nos 55-6 (one example from the Panticapaeum necropolis)

146

Early Imperial
Blown Tableware

Soon after the invention of glassblowing and the establishment of glass production centres in Italy, the Romans quickly adapted to the use of blown-glass tableware.[3] This was apparently sold in matching or co-ordinated groups, and evidence is provided by the presence of such 'dinner sets' in houses excavated at Herculaneum and in a number of well-dated tombs of the first century AD.[4] An important group of early tablewares was also found at the Italian city of Cosa in a destruction level dated AD 40-5.[5] They show not only that glass was already successfully competing with Arretine and thin-walled pottery for a place on the Roman table, but also that glassmakers were already able to produce a wide range of shapes and sizes.

While much of early blown tableware imitates the forms found in cast glass, as well as in metal and pottery services, Roman craftsmen and customers alike soon came to appreciate that glass was especially suitable for making vessels associated with the storing, pouring and serving of liquid refreshments.[6] This gave rise to a long tradition of making wine bottles, decanters and cups in glass – one that finds a persistent echo in the English expression 'a glass of wine/water'.[7]

147   148   149

147 A1880.18.23 Ribbed bowl

Colourless with yellow-green tinge
Mid-first century AD; formerly Piot Collection
H 4.0, D (rim) 11.5, D (max.) 12.6, Th (rim) 0.2-0.1

- Blown into a three-part mould; mould marks visible as two lines on collar; separate mould used for bottom.
- Knocked-off, vertical rim; concave collar below, expanding to angled shoulder; horizontal shallow grooves around collar; sides curving in to moulded bottom; two grooves flanking rounded, broad ridge around outer edge of bottom; convex, curving bottom band; central concave boss with three concentric ridges.
- On exterior, 74 vertical, evenly shaped ribs.
- Intact; two internal cracks. Creamy brown weathering and iridescence.

Compare Stern 1995, 112-13 no. 14 (with discussion and refs). For other examples from the East, see Price 1992, 423, 444 nos 99-104 with pl. 341 (Crete); Lightfoot 1992, 59 no. 21; Lightfoot 1993, 36-7 with figs 52-4 (Asia Minor); Kunina 1997, 276 no. 120

148 A1880.18.22 Ribbed bowl

Pale blue-green
Mid-first century AD; formerly Piot Collection
H 3.9, D (rim) 10.8, D (max.) 12.7

- Blown into a three-part mould; traces of two mould marks on either side of collar; separate mould used for bottom.
- Unworked, knocked-off rim, slightly everted; concave collar below, expanding to angular projecting shoulder; sides curving in sharply to moulded bottom; convex band on bottom around central concavity.
- On exterior, 92 fine shallow ribs, slanting slightly from top right to bottom left; two concentric ridges around exterior of bottom; three more in concave centre.
- Intact, except for one small chip in rim and another in bottom. Brilliant iridescent weathering, partly flaked off; surface pitting, many pinprick bubbles.

Similar to no. 147

149 A1954.53 Deep ribbed bowl

Green with bluish tinge
Mid-first century AD
H 5.5, D (rim) 9.7, D (max.) 10.7, Th (0.3-0.17)

- Blown into a three-part mould; mould marks visible as two lines on collar; separate mould used for bottom.
- Inverted rim, with ground edge; gentle S-shaped collar below; bulging curved sides; outward ridge around edge of bottom with groove inside; another groove near centre and deep, central, pushed-in boss with knob in relief at centre. On exterior, 50 shallow, vertical ribs around sides.
- Intact. Some surface pitting, dulling and faint iridescence; blowing striations; many pinprick bubbles.

Compare Stern 1995, 111-12 no. 13 (with refs); Kunina 1997, 276 nos 121-2 (both from the Panticapaeum necropolis); Lubsen-Admiraal 2004, 334 no. 713 (from Cyprus, 'mould-pressed' [sic]).

ΚΑΤΑΙΧΑΙΡΕ ΚΑΙΕΥΦΡΑΙΝΟΥ

150

151

150 A1880.18.20 Cylindrical cup

Pale yellow-green

First century AD; from Cyprus; Syro-Palestinian, possibly made at Sidon; formerly Piot Collection

H 7.9, D (rim) 7.5

- Blown into a three-part mould; mould marks visible as two lines on sides; separate mould used for bottom.
- Outsplayed, unworked rim; slightly convex cylindrical sides; on bottom, three raised concentric circles.
- Below the rim, two raised horizontal ribs and pairs of palm fronds below, appearing as a wreath encircling the vessel; below this is a Greek inscription: ΚΑΤΑΙΧΑΙΡΕ ΚΑΙ ΕΥΦΡΑΙΝΟΥ, 'Rejoice and be merry!'; three more raised ribs and a narrower band of palm fronds decorate the lower part of the body; the two side seams are concealed by vertical palm fronds, separating the words of the inscription.
- Broken and mended. Encrusted weathering; dulling and pitting.

Harden produced the first catalogue of vessels of this type; see Harden 1935, 171-3. He was able to identify two sub-groups, one (Group Fii) with the inscription given correctly as ΚΑΤΑΧΑΙΡΕ ΚΑΙ ΕΥΦΡΑΙΝΟΥ, the other (Group Fi), as here, with the error of an additional iota, giving ΚΑΤΑΙΧΑΙΡΕ. Harden subsequently published two examples of the ΚΑΤΑΙΧΑΙΡΕ sub-group from tombs at Yahmour in Syria, while he also referred to an example of Group Fi found during excavations on the Greek island of Siphnos; see Harden 1944-5, 82, 84 and 91, pls VI-IX. Further pieces belonging to both sub-groups were listed by McClellan; see McClellan 1983, 72, 76-7. None of these works, however,

noted the existence of the cup in Edinburgh. Although this type of inscribed cup is known from various sites in Italy and the West, it is likely that the Edinburgh example should be added to the list of eastern finds since it came into the Royal Scottish Museum [now part of National Museums Scotland] as part of the Piot Collection. Finally, it should be noted that Harden regarded all of the examples of the ΚΑΤΑΙΧΑΙΡΕ sub-group as being from the same mould; see Harden 1935, 171; Harden 1944-5, 90.8. More recently scholars have noted other distinguishing features. So, for example, the shape of the letter 'A' in the two groups differs; Stern 2000, 166, figs 2-3. It has also be pointed out that one of the two examples in the CMG (both of Harden group F.ii in relation to the inscription; pace Whitehouse 2001a, 22) has only one horizontal rib above the upper band of palm fronds; Whitehouse 2001, 22-3 nos 485-6.

Compare Harden 1935, 172; *Fitzwilliam* 1978, 31-2 no. 51; Oliver 1980, 69 no. 63; Kunina 1997; 275 no. 115; Arveiller-Dulong and Nenna 2005, 194 no. 538

151 A1907.297 Handle of cup, stamped inscription

Pale blue-green

First century AD; probably Italian, and possibly made at Rome itself

H (max. extant) 3.6, W (max.) 2.6

- Body fragment with handle applied as a flat pad to side, drawn out horizontally, then turned down and in to form projecting loop bearing stamped inscription: ARTAS SIDON / APTAC CEIΔW on upper and lower surfaces respectively; drawn downwards in three angled sections, then pressed

in horizontally to body, drawn out again and nipt off below outer edge.
- Small patches of weathering; some dulling and faint iridescence; a few pinprick bubbles.
- Probably from a scyphus of Isings Form 39; see Whitehouse 1997, 91-3 nos 132-4.

For Sidon and glassblowers' signatures, see Stern 1995, 66-74; Whitehouse 1997, 93-4. Six names with the epithet 'the Sidonian' are found stamped on the handles of free-blown cups of Isings Form 39. That of Artas, with the inscription appearing in both Latin and Greek on the top and bottom of the handle, is more common than all of the others put together. By the end of the 19th century as many as 50 had already been recorded; see CIL XV.2/1, 6958. The stamp signifies the name of either the glass-maker or the proprietor of the workshop, while the 'Sidonian' tag indicates Artas' place of origin, not the site of the workshop itself. Since some of the stamps have APTAC CEIΔ WNIOC ЕПОIHCEN̩, there is a greater likelihood that the name refers to the former.

See also Whitehouse 1997, 94 (with refs.); Arveiller 2006, 65; Nenna 2006, 201

Compare Whitehouse 1997, 93-7 nos 135-40; Arveiller 2006, 67 nos F-SKY.001-002, pl. I; Nenna 2006, 206 nos F-MUS.003-011, pls 124-5

152 A1880.18.15 Cup

Deep blue; first century AD; formerly Piot Collection
H 6.6, D (rim) 7.2, D (body) 8.4

- Knocked-off or cut, then ground smooth rim; convex sides to body, curving in to small, concave bottom.
- Wheel-cut decoration, comprising grooves: one 0.3 below rim, less than 0.1 wide; a band of one broad groove, flanked above and below with fine grooves, 3.7-4.1 below rim.
- One crack running down side from rim. Dulling and faint iridescent weathering on exterior; some soil encrustation on interior; pinprick bubbles.

This cup belongs to a large group of Roman cut-glass drinking vessels known as 'Hofheim cups'. Many examples have been found at military sites

152

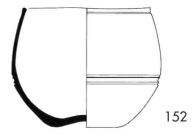

152

in the Rhineland and southern Britain, where they are closely dated by their contexts to the mid-first century AD; see Whitehouse 1997, 221. A fragmentary example has also been found in a Flavian context (c.AD 83-7) at the only Roman legionary fortress in Scotland, Inchtuthil; Price 1985b, 308-10 no. 2, fig. 93.

Isings Form 12; Price and Cottam 1998, 71-3, fig. 21

For other drinking vessels in cobalt blue glass with linear cut decoration, see Kunina 1997, 311 no. 291, 313 no. 297 (both from the Panticapaeum necropolis); Whitehouse 1997, 249 no. 424; *Solid Liquid* 1999, 66 no. 111

Compare Auth 1976, 202 no. 347 (found at Olbia); Platz-Horster 1976, 81 no. 161; *Shining Vessels* 1991, 28 no. 37; Newby 1999, 50 no. 45; *Sangiorgi* 1999, 46 no. 1068; *Solid Liquid* 1999, 67 no. 113

153 A1921.106 Cup

Blue-green; mid-first to second century AD; found in Cyprus
H 8.0, D (rim) 6.9, D (base) 4.5

- Rounded, thickened rim with inward lip; tapering and gently curving sides to body; integral, tubular base-ring; kick and large pontil scar on bottom.
- Intact, except for one small crack in side. Patches of faint weathering and iridescence; some glassy inclusions; very many bubbles.

Isings Form 41b

Compare Lightfoot 1992, 74-6 nos 30-2; Whitehouse 1997, 101-3 nos 150-2

153

155

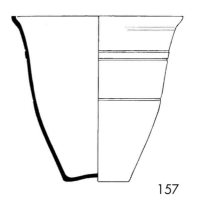
157

154 A1880.18.82   Bowl with trail handles on rim

Colourless
Mid-first to second century AD; formerly Piot Collection
H 3.5, D (rim) 11.0, D (base) 5.8

- Rim folded down, in and pressed on to under-curve of mouth, with inner downward lip; broad mouth; gently curving sides, tapering downwards; tubular base-ring; pushed-in bottom with kick. Two crimped trail handles applied to outer edge of rim.
- Intact. Some large and pinprick bubbles.

Isings Form 43
Compare *Constable-Maxwell* 1979, 79 lot 130; Lightfoot 1987, 36 nos 35-7; Whitehouse 1997, 75 no. 93 (with refs)

155 A1981.416   Bowl

Blue-green
First to early second century AD
H 5.0, D (rim) 10.0, D (base) 5.2

- Thick, rounded rim with inner lip; straight sides tapering downwards; tubular base-ring; almost flat bottom with pontil scar.
- Intact. Black, enamel-like weathering, flaking off to leave dulling, iridescence and pitting; usage scratches.

Isings Form 41b
Compare Whitehouse 1997, 101-3 nos 150 and 152

156 A1880.18.71   Deep bowl

Blue-green
Late first to second century AD; formerly Piot Collection
H 7.4, D (rim) 12.7-12.6, D (base) 7.3

- Horizontal, rounded rim with inward shoulder; straight sides to body, tapering downwards; integral tubular base-ring; convex bottom but with central concavity and pontil mark.
- Intact. Thick creamy brown weathering, mostly flaked off, leaving fine brilliant iridescence and dulling; pinprick and some large bubbles.

Isings Form 41b
Compare Matheson 1980, 37-8 no. 105

157 A1895.277   Cup

Colourless(?)
Probably first century AD; from a tomb at Mount Carmel
H 8.0, D (rim) 8.4

- Knocked-off, uneven rim; short, flaring mouth; convex sides tapering downwards; small, concave bottom.
- Three wheel-cut horizontal grooves around body, 1.6, 2.0 and 3.9 below rim; other faint lines are visible but irregular.
- Intact. Deep pitting and brilliant iridescence over all surfaces; blowing striations.

Isings Form 106c
Compare *Solid Liquid* 1999, 68 no. 116

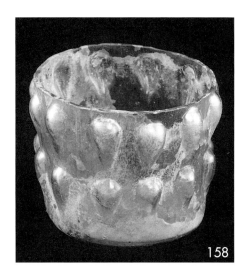

158 A1887.374 Beaker

Pale greenish
Mid- to late first century AD
H (as extant) 4.0, D (max.) 5.2, D (bottom) 4.6

- Blown into a two-part mould, with separate base mould.
- Two rows of twelve knobs with small circular raised bosses at bottom; three raised concentric circles on base.
- Upper part of body missing.

Isings Form 31
Compare *Constable-Maxwell* 1979, 56-7 lots 78-9; von Saldern 1980, 51 no. 44 (with refs); *Benzian* 1994, 56-7 lot 90 (with refs); Ferrari 1998, 171 (no. 1967.115.776, with discussion)

159 A1921.104 Beaker

Blue-green
Mid-first to second century AD; found in Cyprus
H (max.) 8.6, D (rim) 7.25, D (body) 6.6, D (base) 5.75

- Knocked-off rim; short, flaring mouth; slightly convex sides to cylindrical body; thick, flat bottom.
- Five bands of wheel-abraded lines around body: single line 1.2 below rim; another single line 2.6 below rim; another single line 3.45 below rim; then a band comprising two single lines above and below a thicker groove, 0.3 wide; another single line near bottom, 7.3 below rim.

- Intact, except for large chip in rim. Fine limy weathering; iridescence and dulling; many pinprick bubbles.

Vessels of this type are found in the eastern Mediterranean, especially in Asia Minor.

Compare Lightfoot 1989, 27-8 nos 12-14; Lightfoot 1990, 9 pls 4-5; Sternini 1998, 62 no. V13; *Sangiorgi* 1999, 78 no. 196 (right)

160 A1890.1040 Beaker

Pale blue-green
Mid-first to second century AD
H 9.1, D (rim) 7.0, D (base) 6.8

- Knocked-off rim; short, flaring mouth; slightly convex sides to cylindrical body; thick, flat bottom.
- Four bands of wheel-abraded lines around body: single line 3.6 below rim; thicker band 4.2-4.45 below rim; another single line 0.48 below rim; another near bottom, 7.3 below rim.
- Intact. Slight enamel weathering on interior; thicker weathering film covering part of exterior, flaked off elsewhere, leaving brilliant iridescence, dulling and pitting; some large bubbles.

Similar to no. 159

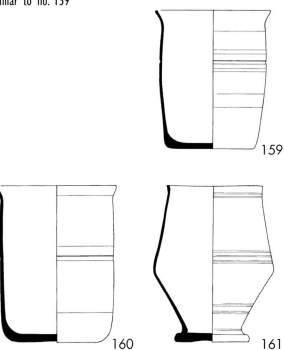

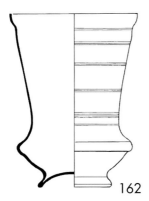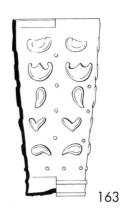

162   162   163   163

161   A1937.521   Carinated beaker

Blue-green; second half of the first century AD
H 9.8-9.5, D (rim) 6.1, D (max.) 7.45

- Knocked-off, unworked and uneven rim; short, slightly flaring mouth; bi-conical sides to body; integral pad base with outward horizontal lip; flat bottom with small hollow at centre.
- Four horizontal bands of wheel-abraded lines around body.
- Intact. Thick limy enamel-like weathering; patches of iridescence and dulling; surface pitting of pinprick bubbles.

Isings Form 34
Compare Hayes 1975, 56-7 no. 136; Lightfoot 1992, 66 no. 25 (with refs); *Shining Vessels* 1991, 34 no. 48

162   A1921.108   Drinking cup ('carchesium' type)

Pale green with yellow tinge
Mid-first to early second century AD; found in Cyprus
H 10.5, D (rim) 7.8, D (body) 7.05, D (base) 4.5

- Knocked-off rim; bulging, shallow mouth; tall, straight sides tapering downwards, then splays to carination; below, slightly concave undercurve; integral tubular base-ring; concave bottom.
- Six bands of wheel-cut lines on body.
- Broken and repaired with three small holes in body. Some limy weathering, dulling and iridescence; a few pinprick bubbles.

Isings Form 36b
Cf. von Saldern 1968, no. 54 (from Crete); *Wolkenberg* 1991, lot

no. 64. *Shining Vessels* 1991, 38 no. 56; Kunina 1997, 313 no. 298 (from the Panticapaeum necropolis); Whitehouse 1997, 228 no. 387

163   A1880.18.19   Beaker

Green with blue tinge
Second half of first century AD; formerly Piot Collection
H 13.5, D (rim) 6.7, D (bottom) 4.6

- Blown into a two-part mould, with separate base mould. Knocked-off rim, slightly thickened and inverted; sides tapering downwards; bottom slightly concave.
- Five horizontal rows of raised decorative elements, interspersed with smaller elements, from top: (a) six horizontal kidneys, hollow at centre, (b) six peltae, (c) eight small bosses, (d) six vertical kidneys, hollow at centre, (e) eight bosses, (f) six heart shapes, (g) eight bosses, (h) six horizontal kidneys, (i) twelve bosses, (j) horizontal rib; on bottom, three concentric circles in relief, with small, central, hollow knob.
- Creamy brown weathering on interior; patches of iridescence, dulling and pitting on exterior.

Stern has pointed out that relatively few conical beakers of this type are known, although they come in a wide variety of designs. Since most of the examples have been found in Italy or the western provinces, it is thought that such vessels were probably made in Italy. Several examples have been recovered from Pompeii and Herculaneum, indicating that they were being produced and used when the eruption of Vesuvius took place in AD 79. An exact parallel to this beaker has not been found.

Isings Form 31 (with discussion and refs)
Compare Stern 1995, 108-10 no. 11

164 A1921.107 Indented beaker

Pale blue-green
Second half of first century AD; found in Cyprus
H 11.0, D (rim) 7.3-7.2, D (base) 4.6-4.55

- Rounded, thickened, vertical rim; sides to body tapering slightly towards bottom; slightly pushed-in bottom with trace of pontil mark.
- Irregular vertical indents and ribs.
- Intact, except for a hole in side. Thick creamy enamel-like weathering; iridescence and pitting; pinprick bubbles.

For discussion of indented beakers, see Whitehouse 1997, 111-12.

Isings Form 32
Compare *Shining Vessels* 1991, 36 no. 50; Kunina 1997, 315 nos 303-4

164

165

165 A1921.105 Indented beaker with cut decoration

Colourless with yellowish tinge
Late first to early second century AD; found in Cyprus
H 9.55-9.3, D (rim) 6.2, W (base) 4.9

- Uneven, knocked-off rim; small, flaring mouth; sloping sides to body; concave centre to square-sided bottom.
- Single wheel-abraded line, 0.9 below rim; four large indents in sides, making star pattern.
- Intact. Thick black enamel-like weathering, mostly flaked off, leaving iridescent and dulled surface; many pinprick and larger bubbles.

Isings Form 32
Compare Oliver 1992, 106-7 and 111 no. T.199/31 (from Amathus); Sternini 1998, 63 no. V16 (with refs); Whitehouse 1997, 112 no. 170

166 A1880.18.75 Indented beaker

Pale blue-green
Second century AD; found in Cyprus; formerly Piot Collection
H 10.35, D (rim) 7.45-7.2, W (max.) 7.2, D (base) 4.2

- Rounded, everted, slightly thickened rim; slightly convex sides to upper body; below, undercurve to integral tubular base-ring; on bottom, kick and traces of large pontil mark.
- Four deep, round indents in sides.
- Intact. Limy weathering, iridescence and dulling; some large and many pinprick bubbles.

Isings Form 35; Compare Vessberg 1956, 143 fig. 44:35

166   167   169

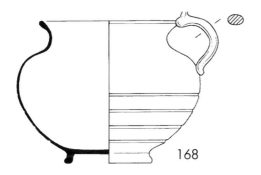

168

167   A1981.417   Beaker

Blue-green
Probably mid-first to second century AD
H 11.1, D (rim) 7.35, D (base) 3.95

- Everted, rounded rim; straight, tapering sides to body, turned-out fold forming edge to base; concave centre to bottom with pontil mark.
- Intact, except for two holes in sides. Thick enamel-like weathering, flaked off on exterior, leaving severe pitting of surface, dulling and iridescence; more weathering on interior; many bubbles.

168   A168.267A   One-handled cup

Colourless with yellow-green tinge
Possibly first century AD; written in ink on body: 'No. 2424 1855'
H (max.) 6.3, H (rim) 5.7, D (rim) 5.9-5.8, D (body) 7.7, D (base) 3.7-3.6

- Rounded rim with flaring mouth; narrow, concave neck; small, sloping shoulder; bulbous body with gentle undercurve; low, flaring base-ring; flattish bottom; rod handle pressed onto upper body and

drawn up in a loop to edge of rim with vertical thumb-rest above.
- Four concentric cut grooves on lower body.
- Broken and mended; some pieces missing.

Compare Whitehouse 1997, 189 no. 331; Kunina 1997, 317 nos 312-15

169   A1970.907   Drinking cup ('modiolus' type)

Light blue-green
Late first to early second century AD; possibly made in Asia Minor
H 11.7, D (rim) 15.3-15.1, D (base) 6.5-6.2

- Everted, horizontal rounded rim; downward tubular fold, forming collar around outside of top of sides; slight inward lip in mouth; bell-shaped sides, curving in to solid, oval base-ring (possibly applied); flattish bottom, concave at centre with tooling cavity; strap handle, applied in three broad claws to side of vessel drawn up as a three-ribbed loop and trailed onto side below collar.
- Intact. Soil encrustation around and under rim; creamy brown weathering, flaking off and leaving iridescence and dulling; black impurities in edge of rim; pinprick and a few larger bubbles.

For discussion of this type of drinking vessel, see Haevernick 1978; Whitehouse 1997, 229.

Compare Bucovala 1968, 33-4 nos 20-1; Hayes 1975, 67 no. 203: 'From western coastal region of Asia Minor (purchased in Istanbul)' (with refs); La Baume 1977, 28 no. 24 and pl. 3,4; *Constable-Maxwell* 1979, 84-6 nos 138-42, esp. no. 141; *Solid Liquid* 1999, 70 no. 122; Sotheby's Sale 7405 (New York, 10 December, 1999), 109 no. 347

170 A1979.131 Skillet (trulla) with winged handle

Yellow-green

Probably first to early second century AD, but possibly fourth century AD; eastern Mediterranean

H 6.0, D (rim) 10.85-10.55, L (body and handle) 17.0, D (base) 4.75-4.5

- Rounded, horizontal rim, slanting up on side opposite handle; exterior fold below rim; sides to body curving in downwards; applied, tooled base-ring; pushed-in bottom, flat at centre; tooled, flattish handle applied to edge of rim with nipt protrusions at ends.
- Crack and area of fill in side. Faint weathering, iridescence and dulling; very few bubbles.

The vessel imitates the shape of metal examples that were widely used in the Roman world; for a silver example, see Kent 1977, 54 no. 106. Such pans were versatile and could be used at religious ceremonies for pouring libations as well as at drinking parties for serving wine. They may also have been used as a dipper at the baths. The uncertainty over the date of this example serves to indicate that some shapes and forms continued in use for a long time.

Isings Form 75b; eastern Mediterranean

Compare MMA 81.10.95; von Saldern 1974, 200 no. 557; Hayes 1975, no. 148; La Baume 1977, 67 no. 232 (found at Krefeld-Gellep, Germany); Harden 1978, 306 pl. I,3 (BM G&R 1851.8-13.470, from Vaison, France); Canav 1985, 84 no. 135; *Napoli* 1986, 224 no. 45 (from Pompeii); Higashi 1991, 56 no. 21; Kunina 1997, 294-5 no. 202 (from the Olbia necropolis); Whitehouse 1997, 198 no. 346

Published: *Constable-Maxwell* 1979, 145 lot 262

170

171 A1937.517 Amphora

Yellow-green

Probably first century AD; H 12.0, D (rim) 4.4-4.3, D (body) 9.3

- Rounded, everted rim; concave neck; sloping shoulder; ovoid body; integral, splayed base-ring, tooled in around inside; flattish bottom with central kick and large circular pontil scar; two rod handles applied in pads on shoulder, curved round and pressed onto underside of rim.
- Intact. Severe surface pitting and iridescence; a patch of dulling on exterior; some soil encrustation and weathering on interior.

Isings Form 15 (with refs)

172 A1880.18.21 One-handled jug

Pale blue-green; first half of first century AD; formerly Piot Collection

H 10.0, D (rim) 2.5, D (body) 7.1

- Blown into a two-part mould. Everted rim, folded round and in; short neck, expanding at base to join imperceptibly with sloping shoulder; bulbous body; flat bottom; rod handle applied below rim, drawn up and then turned down vertically to the shoulder, where it was pinched or cut off.
- Three registers of decoration, divided by two horizontal bands with bosses; on shoulder, two animals, one on each half of the mould, described as either a bull and a crouching lion or a hound pursuing a deer; on body, an acanthus scroll; around bottom, widely spaced tongues or gadroons.
- Intact. Small patches of creamy brown weathering.

Jugs of this type belong to a larger group of vessels attributed to the 'Workshop of the Floating Handles' (Stern 1995, 86-91); they occur in a variety of shapes and sizes, with numerous different forms of moulded decoration. They provide indication of the inventiveness and experimentation of Roman glassmakers.

Cf. Thomas 1976, 19 no. 45; Stern 1995, 88 and ftn 153 (listing four other examples); Lightfoot 2005, 86, fig. 5 (MMA 17.120.243 and 17.194.249). Two further examples from the same mould were sold at auction in 1983; see *Sotheby's Antiquities* sale catalogue, 11-12 July, London 1983, 80 lot nos 266 and 268. See also, from Senj (Senia) in Croatia, incorrectly dated to the late third to early fourth century AD, see Salviati 1999, fig. 2

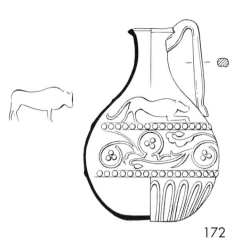

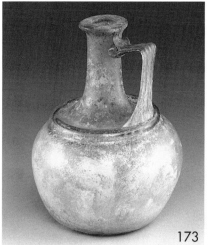

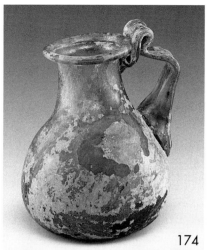

172   173   174

173   A1937.642   Jug with collared shoulder

Pale blue
Second half of first century AD; eastern Mediterranean or Italian
H 10.6, D (rim) 2.55, D (body) 8.15

- Everted rim, folded over and in, flattened on top; cylindrical neck, expanding downwards to join broad shoulder with tubular fold around it; bulbous body; concave bottom; strap handle applied over fold and drawn up, turned in at an acute angle, trailed onto neck and up to rim.
- Trail under rim wound round one and a half times from left to right; a second trail applied around base of neck, also one and a half times from left to right.
- Intact. Patches of weathering and iridescence on exterior and interior; many pinprick bubbles.

For an example decorated with marvered-in chips of opaque white glass, see *Winfield Smith* 1957, 91 no. 153.

Isings Form 53
Compare BM GR1927.2-16.1 and GR1851.3-31.8 (Comarmond Collection); MMA 74.51.43 (from Idalium, Cyprus); Kassel Museum G.123 (Spartz 1967, no. 39 = Boosen 1984, no. 53); *Arch. Deltion* 32 (1977) B'2 Chronika, 180 and pl. 180f (from a tomb on Naxos); Arveiller-Dulong and Nenna 2005, 46-7 nos 46-9

174   A1921.116   Small jug

Blue-green
Late first to second century AD; found in Cyprus
H (rim) 7.3-7.1, D (rim) 3.5, D (body) 6.0-5.9

- Tubular rim; flaring mouth; short neck; squat, bulbous body; thick bottom, slightly concave at centre; strap handle with two trailing pads at edges applied to body, drawn up at an angle and turned in horizontally, then looped upward above rim and trailed down onto and below rim.
- Intact. Faint weathering, iridescence and dulling; purple streak in body; impurities in handle; some bubbles.

Compare Kunina 1997, 303 no. 251 (from the Panticapaeum necropolis)

175   A1921.132   Jug

Pale blue-green
First century AD; found in Cyprus
H (rim) 10.8, D (rim) 2.6, D (body) 8.3, D (base) 4.75

- Everted horizontal rim, folded over and in, flattened on top; conical neck, slightly tooled in at base; sloping shoulder; globular body; integral, splayed base-ring; flattish bottom with faint pontil mark; strap handle with three ribs pressed onto shoulder, drawn up and in, trailed onto neck below rim with vertical fold as thumb-rest rising above rim.
- Intact. Patches of whitish weathering, iridescence and dulling; black impurities in handle; pinprick bubbles.

Isings Form 52
Compare MMA 74.51.133 (from Idalium, Cyprus); Auth 1976, 102 no. 113; Matheson 1980, 32 nos 92-3; Kunina 1997, 303 no. 250

175   176   177

176 A1921.131 Jug

Pale blue
Probably second century AD; found in Cyprus
H 12.0, D (rim) 4.4-4.3, D (body) 9.3

• Folded rim with bevelled outer lip; shallow, flaring
mouth; slightly conical neck; sloping shoulder;
globular body; small, concave bottom; large strap
handle applied to shoulder with three prominent
claws, drawn up and out, turned in at an acute
angle (horizontally), pressed onto neck below rim.
• Intact, except for a crack in shoulder. Patches of
iridescent weathering and surface pitting; one area
of large bubbles near bottom; many elongated
bubbles in handle.

Isings Form 52a
Compare Oliver 1992, 115 no. T.360/7 (from Amathus)

177 A1942.16 Jug

Blue-green
Late first to second century AD; eastern Mediterranean
Bequeathed by Sir William Ramsay.[9]
H 12.25, D (rim) 4.15-4.05, D (body) 7.1

• Everted, partially tubular rim, folded over and in;
shallow, funnel mouth; cylindrical neck; squat,
piriform body; deep kick and large, irregular
pontil scar on bottom; strap handle applied to
body, drawn up vertically, turned round and
down, trailed onto neck and up to edge of rim.
• Intact. Dulling and faint iridescence on exterior;
soil encrustation and enamel-like weathering on
interior; very many bubbles, some elongated.

Compare Kunina 1997, 303 no. 245 (reportedly from Olbia)

178 A1880.18.80 Small jug

Light blue
Late first to second century AD; formerly Piot Collection
H 8.25, D (rim) 3.2-3.15, D (body) 6.0

• Rim, partially tubular and poorly formed; flaring
mouth; short, cylindrical neck with tooling indents
at base; conical body; flat bottom; handle applied
in broad pad, drawn up and round in a loop, then
formed into a smaller, second loop as a thumb-rest
above rim, trailed into mouth with end drawn
back.
• Intact, except for crack from rim down neck
and around base of handle. Some patches of
weathering, iridescence and pitting; very many
pinprick and some larger bubbles.

Similar to no. 177

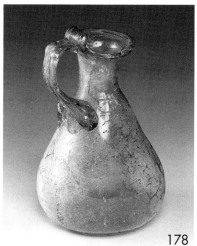

178   180   181

179   A1857.157.3   One-handled jug

Blue-green
Late first century AD; from the necropolis of Tharros, Sardinia
Purchased at the Chevalier Barbetti's Sale (London)
H 16.7, D (rim) 4.0, D (base) 13.2

- Rim folded out, round and in, forming thick, slightly irregular, slanting collar to mouth; cylindrical neck; shallow sloping shoulder; sides tapering in downward; slightly concave bottom; strap handle applied to shoulder in four claws, drawn up vertically, turned in at an acute angle and pressed onto neck with trailing end back along upper surface of handle.
- Intact. Some soil and limy encrustation; dulling and iridescence; some black impurities in neck and handle.

Isings Form 51a

180   A1966.51   Cylindrical bottle

Green
Late first to second century AD; eastern Mediterranean
Bequeathed by Mrs A. W. Acworth; formerly in the Acworth Collection
H 16.6, D (rim) 6.65, D (base) 10.9

- Collared rim with everted rounded lip; short, cylindrical neck; gently sloping shoulder; cylindrical body with slightly slanting sides; slightly concave bottom; broad strap handle with six claws at base, dropped onto shoulder, drawn up and turned in at an right angle and pressed down onto neck below fold of collar.

- Horizontal bands of wheel-abraded lines around body in five registers.
- Intact, except for part of rim; crack in body and shoulder near handle. Patches of enamel-like weathering and brilliant iridescence; some dulling and surface pitting.

For discussion of cylindrical bottles, see Whitehouse 1997, 186-7.

Compare Lightfoot 1992, 51 no. 18; Kunina 1997, 301 nos 231-3 (all from the Panticapaeum necropolis); Sternini 1998, 92-4 no. V74; Arveiller-Dulong and Nenna 2005, 200 no. 559

181   A1921.125   Tall cylindrical bottle

Blue-green; late first to second century AD; found in Cyprus
H 16.85, D (rim) 4.1, D (at top of body) 6.15,
D (at bottom of body) 5.45

- Collared rim with outward horizontal lip and flat upper surface; short, cylindrical and slightly concave neck; gently sloping shoulder; cylindrical body with tapering sides; concave bottom; strap handle applied to edge of shoulder with claws below, drawn up and out, turned in at an acute angle, pressed onto neck and underside of rim.
- Intact. Faint enamel-like weathering, iridescence and dulling; black, streaky impurities in handle; some pinprick bubbles.

Isings Form 51b
Compare Hayes 1975, 59 no. 147; Thomas 1976, 27 no. 106; Welker 1987, 41 no. 49; Barkóczi 1996, 95 no. 299; Kunina 1997, 301-2 nos 235-7 (all from the Panticapaeum necropolis)

Mid-Imperial
Blown Tableware

182 A1936.438   Bowl

Colourless with blue-green tinge
Second to third century AD; found in Syria; transferred
from the V&A
H 5.0, D (rim) 10.0, D (base) 5.6

- Rounded, vertical, thickened rim; slightly convex
  sides, curving in at bottom; tubular base-ring;
  pushed-in bottom with central pontil knob.
- Intact. Patches of faint weathering, iridescence and
  dulling; some glassy inclusions; few bubbles.

Compare Vessberg 1956, 134 figs 42:26-7 (Type B.I.a)

183 A1921.114   Indented bowl

Colourless with pale green tinge
Mid-first to third century AD; found in Cyprus
H 6.0, D (rim) 8.9, D (base) 4.1

- Everted, rounded, thickened rim; slightly convex
  sides; solid, thick pad base; concave bottom with
  pontil scar at centre. Six long, vertical indents,
  placed irregularly around body.
- Intact. Faint weathering and iridescence; pinprick
  bubbles.

184 A1887.372   Indented cup

Pale blue
Mid-first to third century AD
H 7.0, D (rim) 8.3-8.05, D (base) 4.75

- Knocked-off, uneven rim, with slight inward lip;
  bulge below rim; body tapering downwards;
  integral, tubular base-ring; concave bottom.
- Twelve long, vertical indents in sides; above,
  band of wheel-abraded lines around body,
  0.6-0.5 below rim.
- Intact. Faint iridescent weathering and dulling;
  pinprick and larger bubbles.

Isings Form 32
Compare Whitehouse 1997, 113 no. 172; for indented cups found
in Britain, including a fragment from Strageath, Tayside, see Price
and Cottam 1998, 86-8, fig. 29

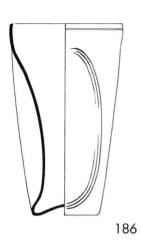
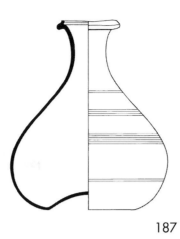

186   187   188

185   A1887.373   Indented beaker

Pale green
Mid-first to third century AD
H 8.7-8.3, D(rim) 10.05-9.65

- Knocked-off, uneven and oval rim; flaring narrow band below; almost vertical sides, curving in at bottom; concave bottom.
- Nine deep elongated indents in sides; above, fine incised groove on exterior below flaring band.
- Intact. Some dulling and iridescent weathering.

Isings Form 32
Compare Whitehouse 1997, 112 no. 171

186   A1957.13   Tall indented beaker

Colourless with pale purple streaks
Mid-first to third century AD
H 11.3, D (rim) 6.7

- Knocked-off, uneven, slightly inverted rim; sides tapering downwards; pushed-in bottom.
- Four deep, long indents, making trapezoidal shape at bottom; wheel-abraded line 0.4-0.5 below rim.
- Intact. Faint iridescence; many bubbles.

187   A1921.130   Flask with cut decoration

Light green
Second to third century AD; found in Cyprus
H 11.9, D (rim) 4.0, D (body) 9.9

- Everted rim, folded round and up, with bevelled outer edge; concave neck, expanding downwards to join imperceptibly with squat, bulbous body; pushed-in bottom.
- Decoration of four bands of wheel-abraded lines horizontally around body; two fine lines at top; four lines below; broader band of six lines at centre and two lines at top of undercurve. Around undercurve horizontal protruding ridge.
- Intact. Brown enamel-like weathering, partially flaked off to leave iridescence and dulling.

Isings Form 26a

188   A1921.117   Large flask

Colourless with green tinge
Second to third century AD; found in Cyprus
H 17.4, D (rim) 4.8, D (base) 13.7

- Everted rim with bevelled lip; slightly funnel-shaped, cylindrical neck; piriform body; concave bottom.
- Decoration comprising many fine horizontal abraded lines in bands around body.
- Intact. Some glassy inclusions; dulling and faint iridescence on exterior; soil and organic material encrusted on side of interior; creamy brown enamel-like weathering, especially on interior; surface pitting; few bubbles.

Such vessels would have been ideal as carafes for wine.

Similar to no. 187

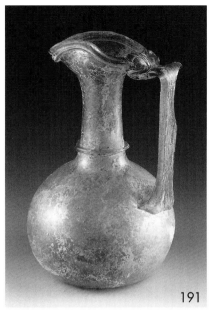

191

193

194

189 A1921.124 Flask

Colourless
Second to third century AD; found in Cyprus
H 10.2, D (rim) 3.7, D (base) 10.2

- Thickened everted rim with bevelled lip and smoothed into mouth; concave neck, curving out to join squat, conical body; bottom concave at centre with slight pontil scar.
- Decoration comprising five registers of wheel-abraded horizontal lines around body: at top and bottom, a fine single line flanking a narrow band to either side of a broad central band.
- Intact. Creamy brown enamel-like weathering, especially on interior; surface pitting; few bubbles.

190 A1880.18.81 Spouted jug

Pale blue
Second to third century AD; from the Grecian archipelago; formerly Piot Collection
H (max.) 9.65, D (max.) 8.2

- Rim folded round and in, drawn out to form spout on one side, pushed down and drawn back on the other; funnel neck below spout; conical body; rounded bottom, pushed in near centre; pad with horizontal crimping at base of handle, drawn up in an elegant loop, pressed onto top of drawn back rim fold with large thumb-rest above, end trailed back along length of handle.
- Intact. Limy weathering on lower part of exterior with faint iridescence and dulling; soil encrustation and enamel-like weathering on interior; some pinprick bubbles.

The rim was formed into a spout in order to facilitate pouring.

For other vessels with similar rims, see Kunina 1997, 309-10 nos 274-7 and 331 no. 392

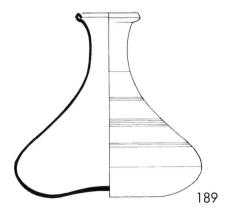

189

191 A1895.280 Jug with trefoil mouth

Pale green
Second to third century AD
H 16.9, L (rim, max.) 7.0, W (rim, max.) 5.3, D (body) 10.9

- Rounded, slightly thickened rim, pushed in at sides to form trefoil mouth; funnel neck below mouth, then cylindrical and expanding downwards to join with sloping shoulder and bulbous sides to body; bottom slightly concave at centre with pontil scar; broad strap handle pressed onto shoulder, drawn up vertically and turned in at an acute handle, then folded under, round and up onto top of rim; fine combed ribbing on exterior of handle.
- Trail wound one and a half times round base of neck from left to right.
- Intact, except for part of handle; crack in body at base of handle. Light soil encrustation and limy weathering, dulling and iridescence; weathering on broken edge of handle (indicating that it is an old, perhaps, ancient break); pinprick bubbles and a few black impurities around neck.

Compare Welker 1987, 45 no. 56

192 Unnumbered Small one-handled bottle

Pale green with blue-green handle
Second to third century AD
H (rim) 8.95, D (rim) 3.4, D (body) 7.35-7.2

- Rounded, everted rim and flaring mouth; conical neck; uneven sloping shoulder; bulbous body; concave bottom; handle applied in large pad to base of neck, drawn up and out, angled in and attached to lip of rim, end trailed back along top of handle. One pinched protrusion in side of body.
- Intact. Some iridescent weathering; faint dulling; some large and many pinprick bubbles.

193 A1927.84 Small cylindrical bottle

Pale green
Second to third century AD
H (rim) 9.5, D (rim) 4.1, D (body) 5.3-5.2

- Everted tubular rim, folded over and in, flattened into sides of flaring mouth; slightly conical neck; sloping shoulder; cylindrical body; slightly convex bottom with prominent pontil scar (causing the vessel to stand aslant and unstable); rod handle applied in large pad on shoulder, drawn up and out, turned in and trailed onto outer and upper edge of rim.
- Intact. Large patches of black enamel-like weathering and brilliant iridescence; surface pitting and dulling; pinprick bubbles.

Compare Oliver 1980, 77 no. 80; Lightfoot 1992, 94 no. 50

194 A1955.14 One-handled bottle

Purple (streaky) with green handle
Second to third century AD
H 9.6, D (rim) 5.2, D (body) 7.0

- Rim folded out, over and in; flaring mouth; concave neck; piriform body; round bottom (stands unstable) with large, round pontil scar; handle applied as thick crimped trail on under-curve of body, drawn up in a slant from right to left to shoulder, then drawn up as a rod, curved in and trailed off below and round rim.
- Intact. Heavily pitted and iridescent exterior surface; many bubbles.

The treatment of the handle recalls a type of bottle commonly found on Cyprus; see Sternini 1998, 97 no. V82. This example, however, may have been made elsewhere.

Late Roman
Blown Tableware

195 A1921.151   Oval dish

Pale blue-green; third to fourth century AD
H 3.4, D (rim) 11.0, D (base) 5.8

- Tubular rim, folded up, round, down and under, uneven and aslant to body; sides curving in gently to integral, tubular base-ring; uneven bottom, pushed-in at centre with pontil mark.
- Intact. Patches of faint, limy weathering, iridescence. Very lopsided.

Isings Form 97a; Compare Merseyside 1979, 17 no. A32; von Saldern 1980, 137-8 nos 138-9; Sternini 1988, 58 no. V5; Whitehouse 1997, 69 no. 80 (with discussion)

196 A1880.18.70   Dish

Colourless with yellow tinge
Third to fourth century AD; formerly Piot Collection
H 4.4, D (rim) 22.3, D (base) 10.7

- Rim folded down and in, forming a broad collar, aslant to body; S-shaped sides; tubular base-ring; almost flat bottom with central pontil scar, thicker towards centre with raised knob on interior.
- Intact. Patches of weathering; elsewhere iridescence and dulling; some pinprick and elongated bubbles.

Similar to no. 195

195

196

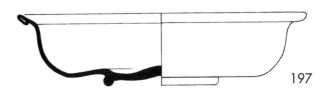

197

198

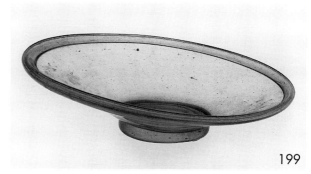

199

197 A1981.415 Dish

Blue-green
Probably fourth century AD
H 3.8, D (rim) 16.0-15.3, D (base) 6.4-6.2

- Tubular rim, folded down and in under lip; S-shaped sides with shallow curves; integral, tubular base-ring; broad bottom with kick and pontil knob at centre.
- Intact. Thick, limy, encrusted weathering covering most of surfaces; patches of dulling and iridescence; one small glassy inclusion.

198 A1957.519 Large dish

Blue-green
Fourth to fifth century AD; found in Syria
Given by Dr G G Allan
H 6.9, D (rim) 23.5, D (base) 10. 2

- Rim folded down and under; broad, slanting sides, curving down to form vertical band, then turned in horizontally above base-ring; tall, applied foot-ring; convex bottom.
- Intact. Faint weathering and iridescence; some pinprick and a few very large bubbles.

199 A1901.547.9 Oval dish

Green
Fifth to early sixth century AD; found at Kôm Ushîm in the Fayyum, Egypt
H 5.0, L (rim) 18.0, W (rim) 11.8, L (base) 6. 2, W (base) 4.2

- Tubular rim, folded up, round, down and under; shallow straight sides slanting in to base; tall,

applied oval foot-ring; slightly concave bottom with pontil scar.
- Intact. Glassy and white, gritty inclusions; many bubbles.

Compare Harden 1968, 82 no. 106; Whitehouse 1997, 71-3, esp. nos 87-9

200 A1926.284 Footed bowl

Blue-green
Perhaps fourth century AD; said to have come from Huainan Province, China
H 5.6, D (rim) 10.05-9.7, D (base) 5.1

- Everted, horizontal, tubular rim, folded round and under; convex, short sides curving in to bottom; integral high base-ring, with tubular edge; almost flat bottom with concave centre and pontil scar.
- Nipt decoration, comprising ten vertical, elongated warts or ribs around undercurve, spaced irregularly.
- Broken around rim and repaired. Small patches of creamy enamel-like weathering; slight iridescence; many pinprick bubbles.

Despite its exotic provenance and unusual shape, this footed bowl has all the characteristics of Roman glass and could be an example of the long-distance trade that took some vessels all the way to China and Korea.[10] Similar tooled ribs are found on a variety of late Roman vessels, including bowls and stemmed cups; see, for example, La Baume 1977, 61 no. 201 and 71 no. 252; Lightfoot 1992, 145 no. 87. The vessel, however, is poorly made and stands so badly aslant that the irregular oval rim is not horizontal. It may, perhaps, be a local product inspired by Roman glass imports.

Compare Watt 2004, 132 no. 42

201 A1922.177 Small bowl

Colourless
Third to fourth century AD
Paper label: 'Amiens 1885'
H 5.7, D (rim) 7.7-7.6, D (base) 5.45

• Everted rim, ground smooth; slightly bulging vertical sides, curving in acutely to slightly concave bottom; base-ring, formed from a separate paraison, with flaring foot with knocked-off edge.
• Decoration of two well-cut grooves set 0.35 and 1.1 below rim.
• Intact. A few gritty white inclusions; dulling and surface pitting; some bubbles.

Compare Whitehouse 1997, 79 no. 102

202 A1895.238.73 Cup

Pale blue-green
Third to fourth century AD; found at Amathus, Cyprus; transferred from the BM
H (max.) 6.7, D (rim) 6.8-6.65, D (max.) 7.0

• Rounded, thickened, slightly inverted rim; slightly convex sides to body; low, pushed-in bottom with pontil scar.
• Intact. Faint iridescent weathering; many bubbles.

Isings Form 96a
Compare Vessberg 1956, 137 figs 44:1, 54:3 and 198-9; Ferrari 1998, 172 no. 1967.115.779

203 A1921.101 Cup

Blue-green
Third to fourth century AD; found in Cyprus
H 7.1, D (rim) 7.1, D (body) 8.1

• Rounded, everted rim; almost straight, conical sides to body, turned in downwards; small bottom with central kick.
• Intact. Iridescence, dulling and deep surface pitting; many bubbles.

Similar to no. 202

204 A1921.112 Cup

Blue-green
Third to fourth century AD; found in Cyprus
H (max.) 5.9, D (rim) 6.3, D (body) 6.85

• Rounded, everted, slightly thickened rim; straight sides to conical body; below, undercurve and rounded bottom with traces of a circular pontil mark and kick near centre. Stands aslant on bottom.
• Intact. Faint iridescent weathering and dulling; some black impurities; few pinprick bubbles.

Similar to no. 202

205 A1921.100 Cup

Blue-green
Third to fourth century AD; found in Cyprus
H 7.9, D (rim) 7.65, D (base) 4.1-3.9

- Rounded and thickened rim; slightly uneven
  bulging sides curving in gently to integral, tubular
  base-ring of irregular, oval shape; uneven, slightly
  pushed-in bottom.
- Intact. Slight iridescent weathering; some glassy
  and white, gritty inclusions; some large and
  pinprick bubbles.

Isings Form 96a

206 A1921.113 Deep bowl

Blue-green
Third to fourth century AD; found in Cyprus
H 5.0, D (rim) 8.3, D (max.) 8.45

- Rounded, vertical rim; straight sides to body, with
  thicker ridge at bottom; below, undercurve and
  rounded bottom with pontil mark at centre and
  large, deep kick.
- Thick-walled, heavy vessel.
- Intact. Faint iridescent weathering and dulling;
  pinprick and a few large bubbles.

Compare Vessberg 1956, 133 fig. 42:24; Oliver 1980, 89 no. 125;
Barkóczi 1996, 28 no. 26 (from Cyprus); Whitehouse 1997, 77
no. 97 (with discussion relating this type of bowl to vessels from
graves in Israel, dating to the third and fourth centuries AD)

207 A1880.18.14 Deep bowl

Patches of pale green and amber-yellow
Third to fourth century AD; formerly Piot Collection
H 5.5, D (rim) 8.8

- Rounded, slightly inverted rim; vertical sides with
  horizontal bulge 1.9 below rim, curving at bottom;
  deep pushed-in bottom with pontil scar.
- Intact; fine enamel-like weathering and iridescence;
  black impurity streaks.

Similar to no. 206

208 A1881.2.4 Deep cup or bowl

Yellow-green
Probably fourth century AD; from Tyre, Lebanon; found
in a tomb in 1876
Label: '1876 Tyre, from ancient tomb'
H 9.3, D (rim) 10.2-10.1

- Knocked-off, vertical rim with flaring mouth;
  slightly convex sides to body; rounded bottom,
  slightly concave at centre.
- Trail applied under rim from right to left for
  almost one and a half turns.
- Intact. Black impurities in rim; patches of
  creamy enamel-like weathering on exterior;
  brown weathering, iridescence and dulling on
  interior; pinprick bubbles.

209

210

211

209 A1961.990 Footed cup

Blue-green with deep turquoise blue trails
Fourth century AD; Syro-Palestinian
Bought from Amie, Lady Noble (of Ardkinglos)
H 7.5, D (rim) 8.3, D (max.) 9.0, D (base) 5.7

- Rounded vertical rim; vertical collar below with tubular hanging fold below; sides curving gently in to integral high base-ring; everted base-ring; deep pushed-in bottom with central pontil scar.
- Trail wound horizontally round body five to six times, then formed into a zigzag below with 15 upwards points and 14 downward angular and uneven points.
- Intact, but internal crack in side. Encrusted, iridescent weathering.

In shape this vessel resembles Isings Form 69a, dated to the first century AD; see Whitehouse 1997, 84 and 87-8 nos 124-6. The deep turquoise trail decoration, however, indicates a later date for this example, showing the popularity of the form through-out the Roman period. The fold below the rim, while causing more work for the maker, served to facilitate the vessel's use since it allowed the cup to be held between thumb and forefinger without fear of it slipping from the drinker's grasp.

Compare Hayes 1975, 103 no. 369

210 A1979.130 Footed cup

Cobalt blue
Fourth century AD; Egyptian
H 7.2-7.4, D (rim) 13.0-13.4, D (base) 5.9

- Rim folded out and down, forming deep collar; tall, S-shaped curve to sides; applied, splayed base, tooled on upper surface; below flat with small central kick and deep pontil scar.
- Intact, except for crack in side below collar. Glassy and white, gritty inclusions; blowing striations; pinprick bubbles.

For this type of vessel, see Harden 1936, 128-9.

Compare Harden 1968, 82 no. 107 (from Egypt); Oliver 1980, 107 no. 174 (with refs); Whitehouse 1997, 82-3 no. 111
Published: *Constable-Maxwell* 1979, 127 lot 228

211 A1961.952 Stemmed bowl

Pale green with bluish tinge
Fourth to fifth century AD; probably made in Egypt
H 8.1, D (rim) 10.35, D (base) 5.7

- Rounded, slightly everted rim; funnel mouth with outward tubular fold below; bell-shaped body with sides tapering in to horizontal under-curve; solid tapering stem; high splayed foot, made from separate paraison, with tooling marks on upper surface and irregular rounded outer edge; deep bottom with prominent central pontil stud.
- Intact. Patches of creamy enamel-like weathering; dulling and iridescence; pinprick and elongated bubbles.

See Harden 1936, 131 no. 358 (Karanis bowl on stem, class IV.B).

Compare Harden 1936, 131 no. 358 (Karanis bowl on stem, class IV.B); *Verres* 1985, no. 283; Whitehouse 1997, 82-3 nos 111-12

212   213   214

212 A1937.520 Footed goblet

Blue-green
Fourth century AD; probably Syro-Palestinian
H 9.5, D (rim) 6.3, D (base) 4.3-4.2

- Rounded, vertical, slightly thickened rim; almost straight sides to conical body, tooled-in to low pedestal and integral tubular base-ring; concave bottom with deep pushed-in centre and pontil scar.
- Three faint horizontal ribs around upper section of body.
- Intact. Brown enamel-like weathering and iridescence on interior; dulling on exterior; some pinprick bubbles.

Fragments of 'Cups with Pushed-in Base' have been found at Jalame in Palestine, although it remains unclear whether the vessels were made at the factory there; see Weinberg 1988, 62-3 nos 187-94.

Compare Hayes 1975, 104 no. 379; Auth 1976, 226 nos 494-5; *Wolkenberg* 1991, lot 76; Kunina 1997, 337 no. 418

213 A1961.988 Footed beaker

Blue-green
Fourth century AD; bought from Amie, Lady Noble (of Ardkinglos)
H 8.9, D (rim) 5.9, D (base) 3.95-3.85

- Rounded, slightly inverted rim; concave sides to body, with acute undercurve; solid pad base; slightly concave bottom with pontil mark.
- Single trail, applied as a broad, leaf-shaped pad and drawn out from left to right slightly more than once around centre of body.

- Intact. Creamy brown, enamel-like weathering, mostly flaked off leaving iridescence and dulling; blowing striations; many pinprick and some large bubbles.

This is a common type of drinking vessel, found at several sites in the Near East. For examples from near Tyre, Lebanon, now in the Ashmolean Museum, Oxford, see Harden 1949a, 153 nos G26-G28. Evidence has been found for the production of 'Cups with Solid Base' at Jalame in Palestine, see Weinberg 1988, 60-2 nos 162-86.

Compare Herbert 1964, 186 no. 980 (from Tyre, Lebanon); Hayes 1975, 103-4 nos 374-7 (with refs); Oliver 1980, 88 no. 123; Arveiller-Dulong and Nenna 2005, 373 no. 989

214 A1927.83 Footed beaker

Pale green
Fourth century AD
H 8.5, D (rim) 7.8, D (base) 4.2

- Thickened, rounded and slightly everted rim; straight sides to body, tapering downwards; solid pad base (possibly added); almost flat bottom with jagged pontil scar.
- Fine trail wound around body in two overlapping circles.
- Intact. One patch of black, enamel-like weathering and iridescence on interior; limy weathering on exterior; some pitting and dulling; pinprick bubbles.

Similar to no. 213

215   A1937.519   Beaker

Blue-green
Third to fourth century AD
H 10.85, D (rim) 6.55, D (bottom) 3.8

- Knocked-off, unworked rim; straight sides, curving slightly and tapering downwards; concave bottom.
- Five bands of wheel-abraded horizontal lines.
- Intact. Creamy brown enamel-like weathering, flaking off to leave iridescence and dulling; surface pitting of pinprick bubbles.

Compare *Shining Vessels* 1991, 32 no. 43

216   A1979.133   Tall beaker

Yellow-green with dark blue blobs
Fourth to fifth century AD
H 10.1, D (rim) 7.4, D (bottom) 4.7

- Knocked-off, unworked and uneven rim with everted lip below; sides tapering towards bottom; integral bulging base-ring; slightly concave bottom.
- Decoration on body: wheel-cut lines and blobs; three large blobs interspersed with groups of three smaller blobs (applied after cut decoration?); abraded horizontal lines in two bands, one 3.3-3.4 and the other 4.8-5.0 below rim.
- Intact, some internal strain cracks. Slight iridescent weathering; several large bubbles.

Isings Form 109c
Compare BM GR1910.4-16.4; Auth 1976, 151 no. 196; Platz-Horster 1976, 90 no. 179 (beaker or lamp); Kunina 1997, 337 no. 423; Arveiller-Dulong and Nenna 2005, 456 no. 1277 (with blue zigzag trail decoration)
Published: Charles Ede, *Important Antiquities* 1978, lot 22

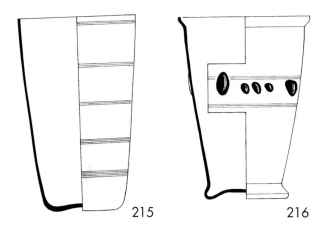

215   216

217   A1957.522   Bowl or lamp

Blue-green
Probably fourth century AD
H 4.6, D (rim) 8.55-8.35

- Rounded, vertical, uneven rim with collar below; sides slightly tapering downwards with undercurve to concave bottom.
- Intact, except for chip and crack in rim. Creamy brown enamel-like weathering on interior with iridescence and pitting; similar weathering on exterior, mostly flaked off leaving dulling and pitting of surface bubbles; many pinprick bubbles.

A vessel in the CMG (79.1.160) has a similar shape but a rim with a folded outer collar. It has been described as a bowl and attributed to the first century AD on account of a parallel from Herculaneum; see Whitehouse 1997, 76 no. 95 (with refs). Compare also a vessel with a ring-base; Kunina 1997, 311 no. 288. Another vessel in the Löffler Collection, however, appears to be a closer parallel to the present example. It is described as a lamp bowl and dated to the fourth century AD or later; see La Baume 1977, 59 no. 194. It is, perhaps, easier to imagine vessels of this distinctive shape as being used as lamps than as lidded containers since the protruding collar would allow the vessel to be suspended either in a solid frame or by means of a chain attachment.

Compare Barkóczi 1996, 28 no. 25; Arveiller-Dulong and Nenna 2005, 190 no. 520 (dated to the end of the first century AD)

217

218 A1895.284   Bowl or lamp

Green with blue tinge
Probably fourth century AD; from a tomb at Tyre, Lebanon
H 6.4, D (rim) 11.35-11.25, D (base) 7.1

- Rounded, everted and slightly thickened rim; concave neck with outward protruding ridge below; vertical sides; concave bottom.
- Intact. Iridescent weathering, dulling and pitting; some pinprick bubbles.

Similar to no. 217

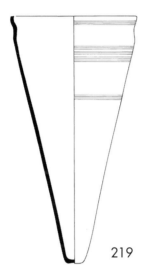

219

219 A1922.176   Conical beaker or lamp

Pale blue-green
Fourth century AD
H 15.7, D (rim) 8.25-8.15

- Knocked-off, unworked rim; slightly indented horizontal band below; straight sides ; small, pointed and rounded bottom.
- Decoration comprising five bands of wheel-abraded horizontal lines around body.
- Intact. Surface pitting and iridescence.

Isings Form 106d; Karanis Class VI.B.1.a
Compare Harden 1936, 162 nos 455-6; Whitehouse 1997, 250 no. 427, Cohen 1997, 408 and pl. III:7-8 (from Hammat Gader, Israel)

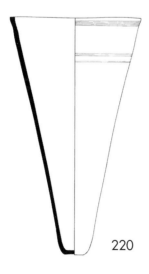

220

220 A1903.374   Conical beaker or lamp

Colourless with green tinge
Fourth century AD
H 17.9, D (rim) 10.2-10.0

- Uneven, ground rim; thick-walled, conical body with slight concave sides; small, flattened bottom.
- Band of wheel-abraded lines, 0.3-0.6 below rim; two further lines, 2.8 and 3.3 below rim, upper more than 0.1 wide, the lower less than 0.1 wide.
- Intact, except for one small chip in rim. Slight surface dulling and faint iridescence; a few bubbles.

Similar to no. 219

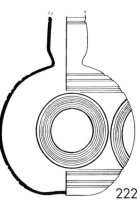

221 A1880.18.18 Flask

Colourless
Third to fourth century AD; formerly Piot Collection
H (as extant) 5.1, D (body) 5.4

- Globular body; slightly flattened, round bottom.
- Decoration of fine engraved lines in bands, approximately 0.6 wide, arranged in a cross-hatch pattern.
- Broken off at top of body. Some surface pitting and faint iridescence on exterior; creamy enamel-like weathering on interior; many pinprick and large bubbles.

222 A1880.18.17 Flask

Colourless
Third to fourth century AD; formerly Piot Collection
H (as extant) 8.3, D (bottom) 6.65

- Vertical rim; slightly funnel-shaped neck, tooled in around base; globular body; slightly concave bottom.
- Decoration of fine engraved lines arranged in matching concentric bands above and below central design of circles; band of engraved lines also around neck where broken off.
- Broken off on neck. White enamel-like weathering, faint iridescence and dulling on exterior; some brownish weathering and iridescence on interior.

Isings Form 103
Compare La Baume 1977, 70 no. 250 (found in Cologne); von Saldern 1980, 80-1 no. 76 (with refs); Matheson 1980, 77-8 no. 203 (with discussion); Kunina 1997, 299 no. 226 (from the Chersonesus necropolis)

223 A1957.520 Indented flask

Light blue
Third to fourth century AD
H 15.7, D (rim) 21.5-20.5, D (body) 9.5

- Fire-rounded and thickened rim; cylindrical neck, tooled in around base; broad, sloping shoulder; globular body; small concave bottom.
- Seven irregular oval indents in sides.
- Intact. Patches of black, enamel-like weathering and iridescence on interior; dulling on exterior; some pinprick bubbles.

Compare *Kofler* 1985, 52 lot 81 (a conical flask with similar indents on the body)

224 A1937.507 Tall flask

Colourless with greenish tinge
Third to fourth century AD
H 22.5, D (rim) 3.4, D (body) 6.6, D (base) 5.6-5.35

- Thickened rim with flattened outer edge; funnel neck with tooled-in groove at base; tall, piriform body; added(?) base-ring, splayed and hollow with flat pad at centre of bottom.
- Single trail wound twice round neck; pre-moulded spiral ribs running from neck down body.
- Intact. Flaking black enamel-like weathering and iridescence, leaving surface dulling; many pinprick bubbles.

9 A1880.18.44 Amphoriskos

1 A1880.18.50 Alabastron

12 A1880.18.38 Aryballos

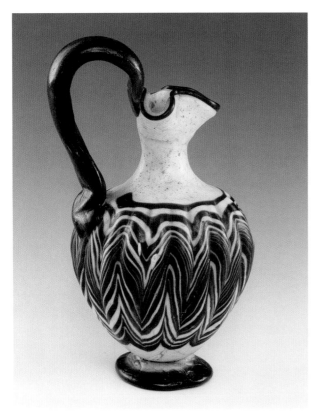

13　A1887.367　Oinochoe

16　A1880.18.43　Oinochoe

17　A1936.435　Alabastron

26　A1880.18.36　Alabastron

41   A1883.22.2   Shallow dish   40   A1883.22.1   Deep bowl

42   A1983.1104   Fragment of cameo glass, head of satyr

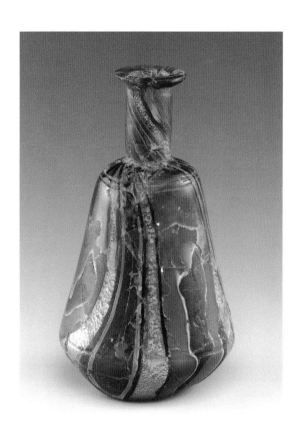

43   A1987.355   Gold-band carinated bottle

47   A1880.18.32   Marbled perfume bottle   46   A1966.358   Marbled perfume bottle

50   A1880.18.76   Flask

141   A1966.64   Small bowl

51   A1983.61   Large jug, with miniature
vessel inside

144 A1921.164 Shallow ribbed bowl

210 A1979.130 Footed cup

235 A1880.18.26 One-handled juglet

237 A1979.30 Small, two-handled jar (amphoriskos)

377 A1880.18.56 Trailed bottle

456 A1911.210.4.M Bottle

492 A1911.286 Floral inlay fragment   493 A1911.285 Floral inlay fragment

499 1960.4 Architectural revetment plaque in sandwich-gold glass

224

225

226

225 A1921.128 Flask

Colourless with green tinge
Third to fourth century AD; found in Cyprus
H 11.4, D (rim) 3.9, D (body) 9.7

- Rounded, thickened rim; flaring mouth above conical neck; broad, bulbous body; solid base-ring; slight kick in bottom, surrounded by pontil scar.
- Trail applied round bottom of neck in three overlapping circles.
- Intact, except for part of trail around neck. Patches of soil encrustation and weathering; faint iridescence; some larger and pinprick bubbles.

Compare Spartz 1967, no. 86 (from Olbia); Auth 1976, 124 no. 154 (with refs); Lightfoot 1992, 130 no. 77; Higashi 1991, 60 no. 29; Weinberg 1992, 133 no. 109

227 A1979.132 Flask

Pale blue-green
Fourth to fifth century AD
H 20.1, D (rim) 3.7, D (body) 6.6, D (base) 4.4

- Rounded and slightly thickened rim; funnel mouth; slender, conical neck; tall, piriform body; short, hollow pedestal and integral tubular base.
- Grozed decoration of five stylised arches with capitals containing hollow rings; above, 19 blobs.
- Intact. Some faint iridescent weathering; many pinprick and elongated bubbles.

For discussion of this and other similar vessels, see Whitehouse 1997, 256-7 no. 438.

Published: *Constable-Maxwell* 1979, 146 lot 266

226 A1937.643 Trailed flask

Blue-green
Third to fourth century AD
H 14.4, D (rim) 2.8, D (body) 8.4

- Thick, rounded rim, vertical to flaring mouth; concave neck, expanding downwards to bulbous body; integral base-ring; flat bottom with small kick at centre.
- Trail applied round neck in two irregular circles and trailed off.
- Intact. Thick, creamy brown weathering, mostly flaked off leaving deep pitting and brilliant iridescence.

227

228 A1961.987 One-handled jug with trefoil mouth

Green with blue tinge
Fourth century AD; bought from Amie, Lady Noble (of Ardkinglos)
H 17.7, L (rim) 7.6, W (rim) 6.6, D (body) 9.25

- Rounded, slightly thickened rim; broad, flaring mouth with sides folded over and in, forming an elegant trefoil mouth; cylindrical, slightly conical neck; sloping shoulder joining imperceptibly with globular body; separate, splayed pad base with tooling marks on upper surface in two layers; concave bottom with central pontil mark.
- Trail applied under rim from left to right, slightly more than one turn; another trail applied as a broad pad at base of neck and trailed around horizontally; handle applied as a broad pad on shoulder, drawn up and out at an acute angle, then curved in and pressed onto underside of rim and on outer lip, nipt off above.
- Intact, except for section of trail around neck. Dulling and pitting on exterior; enamel-like, iridescent weathering on interior; large black impurity in handle; some bubbles.

Compare Welker 1987, 46 no. 57 (from Lebanon)

229 A1899.306 One-handled jug

Pale green with yellow tinge; Fourth century AD; from Tyre, Lebanon
Bought from G. F. Lawrence
H 17.8, D (rim) 5.5-5.15, D (body) 6.7, D (base) 5.0

- Rounded rim; flaring mouth; slender, conical neck, expanding downwards to join slanting shoulder; straight, tapering sides to body; pushed-in curve below; outsplayed tubular base-ring; pushed-in bottom with pontil scar; handle applied as round pad on shoulder, drawn up and outwards as a slender rod, turned in and trailed on under and around rim, trailed off above.
- Trail under rim wound round one and a half times from left to right; a second trail applied around base of neck, also 1½ times from left to right.
- Intact. Creamy enamel-like weathering and iridescence; some limy encrustation; some black impurities and bubbles in rim.

230 A1899.305 One-handled jug

Pale green; fourth century AD; from Nazareth
Bought from G. F. Lawrence
H 19.6, D (rim) 6.2, D (body) 7.5

- Rounded rim; flaring mouth; cylindrical neck; tall, slender body with S-shaped curve to sides; pushed-in bottom with pontil mark near centre; rod handle applied in large pad to edge of shoulder, drawn up and outwards, then turned in horizontally, trailed onto neck and edge of rim with upward fold forming thumb-rest, tooled flat.
- Fifteen pre-moulded slender ribs extending downwards from shoulder, some straight, others curved.
- Broken and mended; one hole in side. Some weathering.

For other vessels decorated with pre-moulded ribs, see Kunina 1997, 333 no. 401.

Compare Oliver 1980, 102 nos 160-1; Lightfoot 1992, 134 no. 81; Arveiller-Dulong and Nenna 2005, 384 no. 1030

231 A1903.263 Jug

Blue-green; sixth century AD; found at Mount Carmel
H 12.7, D (rim) 5.5

- Body blown into a mould. Partially tubular rim, everted, folded round and in, pressed flat into flaring mouth; cylindrical neck; sloping shoulder, broader on side where handle was applied; body divided into six panels; deep, pushed-in bottom with pontil scar; strap handle applied in thick pad, drawn up and curved outwards, round and in, then trailed onto edge of rim, with downward fold.
- Panels are decorated with three different designs: (1) cross-hatch pattern; (2) tree/branch with long slender leaves; and (3) lozenges with circular knobs.
- Intact. Patches of creamy brown weathering; iridescence, dulling and pitting of surface bubbles; some black impurities in handle; elongated and pinprick bubbles.

Compare MMA X243 and X244; Merseyside 1979, 14 no. A25 (probably also from Mount Carmel); *Luzern* 1981, 328; Weinberg 1992, 134 no. 110

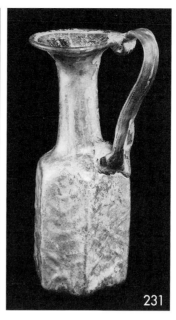

228 230 231 232

232 A1948.407 Jug

Pale blue-green
Sixth century AD
H 21.0, D (rim) 6.1-5.8

- Body blown into a mould. Partially tubular, everted rim, folded over and pressed into broad, flaring mouth; cylindrical neck, expanding downwards; curved, concave shoulder with bulge around edge above moulded sides; six panels on body; deep pushed-in bottom, with kick and jagged pontil scar; rod handle made from part of trail decoration.
- Mould-blown panels are decorated with three different designs: (1) lattice or cross-hatch pattern, (2) palm branch with numerous leaves on either side of a central stem, and (3) lozenges with central circular bosses; on hexagonal bottom, pattern of radiating lines. Trail applied to centre of neck, wound round and down in a spiral three times, trailed across shoulder and pressed as a pad onto edge, then drawn up as rod handle in elegant outward curve and pressed onto rim with upward trail-off.
- Intact, except for part of trail around neck and crack around base of neck and shoulder. Some faint weathering; patches of iridescence, pitting and dulling.

Compare Hayes 1975, 112-13 nos 426-7 (with refs); Oliver 1980, 130 no. 227; *Luzern* 1981, 329; Stern 1995, 260-1 nos 178-9 (with discussion of the group on p. 250-1)

Notes

1   Grose 1989, 244-6.
2   See Fleming 1996b, 16 and fig. 5 (from China); In addition to the complete vessels, the NMS collection also includes a rim fragment, recorded as coming from Cyprus – see no. 39.
3   See Crawford 1987.
4   Höricht 1986; Stern 1999a, 471 with references in no. 175.
5   Grose 1974.
6   Stern 1999a, 479.
7   For the prevalence of drinking vessels among glass produced in the West from the third century AD onwards, see Stern 1999a, 481 and no. 256. By contrast to the English use of the word 'glass' to mean an actual drinking cup and, indeed, of the word 'bottle' to be generally taken to signify a container made of glass (as in wine, beer or milk bottle), 'water bottle' as in 'canteen' or personal heater implies a vessel made in various materials other than in glass.
8   Not having had the opportunity to study the various vessels in detail, I am unable to confirm or refute Harden's assertion.
9   For Ramsay and Cyprus, see Goring 1988, 23.
10 See Watt 2004, 57-65 [An Jiayao], and above p. 20 with footnote 84.

Roman Utilitarian Glassware

Once the skill of glassblowing had been mastered and had been generally adopted by glassmakers, they started to produce vessels in great quantities and in a large number of different shapes. The quality of these products varies widely; some are well made and are of an attractive appearance, but others are crudely formed and of little intrinsic value. Nevertheless, the sheer size of the industry that was required to produce this mass of material underlines how glass became both popular and ubiquitous in the Roman world. Indeed, certain types of common ware almost disappear from the ceramic repertoire in Roman times, replaced by glass equivalents. This is particularly true in the case of pottery bottles (unguentaria) and jars (ampullae).[1]

In addition to a wide range of containers, glassmakers produced other objects associated with the storage and dispensing of foods, liquids, perfumes, ointments, etc. So, for example, lids and funnels were made of glass (see cat. nos 248, 250, 252, 277 and 279), while stoppers were also produced to fit flasks and bottles.[2] Certain vessels were made as sealed phials, implying a very close relationship between the producer of the contents and the glass-worker.[3] Epigraphic evidence from Pompeii reinforces the view that glassmakers and perfume sellers worked closely together, for one quarter of the city was known as the *regio clivi vitrari sive vici turari*.[4] Other glasses were specifically shaped to act as pourers or fillers (gutti), having both a neck and rim at the top for filling and a spout on the side for pouring.[5] Remarkable as it may seem, some of these fillers are regarded as baby or infant feeding bottles.[6] In addition, a variety of utensils were also made from glass; these include siphons, ladles, spoons, spatulas and stirring rods (see cat. nos 457-61).[7]

Mould-blown Vessels

233 A1880.18.27 Flask ('Temple' series)

Translucent dark blue
First half of first century AD; formerly Piot Collection
H (as extant) 6.2, D (base) 2.3

- Blown into a three-part mould, with separate base mould. Cylindrical neck, tooled and pinched in on one side at base; convex sloping shoulder; slightly bulbous cylindrical body; low, circular base with flat underside.
- On shoulder, six pointed arches, each containing a large egg-shaped object; on body, six rectangular panels divided by columns, each with an abacus and torus capital, slender shaft and high double torus base; in the panels, six vessels – (1) a spouted jug (oinochoe) with handle to right, (2) a footed bowl (cylix) with wide opening and two curving handles from shoulder to rim, the opening containing fruit piled up above rim, (3) a footed wide-mouthed vessel (hydria) with two vertical handles on the shoulder, (4) a footed bowl with tall cylindrical neck, (5) a footed jug, similar to panel 1, with high handle to the right, and (6) a second footed vessel as in panel 3; around the bottom, fillets suspended from the centre of one

panel to the centre of the adjacent panel, with alternating large and small fruits with knobbed surfaces below each column; on bottom, two poorly formed raised concentric circles.
- Rim and upper section of neck missing. Patches of faint weathering and dulling.

A large number of vessels of this type are known. They are attributed to workshops that were operating along the Syro-Palestinian coast during the first century AD, although their find-spots indicate that they were traded widely throughout the eastern Mediterranean. For a full discussion, see Stern 1995, 74-86.

Compare BM GR 1913.5-22.15; Thomas 1976, 19 no. 47; Stern 1995, 122-7 nos 26-33 (Series A3); Kunina 1997, 279 nos 134-6; Arveiller-Dulong and Nenna 2005, 224-5 nos 655-6

234   235   237

234 A1880.18.25 One-handled juglet

Pale bluish-green, with colourless handle
Second quarter of first century AD; Syro-Palestinian;
formerly Piot Collection
H (max.) 9.9, H (to rim) 9.6, D (rim) 2.7-2.5

- Blown in a three-part mould, with separate base
  mould. Everted rim, folded round and in; cylindrical
  neck; convex shoulder and bottom above and
  below an indented cylindrical body; flat base with
  three raised concentric circles; handle attached
  in pad to shoulder, drawn up and turned in
  horizontally with pinched thumb-rest above rim.
- On shoulder, elaborate but indistinct design
  representing six different animals divided into
  pairs by plants; on body, six square panels framed
  by beaded ribs and topped by alternating triangular
  pediments and arches, again in beaded outline;
  each panel contains an object in relief, four of
  which are plant motifs, while the two remaining
  panels contain a footed, one-handled jug and a
  pair of strigils; around the bottom, a design of
  tightly packed tongues or gadroons.
- Intact. Creamy whitish weathering, brilliant
  iridescence and pitting.

Stern has argued that, despite the similarity of the
decoration on these vessels to that on products
signed by Ennion, it is unlikely that any of them
were made in his workshop. Nevertheless, it is
clear that they drew their inspiration from the
famous glassmaker and were probably produced
in the same area.

Compare Matheson 1980, 45-6 nos 119-20 (with refs; no. 120 is
a close parallel and may be from the same mould); Stern 1995,
146-8 no. 48

235 A1880.18.26 One-handled juglet

Translucent blue, with greenish colourless handle
Second half of first century AD; formerly Piot Collection
H (max.) 9.1, H (to rim) 8.5, D (rim) 2.8

- Blown into a two-part mould, with separate
  base mould. Rim folded out, up and in; cylindrical
  neck; convex shoulder, curving down and out to
  cylindrical body; convex undercurve; flat, circular
  base pad; bifurcated handle applied to shoulder,
  drawn up and outward in a gentle curve, then
  formed into projecting thumb-rest as loop above
  rim, and trailed onto edge of rim and top of neck.
- On the shoulder, a frieze of indistinct ribs; on the
  body, two floral sprays arranged horizontally, each
  with single-pointed leaves alternating with stems
  ending in round knobs, probably representing an
  olive wreath; above and below this central panel
  runs a single horizontal raised rib; around the
  bottom, another frieze of ribs.
- Intact. Faint iridescence; small patch of dulling.

Compare Auth 1976, 198 no. 323; *Benzian* 1994, 48 lot no. 79;
Verres 1985, 61 no. 129; Heisserer 1986, 106 no. 168; Stern 1995,
169 no. 78

238

236 A1880.18.30 One-handled juglet

Pale purple with opaque handle
Second half of the first century AD; Syro-Palestinian;
formerly Piot Collection
H 6.0, D (rim) 2.5, D (body) 3.8

• Neck free-blown; body blown into a two-part with
  prominent mould marks down sides of body and
  across bottom. Rim folded out, round and in; short,
  cylindrical neck; ovoid body; small, round pad
  base; rod handle applied to shoulder, drawn up
  and out, then curved in and trailed onto and under
  rim, with loop above rim forming a miniature
  thumb-rest.
• Moulded decoration on body in three registers; at
  top, band of downturned tongues in raised outline;
  similar upturned tongues on lower body; at centre,
  a frieze of lozenges forming a pattern of Xs
  around body.
• Intact, except for one hole in body. Iridescence;
  small patches of dulling and surface pitting.

Bulbous bottles decorated with a central band of
lozenges were clearly made either in a number of
different workshops or, at least, by craftsmen using
a variety of moulds. Most examples with known
provenances have been found in the East, even
beyond the Roman frontier in Georgia and
Armenia; see Lightfoot 1989, 25-6 no. 8; Stern
1995, 150-1 nos 53-4 (with refs).

Compare a similar one-handled juglet in the Adana Regional
Museum, Turkey (inv. no. 24.1.72, unpublished)

237 A1979.30 Small, two-handled jar (amphoriskos)

Dark manganese purple
Second half of first century AD
H 8.8, D (rim) 2.8

• Blown into a two-part mould. Partially tubular
  rim, folded out, round and in; short, cylindrical
  neck; elongated piriform body; pointed, nipple
  bottom; two rod handles attached to upper part
  of body, drawn up and out, then curved round, in
  and down onto neck, and trailed off above.
• Body decorated with 19 concentric, horizontal ribs.
• Faint weathering and iridescence on interior;
  some bubbles.

Stern has suggested that, since there are numerous
variations in size and shape, such vessels were produced in a number of different workshops, probably
located somewhere in the eastern Mediterranean.
No exact parallel for this example has been found.

Compare von Saldern 1974, 146-7 nos 418, 420-5; Stern 1995, pp.
157-9 nos 64-8 (with discussion and refs); Kunina 1997, 280 nos
142-4; Arveiller-Dulong and Nenna 2005, 266 no. 804 (from Cyrenaica)
Published: Charles Ede, *Roman Glass* 1979, lot. 1

238 A1979.128 Multi-sided bottle (amphoriskos)

Dull blue-green
Second half of first to early second century AD
H 6.6, D (body) 3.8, D (rim) 2.9

• Blown into a two-part mould. Partially tubular
  rim, folded out, round, up and in; cylindrical neck;
  nine-sided body; square, slightly convex bottom;
  two rod handles applied to shoulder above main
  panel on each side in a wide claw, drawn up and
  folded in onto neck.
• Intact. Dulling and faint iridescence.

Several examples have been found in the Black Sea
region, suggesting that this type of vessel was produced somewhere in the eastern half of the Empire.

Compare Stern 1995, 150 no. 52 (listing 16 other examples, with
refs); Kunina 1997, 279 no. 137; Arveiller-Dulong and Nenna 2005,
224 no. 653
Published: *Constable-Maxwell* 1979, no. 104

239   240   241

239   A1880.18.28   Date flask

Amber brown
Mid-first to second century AD; formerly Piot Collection
H 7.0, D (rim) 1.3, W (max.) 3.1

- Body blown into a two-part mould of two vertical sections. Everted rim, folded round and in; flaring neck; body shaped like a date with wrinkled surface.
- Creamy weathering, flaking off in patches to leave iridescence and dulling.

For a full discussion of this type, see Stern 1995, 91-4.

Isings Form 78d
Compare Stern 1995, 172-9 nos 84-107; Kunina 1997, 281 nos 147-8 (both from the Panticapaeum necropolis); Sternini 1998, 70-1 no. V20 (with refs); Arveiller-Dulong and Nenna 2005, 227 nos 661-3

240   A1880.18.24   Janiform head-flask

Pale yellow-green
Third century AD; eastern Mediterranean, possibly Syro-Palestinian; formerly Piot Collection
H 8.5, D (rim) 4.0, D (body) 4.9

- Rim and neck free-blown; body blown into a two-part mould. Tubular rim, folded round and into flaring mouth; cylindrical neck; body in the shape of a double head; flat bottom.
- The moulded decoration comprises two heads, back to back with similar features, resembling chubby, childlike faces: large round eyes, fat cheeks, large nose, small mouth with dimples at the corners, and prominent chin. The hair is rendered as rows of distinct, evenly spaced knobs that frame the face to chin level.
- Intact. Enamel-like weathering and iridescence.

For a general discussion of 'head-shaped vessels', see Stern 1995, 201-15.

Compare Stern 1995, 234 no. 150

241   A1921.123   Square bottle

Light blue
Second half of first century AD; found in Cyprus
H 16.4, L (at top of body) 7.6, W (at top) 7.6, L (at bottom of body) 7.5, W (at bottom) 7.35, D (base) 13.9

- Collared rim with bevelled upper lip; cylindrical neck with tooling marks around base; sloping shoulder; flat sides, tapering slightly downwards; flat bottom with slight hollow towards centre; strap handle applied to shoulder with two claws below, drawn up and turned in at an acute angle, pressed onto neck.
- Broken and mended. Faint enamel-like weathering and iridescence; some dulling and pitting; pinprick bubbles.

Cf. *Shining Vessels* 1991, 66 no. 119; Kunina 1997, 285 nos 163-4

242

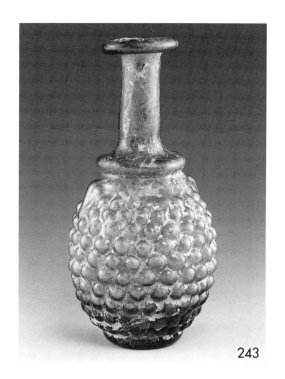

243

242 AI882.28.3 Square bottle

Blue-green
Second half of first to second century AD
H 10.5, D (rim) 3.1, W (body) 5.4, W (bottom) 4.5

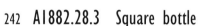

- Rim everted, folded round and in; neck expanding
  downwards, pushed into body, forming hollow
  circle around square shoulder; flat sides formed in
  a mould; flat bottom; ribbed handle dropped on to
  edge of shoulder, drawn up vertically and curved
  in and down, then pressed onto neck below rim.
- Intact, except for one crack in side. Soil-encrusted
  weathering, flaking off, on interior; iridescence
  on exterior; streaky black impurities in handle;
  elongated bubbles in neck.

Isings Form 50a
For a general discussion of square bottles, see Charlesworth 1966
(mainly finds from Roman Britain); Whitehouse 1997, 183 no. 322
(with refs); Rottloff 1999

243 AI903.265 Large grape flask

Yellow-green
Late second to early third century AD; found at Mount Carmel
H 13.0, D (rim) 3.3, D (max.) 6.7

- Blown into a two-part mould, with separate base
  mould. Tubular rim, folded out, down, round and
  in; tall, cylindrical neck, with tooled indent around
  base, then flaring out to hollow projecting roll
  around shoulder; bulbous body; slightly concave
  base with central pontil mark.
- On the body, stylised pattern of grapes, arranged
  in ten horizontal rows of hemispherical knobs; at
  the top to each side, a small triangular leaf with a
  raised central stem.
- Intact. Patches of iridescent weathering and
  dulling; elongated bubbles on neck.

Blown in the same mould as no. 244 and belongs
to Stern's Series A. Numerous examples of this type
of vessel are recorded from the Near East, and this
flask may now be added to the list. They vary in
height because after the body had been blown into
the mould the vessel was finished off by applying the
pontil to the bottom and then working the neck and
rim free-hand. These grape flasks are closely related
to other mould-blown vessels with a decoration of
overlapping circles and dimples (Fleming 1996b,
fig. 2) that bear comparison with the patterns
found on Roman silverware.

Compare MMA 30.115.79; UPM no. MS 5114 (Fleming 1996b, fig.
3c); Merseyside 1979, 13 nos A23-A24 (the latter from Jaffa); Auth
1976, 73 no. 72 (with refs); 200 nos 335-6; *Constable-Maxwell*
1979, 55 lots 76-7; Stern 1995, 191-5 nos 120-8 (with discussion
and refs); Kunina 1997, 281, nos 149-51; Arveiller-Dulong and
Nenna 2005, 397-8 nos 1074-6

244 A1957.369 Large grape flask

Pale yellow-green, with opaque blue blobs
Late second to early third century AD; Syro-Palestinian
H (as extant) 9.6, D (max.) 6.7

- Blobs on top edge of shoulder bulge above leaves.
  Pontil mark on concave bottom.
- Rim and upper section of neck missing.
  Weathering on interior.

Blown in the same mould as no. 243

245 A1955.13 Large sprinkler flask

Pale green with purple streak in rim
Third to fourth century AD
H 10.3, D (rim) 5.7, D (body) 7.9

- Made in two separate parts; body blown into a two-
  part mould; neck free-blown and tooled. Rounded
  rim with rib on undercurve; broad, flaring mouth;
  cylindrical neck, tooled in to top of globular body;
  rounded bottom with jagged pontil scar.
- Body decorated with pattern of circular bosses
  and concentric circles, of which only two are now
  discernible.
- Broken and mended around mouth. Deep pitting
  and brilliant iridescence covering most of surfaces.

The moulded design is similar to that found on some cut-glass
and silver vessels; see above no. 222

246

246 A1888.378 Small cylindrical bottle

Deep blue-green
Probably third to fourth century AD, but possibly Islamic
H 9.7, D (rim) 3.4-3.3, D (max.) 6.9

- Everted rim with bevelled lip; cylindrical, slightly
  bulbous neck; curving shoulder; cylindrical body
  with almost vertical sides; pushed-in bottom with
  jagged pontil scar.
- Mould-blown decoration around body in four
  panels: four circular raised bosses between vertical
  raised ribs with eight small circular indents below
  and forming a rosette pattern on bottom. No
  visible trace of mould marks.
- Intact. Deep pitting of surfaces with some
  iridescent weathering.

No clear parallel has been found

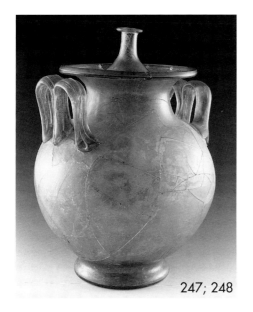

247; 248

247 A1881.32 Cinerary urn

Light blue-green

Mid-first to second century AD; said to have been found in the ancient city of Libarna; discovered in 1846 during the construction of a railway line in the Serraville district

H 29.8, D (rim) 19.8-19.5, D (body) 26.0, D (bottom) 14.1

- Thick, tubular rim, folded up, round and in, with flattened outer edge; flaring mouth; neck expanding downwards; sloping shoulder; bulbous body, tapering downwards; pushed-out, splayed integral base-ring; concave bottom; two large handles, applied to shoulder from left to right, worked into vertical, M-shaped loops and trailed off back along top of handle.
- Broken and repaired; some areas of fill in sides. Faint iridescence and dulling; some black impurities in rim and handles; very many bubbles.

Large glass vessels frequently found a secondary use as receptacles for the cremated remains of the deceased.[8] Most examples have been found in Italy and the western provinces.[9] Like the two examples here, the glass urn with lid in the Hunterian Museum in Glasgow (D.1969.3) probably came from Italy.[10] However, examples are also known from sites in North Africa, and one urn in the MMA is said to be from Alexandria in Egypt, but very few have been recorded from Greece and Asia Minor – an unpublished example in the Çankırı Museum, Turkey probably represents a local find from the Roman city of Gangra in Paphlagonia.[11] For examples found in the Roman cemeteries in Albania (principally from

Vessels used for Specific Purposes

Dyrrachium), see Tartari 2005, 26-7, 149-54 nos 266-76, figs 1 and 7a. For further discussion, see Whitehouse 1997, 171; Foy and Nenna 2003, 266.

Isings form 63

Compare BM P&RB 1836.2-13.18; MMA 91.1.1297; *Fitzwilliam* 1978, 38-9 nos 72-3; Harden 1978, 306 pl. I,7 (BM G&R 1851.8-13.511, from Orange, France); Merseyside 1979, 16 no. A30; Whitehouse 1997, 172 no. 302; Arveiller-Dulong and Nenna 2005, 168-9 nos 473-7; Page 2006, 37 no. 11 (possibly from Cologne)

248 A1881.32A Funnel lid

Light blue-green

Mid-first to second century AD

H 6.9, D (knob handle) 3.75-3.65, D (max.) 14.3-14.1

- Everted rim, folded round and in, flattened on top and forming constriction at top; cylindrical neck at top, then flaring out into conical shoulder; flat body; outer edge folded, partially tubular, round and under, on one side pressed flat (probably when held by maker to form rim), forming rounded and slightly bulging edge.
- Intact. Faint iridescent weathering on upper surface; dulling on underside; blowing striations; some pinprick and large bubbles.

Usually described simply as 'lids', these objects also served as libation funnels through which offerings could be made to the dead; see Whitehouse 1997, 172.

Found with no. 247

249; 250

250 A1887.371A Oval lid

Pale green with blue tinge
Mid-first to second century AD
H 5.9, D (knob handle) 3.85-3.8, D (max.) 10.9-10.55

- Knob at top folded out, down, round and in, as if vessel rim but without mouth; upper surface of knob irregular and bevelled with central tooled hollow; cylindrical neck, flaring downwards to broad, shallow, conical body; thick, solid, down-turned lip, rounded and with bevelled outer edge.
- Intact. Some soil encrustation and weathering under rim and inside knob; elsewhere faint iridescence and dulling; a few gritty and black impurities; many bubbles, some elongated horizontally.

Found with no. 249

249 A1887.371 Cinerary urn

Pale green with blue tinge
Mid-first to second century AD; from Puteoli (Pozzuoli), Italy
H 29.8, D (rim) 14.2-13.9, D (body) 20.2, D (bottom) 11.4

- Tubular rim, folded out, over and in; tall, flaring mouth; short, concave neck; broad, sloping shoulder; ovoid body, tapering downwards; vertical foot band above concave bottom; two handles applied to shoulder in large circular pads and drawn across from left to right, tooled into upright M-shaped loops.
- Intact, except for internal strain cracks around body. Brilliant iridescent sheen to part of exterior; elsewhere yellowish-brown weathering and dulling; blowing striations; two white, gritty inclusions in side; few bubbles.

Similar to no. 247

251 A1956.450 Cinerary urn (olla)

Pale blue-green
Second half of first to early third century AD
H 21.9, D (rim) 17.0, D (body) 22.0, D (bottom) 11.0

- Broad, everted, tubular rim, folded down, under and round; broad, piriform body, tapering downwards; concave bottom.
- Intact. One large glassy inclusion in side, forming protruding blob. Creamy brown weathering, partially flaked off, on interior; slight dulling on exterior; soil encrustation and thick weathering in fold under rim; blowing striations; many pinprick bubbles.

Isings Form 67a
Compare Thomas 1976, no. 71; *Fitzwilliam* 1978, 38 nos 71; Merseyside 1979, 17 no. A31 (from Ventimiglia, Italy); Kunina 1997, 331 no. 387; Whitehouse 1997, 175 no. 307 (with discussion); Newby 1999, 62 no. 53; Arveiller-Dulong and Nenna 2005, 158-64 nos 433-58

252 A1956.450A Lid

Pale blue-green
Second half of first to early third century AD
H 7.3, D (knob handle) 4.05, D (max.) 14.7

- Rim folded out, round and in, pressed into side, forming constriction; cylindrical neck, expanding downwards; concave sides; bevelled, slanting edge, with rounded lower lip. Formed originally like a vessel, but with the body cut off and lower edge turned into the rim of the lid.
- Intact. Iridescent weathering on underside; slight soil encrustation and dulling on upper surface; creamy weathering, partially flaked off, on rim; few bubbles.

Isings Form 66b
Found with no. 251

251; 252

253 A1857.157.2 Cinerary urn

Light blue-green
First to second century AD; from the ancient necropolis at Tharros, Sardinia
Purchased at the Chevalier Barbetti Sale (London)
H (max.) 19.9, D (rim) 21.7-21.4, D (body) 26.0, D (bottom) 13.1

- Broad, round, everted rim, with tubular fold at edge, turned down and in, then back out another tubular fold under rim; globular body; concave bottom.
- Intact. Patches of weathering and brilliant iridescence on interior; faint weathering, iridescence and dulling on exterior; one jagged glassy inclusion in side; blowing striations; pinprick bubbles.

Similar to no. 251

253

254

255

254 A1880.18.77 Oil bottle (aryballos)

Blue-green
Late first to mid-second century AD; formerly Piot Collection
H 7.2, D (rim) 2.6, D (body) 7.1

• Collared rim, folded out, down, round and up; short neck; bulbous body; rounded bottom; two trailed loop handles on shoulder, pressed on to body in a large pad, drawn up and in and pressed down. One handle shows tooling marks very clearly. Uneven and carelessly made.
• Intact. Slight iridescence and pitting.

Glass aryballoi are a common type of vessel, used for carrying oil to the baths or gymnasium. Several examples have survived complete with their bronze suspension chain or carrying apparatus; see, for example, von Saldern 1968, no. 60; von Saldern 1974, 188 no. 518; Auth 1976, 118 nos 142-4; Matheson 1980, 32 no. 91; Welker 1987, 27 no. 25; Whitehouse 1997, 201 no. 351. The present example is unusual in that the handles are attached to the shoulder and do not extend as far as the neck; see Sorokina 1987, 41 and figs 2-3.

Compare Higashi 1991, 57 no. 23

255 A1881.2.2 Oil bottle (aryballos)

Colourless
Late first to mid-second century AD; from Tyre, Lebanon
H 9.5, D (rim) 6.5, D (body) 9.8

• Collared rim with horizontal outer lip and prominent downward fold; short, cylindrical neck; globular body; small, concave bottom; two thick handles applied to shoulder, drawn up and turned in, pressed onto neck and underside of rim.

• Intact, except for repair in rim. Limy weathering on most of vessel; some dulling and iridescence on exterior; pinprick and elongated bubbles.

This vessel belongs to Sorokina's 'Second Group', which may have been made in western Asia Minor; see Sorokina 1987, 41-3 and figs 2-4.

Isings Form 61

256 A1899.303 Kohl bottle

Yellow green
Fourth century AD; found at Mount Carmel (with nos 258 and 302)
Bought from G. F. Lawrence
H 13.2, D (rim) 3.8, D (body) 3.5, D 4.1 (base)

• Everted rim, folded over and in; tall neck, expanding downwards; squat, globular body, tooled in below; high, integral, tubular base-ring; deep kick in bottom with pontil scar; two 'ear' loop handles applied to neck, drawn out and up, and trailed onto rim and neck under rim; one thicker and straighter, the other more rounded.
• Nine tooled ribs drawn down body from top left to bottom right in gentle S-shaped curve from underside of rim.
• Intact, except for cracks in rim. Creamy enamel-like weathering, flaking off in patches to leave iridescence; few pinprick bubbles.

For the use of kohl in antiquity as make-up, especially for painting the upper eyelids and the eyebrows, see Dayagi-Mendels 1989, 36-44 (with examples of glass kohl bottles from Eretz Israel illustrated on p. 49).

Compare Vessberg 1956, 167 fig. 47:28; Welker 1987, 56 nos 74-5; Kunina 1997, 335 no. 409; Arveiller-Dulong and Nenna 2005, 412 no. 1132

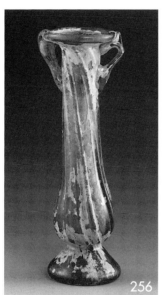

256 257 258 259

257 A1899.310 Single kohl bottle

Blue-green
Fourth to fifth century AD; from Hebron, Palestine
Bought from G. F. Lawrence
H (rim) 10.2, D (rim) 3.3, D (body) 2.9, D (base) 3.25-3.15

- Tubular rim, folded over and in; flaring mouth; long and slender cylindrical body, curving out to join imperceptibly with squat, slightly bulbous body; integral tubular base-ring, crudely tooled in; pushed-in, uneven bottom with pontil mark; two claw-pad handles applied to neck, drawn out and up, pinched off on rim.
- Fine spiral trail applied on base-ring and trailed around body many times, ending under rim.
- Hole in bottom of body; parts of trails missing, especially on lower section of neck and body. Enamel weathering, brilliant iridescence and pitting.

Compare *Verres* 1985, nos 437 and 439; Higashi 1991, 70 no. 43; Barkóczi 1996, 42 no. 77

258 A1899.302 Single kohl bottle

Yellowish-green
Fourth century AD; found at Mount Carmel (with nos 256 and 302)
Bought from G. F. Lawrence
H (with handle) 13.5, D (rim) 4.9, D (body) 3.95-3.8, D (base) 3.15-2.9

- Tubular rim, folded out, over and in; flaring mouth; long, cylindrical body, curving out to squat, slightly bulbous body; tubular base-ring, crudely tooled into bottom of vessel with deep kick and pontil scar. Vessel stands unstable on base-ring.
- Trail applied to neck in pad and then wound round in zigzag pattern with six matching upward and downward points; a second, fine trail runs across this zigzag would twice round body in a spiral.
- Intact, except for part of trail in rim below loop handle; part of spiral trail missing. Patches of iridescent weathering and pitting; few bubbles.

Compare Barkóczi 1996, 41-2 nos 74-6

259 A1899.309 Single kohl bottle

Blue-green
Fourth century AD; Sidon, Lebanon
Bought from G. F. Lawrence
H (with handle) 16.4, D (rim) 3.8, D (base) 3.8

- Everted tubular rim, folded over and in; cylindrical body, bulging slightly towards bottom; thick-walled, flaring base with concave bottom and pontil scar; strap handle in loop, applied to outer edge of rim.
- Spiral trail wound round centre of body five times, then two vertical zigzag trails applied to sides in large pads at bottom and trailed off on upper edge of rim.
- Intact, but crack in rim below loop handle; part of spiral trail missing. Patches of iridescent weathering and pitting; a few bubbles.

260 A1950.43 Double kohl bottle

Greenish colourless with deep blue trails
Second half of fourth century AD; Syro-Palestinian
H 11.2, L (rim) 3.9, W (max.) 2.2

- Tubular rim, folded round and into mouth; tall, cylindrical body with two compartments; one side bulbous, the other more pointed; thick, uneven bottom.
- Crimped trails applied at bottom of sides and drawn up with loop handles at top, trailed onto outer edge and top of rim.
- Broken and mended. Limy weathering, iridescence, pitting and dulling on body.

Compare Merseyside 1979, 23-4 nos A44 (b) and (d), from Nazareth and Tiberias respectively; Fleming 1997, 31 fig. 15 (UPM no. 32-15-68, from the north cemetery at Bet Shean, ancient Scythopolis, Israel)

261 1895.278 Double kohl bottle

Blue-green
Late fourth to fifth century AD; from a tomb at Mount Carmel
H 12.15, L (rim) 3.65, W (rim) 2.25, W (max.) 4.7

- Tubular rim, folded round and in, partly blocking mouth; tall, slight concave sides to body with two compartments, flaring outward at bottom; thick, uneven, round bottom with central pontil scar.

- Zigzag trail applied below rim and drawn up to outer edge of rim with four upward and three downward points, then trailed round body seven times in a spiral.
- Intact, except for small lengths of trail. Iridescent weathering and pitting; pinprick bubbles.

Compare Spartz 1967, nos 131-2 (with refs); Barkóczi 1996, 40 no. 67; Fleming 1997, 34 fig. 21 (UPM no. MS 5105); Ferrari 1998, 181 (no. 1967.115.815, with discussion)

262 A1958.95 Double kohl bottle

Colourless with blue-green tinge
Late fourth to fifth century AD
H (body) 11.7, L (rim) 3.9, W (rim) 2.2, L (max.) 4.95

- Poorly and partially formed tubular rim; cylindrical sides to body; slightly flattened pad on bottom with pontil scar; two small handles applied to sides, drawn up and out at an angle, turned in horizontally and trailed off on top edge of rim.
- Trail applied at bottom and wound round body in spiral of 16 turns; decoration apparently applied before fusion of the two compartments.
- Intact. Some soil encrustation; weathering and dulling; elongated, vertical bubbles.

Similar to no. 261, but also compare *Kofler* 1985, 21 lot no. 23; Higashi 1991, 70 no. 44

263 A1950.44 Double kohl bottle

Green
Fourth to fifth century AD
H 10.75, W (rim) 2.9, L (max.) 7.25

- Tubular, everted rim, folded round and into mouth; tall, cylindrical body with two compartments, broadening and curving in at bottom; flattened bottom. The two tubes are joined by a single sheet or layer of glass.
- Wavy trails applied to sides, dropped on at bottom and trailed up to top of rim and trailed off.
- Metal (bronze or iron?) spatula embedded in one compartment.
- Intact, but internal crack in side. Iridescent weathering on handles; dulling and slight iridescence on body.

264 *A1966.61* Double kohl bottle

Blue-green with dark blue handles and loop
Fourth to fifth century AD
Bequeathed by Mrs A. W. Acworth; formerly in the Acworth Collection
H (body) 11.5, H (max.) 17.0, L (rim) 5.5, W (rim) 3.5

- Large tubular rim, folded over and in with broad collar inside mouth; cylindrical sides to body; one compartment more bulbous, the other more pointed at the bottom; thick, slightly flattened bottom with smooth pontil mark; claw-pad handles applied to sides, drawn out and up at an angle from body and turned in acutely to outer edge of rim; further loop pressed onto top of handles.
- Trail applied near bottom and drawn up in spiral of eight and a half turns; decoration apparently applied before the two compartments were fused together.
- Intact, except for chip in loop handle. Brilliant iridescence on handles and loop; some patches of thick limy weathering; elsewhere iridescence and pitting of surface bubbles.

Although this bottle was accessioned together with a glass rod applicator (below no. 460), the two objects should probably not be associated.

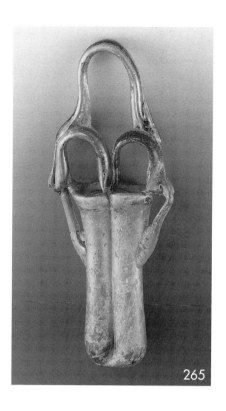

265

Compare Merseyside 1979, 24 no. A44 (c), from Nazareth; Heisserer 1986, 109-10 no. 177 (reportedly found at Hama, Syria); Welker 1987, 54 no. 71 (from Palestine); Kunina 1997, 335 no. 413

265 A1961.953 Double kohl bottle ('saddle-flask' type)

Blue-green; trail handle in pyramid of three loops
Fifth to sixth century AD
H (body) 12.4, H (total) 21.6, L (rim) 5.6, W (rim) 3.75

- Tubular rim, folded out, over and in, forming deep collar inside mouth; long, slightly concave sides to body; small, narrow bottom with scar from pontil at end.
- Handles trailed onto sides of body, drawn up and out, turned in at acute angle to edge of rim; second double loop applied on top of handles and to rim of central partition; third tall loop applied above.
- Intact, but cracks in sides and bottom. Iridescent weathering and dulling.

Compare Higashi 1991, 71-2 no. 45; Arveiller-Dulong and Nenna 2005, 484 no. 1322

General Purpose Storage Vessels

266

266 A1954.54 Jar or small olla

Purple
Probably first century AD
H 6.2, D (rim) 5.5, D (body) 6.0

- Rim folded out, under and round, with broad, sloping upper edge and folds underneath; globular body; small, concave bottom.
- Intact. Dulling and iridescence; some pitting of surface pinprick bubbles.

For a large version, decorated with marvered blobs, see Harden 1987, 111 no. 44 (from Arles, France); compare also *Sangiorgi* 1999, 55 no. 123.

Isings Form 68
Compare Spartz 1967, no. 44

267 A1880.18.60 Ribbed flask

Deep purple, appearing opaque black
First century AD; formerly Piot Collection
H (as extant) 11.3, D (max.) 9.0, D (body) 8.75

- Slightly conical neck; broad, sloping shoulder; bulbous body; concave bottom.
- Thirteen tooled ribs running from lower part of neck down sides with pronounced curving fins.
- Broken around neck; rim missing. Enamel-like weathering, flaking off to leave brilliant iridescence and pitting.

Isings Form 26b
Compare MMA 74.51.37 (from Cyprus); Winfield Smith 1957, 91 no. 152; Hayes 1975, 52 no. 109; Kunina 1997, 294 no. 199; see also Matheson 1980, 27 nos 72-3 (with refs)

268 A1944.1 Flask

Pale yellow green
Probably mid- to late first century AD
H 10.8, D (rim) 3.5, D (body) 5.1

- Rounded and slightly thickened rim; flaring mouth; cylindrical neck; sloping shoulder; bulbous body; concave bottom.
- Intact. Creamy brown enamel-like weathering, flaking off to leave brilliant iridescence; pitting of surface bubbles.

269 A1927.610 Tall conical flask

Pale manganese purple
Probably first century AD
H 15.6, D (rim) 3.1, D (body) 5.4

- Everted, tubular rim, folded over and in; flaring, funnel mouth; neck tapering downwards, with indent at base; tall, conical body; slightly concave bottom.
- Intact. Creamy weathering and iridescence on interior; dulling and faint iridescence on exterior; some black impurities around rim and mouth; some large and smaller, elongated bubbles.

271

270

270 A1880.18.78 Amphoriskos

Blue-green

Second half of first century AD; probably Cypriot; formerly Piot Collection

H 13.35, D (rim) 2.6, D (max.) 5.8, D (base) 3.2

- Tubular rim, folded out, over and in; cylindrical neck curving out and joining imperceptibly with piriform body; integral base-ring; slightly concave bottom; two loop, ear-shaped handles.
- Two crimped trails on upper body, formed into handles at top, applied onto and below rim. Two crimped trails down sides with small handles formed as triangular loops at top.
- Intact. Purple streak in one handle. Pitting of surface bubbles; gritty white and black inclusions, with one large black impurity in handle; some large bubbles.

Although this vessel bears some resemblance to flasks with ornamental handles dating to the fourth century AD (see, for example, Kunina 1997, 333 nos 404-5), it should probably be seen rather as a product of a workshop that principally made one-handled jugs (see Kunina 1997, 302-3 nos 242-4, examples from Kertch and Panticapaeum).

Compare Vessberg 1956, 166-7 figs 47:23 and 58:4

271 A1880.18.61 Cylindrical jar

Semi-translucent blue

First to second centuries AD; formerly Piot Collection

H 5.3, D (base) 4.2, D (rim) 3.5 cm

- Rounded, vertical rim; outward fold below, slanting downwards and forming shoulder; cylindrical body, with outward fold around base; slight kick in centre of bottom with off-centre pontil scar.
- Intact, but originally had a lid. Thick enamel-like creamy brown weathering film and iridescence on interior and exterior; pitting of surface bubbles.

The vessel may be identified as an inkwell but could equally as well have been used as a container for any other liquid or paste.

Compare *Winfield Smith* 1957, 55 no. 64; Auth 1976, 119 no. 145; Platz-Horster 1976, 77 no. 153; Thomas 1976, 22 no. 68; *Constable-Maxwell* 1979, 43 lots 44-5; Oliver 1980, 54 no. 42; Kunina 1997, 329 nos 382-3; Whitehouse 1997, 199 no. 348 and 209 no. 360

272 A1887.376 Bottle

Pale dull green

Second century AD

H 8.4, D (rim) 2.2, D (body) 3.6

- Rim folded out, round and up, forming groove around mouth; short, cylindrical neck; curving shoulder; tall, slightly convex body; small, concave bottom.
- Intact. Dulling and slight surface pitting on exterior; soil encrustation and iridescent weathering on interior; glassy inclusions; pinprick and large bubbles.

For an amphoriskos with a very similar shape but with handles (now missing) and coil base, dated to the first century AD, see Weinberg 1992, 118 no. 85. Also compare four bottles from an 'apothecary's set', probably from Egypt; see *Benzian* 1994, 86 lot 145.

Compare Lightfoot 1992, 183 no. 118; Sternini 1998, 79-80 no. V52 (with refs); Arveiller-Dulong and Nenna 2005, 353 nos 953-5

273   275   278; 279

273 A1921.127 Small square jug

Green

Probably second century AD; eastern Mediterranean

H 9.5, D (rim) 3.3, L (body) 5.8, W (body) 5.65, L (bottom) 5.6, W (bottom) 5.5

- Everted rim, folded round and in; bevelled outer lip on one side of rim; cylindrical neck, tooled in slightly at base; broad, gently sloping shoulder; square sides to body, tapering downwards; slightly convex bottom; strap handle with two prominent claws at edges, pressed onto shoulder, drawn up and turned in at an acute angle and pressed onto neck with downward pad.
- Intact. Some black and gritty inclusions in handle; faint iridescence; pitting of surface bubbles; many bubbles, elongated in neck.

It remains uncertain whether square bottles such as this were blown in a mould or whether they were shaped by hand after inflation. The latter seems eminently more likely since their shape is much more rounded and irregular than those examples, such as bottles with stamped bases, that were clearly mould-blown; see, for example, above no. 242.

Compare Vessberg 1956, 149 figs 47:3 and 57:5; Charlesworth 1966, 37 Appendix I, 9, fig. 4 (V&A, from Cyprus)

274 A1880.18.72 Jar

Colourless with pale blue-green tinge

Second to third century AD; from the Grecian archipelago; formerly Piot Collection

H 7.6, D (rim) 8.9, D (body) 10.1

- Knocked-off rim with flaring mouth; bi-conical, slightly convex sides to body, curving in to irregular convex bottom with deep, pointed kick near centre.
- Two wheel-cut lines around bottom of body, 4.8 and 5.0 below rim.
- Intact. Deep pitting and brilliant iridescence on exterior and upper part of interior.

Numerous examples have been found on Cyprus, see Vessberg 1956, 139 and 198 (esp. Cyprus Museum D1129, fig. 44:13).

Compare Whitehouse 1997, 249 no. 425; Kunina 1997, 291 no. 182 and 313 no. 292; Ferrari 1998, 178 (no. 1967.115.785, also decorated with fine incised lines but not described)

275 A1921.94 Jar

Colourless with bluish tinge

Second to third century AD; found in Cyprus

H 7.1, D (rim) 7.05, D (max.) 9.2

- Knocked-off, uneven, vertical rim; short, flaring mouth; bi-conical body with projecting ridge at point of greatest diameter; small, slightly concave bottom.

- Two fine wheel-abraded lines around upper section of body, 3.9 and 4.1 below rim.
- Intact. Patches of whitish enamel-like weathering and iridescence; few pinprick bubbles.

Similar to no. 274

276 A1914.107 Jar

Pale blue-green
Second to third century AD
H (rim) 6.2, D (rim) 7.1, D (body) 7.75

- Rounded, vertical and thickened rim with inner lip; slightly convex sides; very shallow, round bottom, concave at centre, with pontil scar.
- Intact. Iridescence and dulling; many pinprick bubbles.

Lidded jars are well known from Cyprus and so have come to be regarded as products of a local Cypriot workshop; see Vessberg 1952, 119 (type A.II, pl. III, 9-18); Oliver 1992, 107. However, examples are also known from sites in Israel and Syria; see Sternini 1998, 98-100 nos V85-V87. Many of the lids are decorated with cold-painted figures, usually depicting Aphrodite or Eros; see, for example, Harden 1987, 270 no. 148 (with refs); Kunina 1997, 291 no. 182 (with refs). It seems likely, therefore, that these jars were used principally by the women of the house as containers for cosmetics and toiletries.

Compare Vessberg 1956, fig. 56.2 (Ny Carlsberg Glyptotek no. 2873)

277 A1914.107A Lid for jar

Pale blue-green
Second to third century AD
H (max.) 1.35, D (max.) 8.2

- Knocked-off, inverted edge to rim; rounded upward fold; deep, concave top.
- No trace of painted decoration on upper surface.
- Intact, except for chip and crack in edge. Iridescence, dulling and pitting; few bubbles.

Found with no. 276
Compare Whitehouse 1997, 204 no. 356

278 A1914.108 Indented jar

Colourless with pale bluish tinge
Second to third century AD; eastern Mediterranean
H 8.55-8.35, D (rim) 6.05, D (base) 5.1

- Knocked-off, unworked rim; flaring mouth; slightly concave sides to body; outward fold at edge of base; almost flat bottom.
- Four elongated, shallow indents in sides; above, wheel-abraded horizontal line around body, 1.5 below rim.
- Intact. Thick brown weathering on bottom on interior; limy weathering, mostly flaked off leaving iridescence and dulling; pinprick bubbles.

Very similar to an indented beaker from Cyprus, above no. 165.

Compare Vessberg 1953, 163 and 166, fig. 1,b (from Amathus Tomb 17); Vessberg 1956, 142 figs 44:28-30 and 54:8; Whitehouse 1997, 112 no. 170

279 A1914.108A Lid

Pale yellow
Second to third century AD
H 1.2, D (max.) 7.0

- Inverted, knocked-off edge; above, rounded fold; deeply concave upper surface.
- No trace of any decoration on upper surface.
- Intact. Iridescence and dulling; some black impurities; pinprick bubbles.

Associated with no. 278. The fact that the lid does not fit the jar very well may give rise to doubts about whether the two objects were originally intended to go together or whether in fact they were found together. For another ill-fitting jar and lid, see Vessberg 1956, 208-9 fig. 56:3 (Ny Carlsberg Glyptotek no. 2874).

Similar to no. 277

280   281   284

280   A1966.68   Small indented jar

Pale green
Second to third century AD
Bequeathed by Mrs A. W. Acworth; formerly in the Acworth Collection
H 4.4, D (rim) 3.6, W (max.) 3.8

- Everted rim, folded over and in, flattened into sides of mouth; slightly concave neck; bulbous body; round bottom.
- Six flattened, shallow indents in sides.
- Intact. Black enamel-like weathering, flaking off and leaving brilliant iridescence; surface pitting; pinprick and some larger bubbles.

Compare Auth 1976, 221 nos 465-6; Arveiller-Dulong and Nenna 2005, 421 nos 1169-70

281   A1927.85   Small indented jar

Colourless
Second to third century AD
H 6.0-5.85, D (rim) 4.05-3.95, W (max.) 4.65

- Rim folded round and in, flattened into broad, flaring mouth; concave neck; narrow shoulder; tapering sides to body; concave bottom.
- Eight irregular, vertical indents in sides.
- Intact. Enamel-like weathering, flaking off and leaving patches of brilliant iridescence; surface pitting; some bubbles.

282   A1895.286   Indented jar with collared rim

Blue-green
Second to third century AD; from a tomb at Tyre, Lebanon
H 6.8, D (rim) 6.4, D (body) 7.25

- Collared rim with everted, rounded outer lip; short, concave neck; squat body; slightly pushed-in, thickened bottom with raised pontil scar at centre.
- Four indents in sides of body.
- Intact. Some patches of weathering, dulling and pitting; some bubbles.

283   A1882.28.2   Square indented bottle

Greenish colourless
Second to third century AD
H 6.27, D (rim) 2.3, L (body) 4.35, W (body) 4.2

- Everted rim with bevelled upper lip; slightly flaring, cylindrical neck with tooling marks around base; sloping shoulder; square sides to body; pushed-in bottom with pontil scar.
- Four indents in centre of sides.
- Intact. Brownish weathering; some deep pitting; pinprick bubbles.

Compare Hayes 1975, 76 no. 269

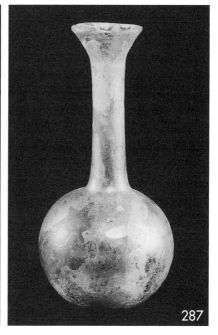

285

286

287

284 A1921.147 Bottle with cut decoration

Colourless
Second to third century AD; found in Cyprus
H 9.7, D (rim) 2.2, D (body) 7.6

- Vertical, rounded rim with bulging collar below; cylindrical neck, with slight indent around base; spherical body; small, almost flat bottom.
- Wheel-cut line forming groove around upper body.
- Intact. Patches of soil encrustation, weathering and iridescence; pinprick bubbles.

285 A1921.119 Flask

Pale blue-green
Second to third century AD; found in Cyprus
H 8.9, D (rim) 5.8, D (body) 7.2

- Rounded, thickened rim; tall, flaring mouth; globular body; pushed-in bottom with pontil scar.
- Intact. Some soil encrustation on interior; dulling and faint iridescence on exterior; a few pinprick bubbles.

286 A1921.121 Flask

Blue-green
Probably second century AD; found in Cyprus
H 11.1, D (rim) 4.2, D (body) 7.9

- Rounded, thickened rim; flaring mouth; bulge in side of concave neck; bulbous body; deep kick in bottom with pontil ring.
- Intact. Soil-encrusted weathering on interior; faint iridescence on exterior; many bubbles.

Compare Lightfoot 1992, 119 no. 66

287 A1937.514 Flask

Pale green
Second to third century AD
H 12.1, D (rim) 3.1, D (body) 6.2

- Rounded, slightly thickened rim; flaring mouth; slender, cylindrical neck; globular body; small, concave bottom.
- Intact. Black weathering and ash-like encrustation with brilliant iridescence on interior; dulling on exterior; blowing striations; large and pinprick bubbles.

288   289   290
291   292   293

288 A1955.17 Squat jar

Blue
Probably third to fourth century AD
H 5.9, D (rim) 4.1, D (body) 5.1

- Rounded, flaring rim, folded over and into mouth, forming a collar, partially flattened into neck; concave neck; bulbous body; slightly concave bottom.
- Intact. Brownish enamel-like weathering, faint iridescence and dulling; deep pitting of surface bubbles; very many bubbles.

Compare Whitehouse 1997, 164-5 no. 286 (with refs)

289 A1895.283 Small jar

Blue-green
Third to fourth century AD; from a tomb at Tyre, Lebanon
H 6.4, D (rim) 5.0-4.65, D (bottom) 5.0

- Rounded, everted, thickened rim; slightly convex sides to conical body, curving in at bottom; flat bottom with small pontil scar.
- Single trail in same colour glass wound round body horizontally below rim, slightly more than one turn; end smoothed into body.
- Intact. Creamy brown enamel-like weathering; iridescence and pitting; many pinprick bubbles.

Compare Vessberg 1956, 168-9 (Form A.II), figs 45:24-5 and 55:7; Hayes 1975, 121 no. 475 (with refs); Oliver 1980, 87-8 nos 119-22

290 A1923.353 Trailed jar

Pale yellow-green
Third to fourth century AD
H 7.4, D (rim) 5.25, D (max.) 8.1

- Rounded, slightly everted, thickened rim; bi-conical sides to body; integral tubular base-ring; low kick in bottom with circular pontil mark.
- Single trail in same colour glass wound three times round upper section of body, 1.0 below rim.
- Intact. Thick, creamy brown weathering on interior; similar on exterior, mostly flaked off leaving iridescence, dulling and surface pitting; many bubbles.

Compare Matheson 1980, 98-9 no. 264; Kunina 1997, 318 no. 320; Arveiller-Dulong and Nenna 2005, 372 no. 985

291 A1921.115 Trailed jar

Colourless
Third to fourth century AD; found in Cyprus.
H. 7.5, D. (rim) 5.5, D. (body) 7.7

- Rounded, slightly thickened rim; flaring mouth; short, concave neck; body expanding downwards, then curving in to pushed-in bottom.
- Single trail of same glass around body below neck.
- Intact. Patches of creamy brown weathering; faint iridescence and surface staining; some glassy, white inclusions and pinprick bubbles; usage scratches.

Vessberg commented that since this type of sack-shaped jar is found in large numbers in Cyprus, most examples were made there in a single workshop; see Vessberg 1956, 209. Some may indeed be Cypriot, but the type is more widespread in the eastern Mediterranean and Near East than Vessberg envisaged and was presumably made at a number of different centres not just on Cyprus but also in Syria and Asia Minor; see Lightfoot 1989, 39-40; Lightfoot 1992, 143 no. 85.

Similar to no. 289; see also Arveiller-Dulong and Nenna 2005, 371-2 nos 983-4

292 A1955.16 Nipt jar

Green with bluish tinge
Fourth century AD; eastern Mediterranean
H 8.9, D (rim) 4.9-4.8, D (max.) 6.4

- Thickened, rounded rim, tooled flat on inside of mouth; short, concave neck; piriform body; slightly concave bottom.
- Decoration comprising three uneven rows of warts, pinched out on body, ten in top row, nine in middle row and eight in bottom row; above, fine trail applied around rim and then drawn in a spiral down neck in three and a half turns.
- Intact. Dulling and pitting on exterior; thick enamel-like black weathering and iridescence on interior; many pinprick and large bubbles.

Compare Canav 1985, 83 no. 132; Lightfoot 1989, 44-5 nos 53 and 59

293 A1937.524 Small flask with nipt decoration

Purple and colourless
Possibly fourth century AD
H 8.6, D (rim) 2.7, D (body) 6.55-6.35

- Rounded, vertical rim; flaring neck; globular and lentoid body; round bottom with pontil scar; two handles dropped onto shoulder and drawn up, turned in and trailed onto top of neck and rim, with ends nipt off above rim.
- Single trail in same colour glass applied below rim, wound round once horizontally, then trailed down in spiral to base of neck and wound round twice; another trail in darker glass wound three times round body and then formed into a zigzag pattern below.
- Intact. Faint iridescence and slight dulling; some soil encrustation; pinprick and elongated bubbles.

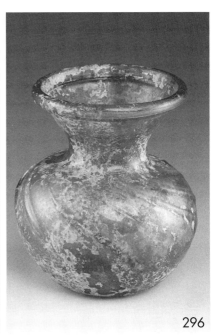

294

295

296

294 A1966.69 Small nipt jar

Pale blue-green
Fourth to fifth century AD
Bequeathed by Mrs A. W. Acworth; formerly in the Acworth Collection
H 4.4, D (rim) 2.5, D (body) 3.9

- Rim folded out, round and in; neck tapering down-wards; narrow, sloping shoulder; squat, rounded body; deep kick in bottom.
- Six pinched, horizontal projections around body.
- Intact. Creamy brown weathering, flaking off to leave iridescence; some surface pitting; bubbles.

Compare Matheson 1980, III no. 289; Whitehouse 1997, 181 no. 318 (with refs)

295 A1981.419 Small jar with four handles around rim

Pale blue
Fourth to fifth century AD; Syro-Palestinian
H 4.2, D (rim) 3.7-3.6, D (body) 3.65-3.55

- Everted tubular rim, folded over and in, smoothed into mouth; funnel neck; slightly concave shoulder; rounded, tapering sides to body; deep kick in

bottom; four rod handles applied on edge of shoulder, drawn up and pressed onto top of edge.
- Intact, but one handle restored. Some soil encrustation; faint, iridescent weathering; pinprick bubbles.

Compare Merseyside 1979, 19 no. A36 (from Tyre, Lebanon); Matheson 1980, 118 no. 313; Kunina 1997, 333-5 no. 408; Whitehouse 1997, 170 no. 299

296 A1895.276 Jar

Blue-green
Third to fourth century AD; from a tomb at Mount Carmel
H 8.4, D (rim) 6.45, D (body) 7.6

- Everted rim, folded over and in, with lip tooled and flattened into side of mouth; tapering neck; squat, bulbous body; slightly concave bottom.
- Ten pre-moulded ribs on body, running diagonally from top right to bottom left.
- Intact. Faint enamel weathering and iridescence; some patches of dulling; pinprick bubbles.

Compare von Saldern 1974, 178 nos 493-4; Heisserer 1986, 107-8 no. 172 (reportedly from Bet Shean, Israel)

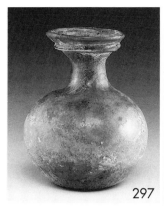   

297 A1881.2.3 Flask

Light green
Third to fourth century AD; from Tyre, Lebanon
H 10.7, D (rim) 5.8-5.65, D (body) 9.2

- Rounded, thickened rim with deep, funnel mouth; short, slightly conical neck; globular body; concave bottom.
- Trail applied under rim from right to left for almost one and a half turns.
- Intact. Soil encrustation; brown enamel-like weathering; faint iridescence and dulling; few pinprick bubbles.

298 A1966.57 Small flask

Colourless, with deep blue-green trail
Fourth to fifth century AD
Bequeathed by Mrs A. W. Acworth; formerly in the Acworth Collection
H 8.35, D (rim) 2.95-2.8, D (base) 5.6

- Vertical, rounded rim; cylindrical neck, slightly tapering downwards, sloping shoulder; squat bulbous body; pushed-in bottom.
- Trail applied around rim and then drawn in a spiral down neck in four and a half turns.
- Intact. Dulled surface on exterior; creamy brown weathering and iridescence on interior; pinprick and some large bubbles.

Compare Vessberg 1956, 155-6 fig. 48:20 (Class A.II.b, Group 2)

299 A1966.56 Trailed flask

Pale green
Fourth to fifth century AD
Bequeathed by Mrs A. W. Acworth; formerly in the Acworth Collection
H 11.45, D (rim) 2.7, D (base) 7.1

- Rounded, slightly inverted rim; cylindrical neck tapering downwards; small shoulder; squat globular body; deep concave bottom.
- Trail applied on neck in spiral of six turns.
- Intact. A few black impurities in neck. Faint iridescent weathering and dulling; some large and pinprick bubbles.

Compare Neuburg 1949, pl. XXVI no. 85c (left)

300 A1937.510 Trailed flask

Pale blue-green
Fourth to fifth century AD
H 13.1, D (rim) 3.6-3.5, D (base) 7.15

- Rounded, vertical rim; cylindrical neck, tapering slightly and tooled in at base; broad shoulder, curving to squat tapering body; pushed-in bottom with pontil ring at centres.
- Broad band, 2.5 wide, of fine spiral trail on neck applied from top to bottom, beginning in bulbous pad.
- Intact. Iridescent weathering and dulling on exterior; creamy weathering on interior; some small black impurities; pinprick bubbles.

Similar to no. 299

301 A1957.521 Trailed flask

Pale green with blue tinge; opaque dark brown trail
Fourth to fifth century AD
H 12.6, D (rim) 3.2-3.15, D (max.) 6.65

- Rounded vertical rim; cylindrical neck with
  narrower section below; squat, globular body;
  concave bottom.
- Thirty-two pre-moulded ribs on body, roughly
  vertical, but slanting slightly from left to right; trail,
  appearing black, on neck; thick trail at top and
  bottom, trailed from top, forming a broad band,
  2.1 wide.
- Faint iridescent weathering; many large and
  pinprick bubbles.

For a larger, plain flask with a similar neck shape, see Whitehouse
1997, 178 no. 313 (with discussion)
Compare Merseyside 1979, 15 no. A27; *Solid Liquid* 1999, 90
no. 162

302 A1899.304 Flask

Pale blue-green
Fourth century AD; found at Mount Carmel (with nos 256 and 258)
Bought from G. F. Lawrence
H 16.4, D (rim) 3.0, D (max.) 5.0, D (base) 4.35

- Everted, partially tubular rim, folded over and in,
  smoothed into mouth; cylindrical neck with tooling marks around base; elongated piriform body;
  integral tubular base-ring; pushed-in bottom with
  central pontil mark; two small handles between
  neck and body.
- Two crimped trails down sides with small handles
  formed as triangular loops at top.
- Intact. Purple streak in one handle. Faint iridescent
  weathering and dulling; few pinprick bubbles.

Compare MMA X.21.201 and 32.132.46; UPM no. 86-35-32 (cf.
Fleming 1997, 27 fig. 4); Auth 1976, 219 no. 453; Thomas 1976,
32 no. 141 (perhaps made in Hebron, Jordan); Auth 1976, 132
no. 165; *Kofler* 1985, 37 lot 55; *Wolkenberg* 1991, lot 82; Kunina
1997, 333 nos 404-5

303 A1937.508 Large sprinkler flask

Olive green
Third to fourth century AD
H 12.9, D (rim) 5.6, D (body) 7.9

- Rim folded out, over and in, tooled into mouth;
  wide flaring mouth; cylindrical, funnel neck; tooled
  and twisted at base to form constriction; globular
  body; concave bottom.

303

304

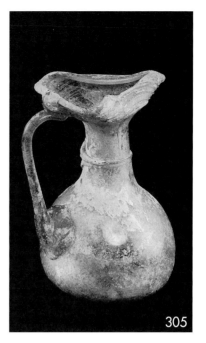

305

- Six tooled ribs of varying length arranged vertically around body.
- Intact, except for crack in bottom. Thick, black, enamel-like weathering on exterior, flaking off to leave iridescence; black impurities; pinprick bubbles.

304 A1970.908 Handled jar

Pale yellowish-green
Fourth century AD; Syro-Palestinian
H 8.9, D (rim) 7.2, D (base) 9.2

- Rim folded over and in, mostly smoothed in inside of flaring mouth; concave funnel neck; sloping shoulder; globular body; flattened, slightly concave bottom with pontil scar; three rod handles applied as thick pad on shoulder, drawn up and out, turned in and trailed onto and above rim.
- Single trail applied from right to left on underside of rim.
- Two handles broken off and repaired. A large patch of deep pitting, enamel-like weathering and brilliant iridescence; some black impurities; many bubbles.

Compare *Shining Vessels* 1991, 82 no. 150 (allegedly from Palestine)

305 A1899.311 One-handled jug with trefoil rim

Blue-green
Third to fourth century AD; from Sidon, Lebanon
Bought from G. F. Lawrence
H 8.6, D 5.8

- Rim folded over and tooled into mouth, pushed in at sides to form trefoil mouth; slightly conical neck; steeply sloping shoulder, joining imperceptibly with squat, bulbous body; pushed-in bottom with central pontil scar; rod handle applied in large pad on shoulder, drawn up and slightly outwards, trailed under rim and pinched off on top edge of rim; applied after decoration.
- Single trail in same coloured glass applied around neck in two turns; another, finer trail applied (before the trefoil mouth was fashioned) on under-curve of rim and wound in spiral upwards in five and a half turns.
- Intact. Limy encrusted weathering, faint iridescence and dulling; elongated bubbles in handles.

Isings Form 88b
Compare von Saldern 1974, 228 no. 670; Canav 1985, 69 no. 103; see also *Sangiorgi* 1999, 78 no. 203

306   307   308

306   A1937.528   Footed flask

Yellow with olive green tinge
Probably third century AD
H 8.2, D (rim) 2.9, D (body) 4.5

- Thickened, rounded rim; tall, flaring mouth; neck expanding downwards to globular body; tubular, integral base-ring; flattish bottom with small kick at centre.
- Intact. Thick, soil-encrusted weathering, mostly flaked off, leaving dulling and iridescence on exterior; similar weathering on interior; some larger and pinprick bubbles, especially in mouth.

Isings Form 104a

307   A1903.264   Two-handled flask

Purple with purple-streaked greenish handles.
Fourth century AD; found at Mount Carmel
H 16.8, D (rim) 3.0-2.9, D (body) 7.4, D (base) 5.05-4.9

- Rim folded out, over and in, forming broad lip on one side; short, funnel mouth; conical, cylindrical neck; globular body; splayed integral tubular base-ring; small bottom with pontil scar; two handles applied as pads onto shoulder: one looped round and onto neck with flat thumb-rest above; the

other drawn up vertically and curved into neck with trailing-off end above.
- Intact. Small patches of iridescent weathering; black impurities; some bubbles.

For similar handles, see Arveiller-Dulong and Nenna 2005, 387 no. 1037.

308   A1922.541   Two-handled flask (amphora)

Yellow green
Third to fourth century AD
H 20.6, D (rim) 3.5-3.2, D (body) 8.7-8.6, D (base) 5.0

- Oval rim, folded slightly out, over and in, flattened on top edge; tall, slightly concave neck; broad, gently sloping shoulder; sides to body tapering downwards, then flaring at bottom; pushed-in bottom with pontil scar at centre; surviving handle pressed onto shoulder with crimp on top of pad, drawn up at an angle and pressed onto neck with vertical trail-off.
- Broken and mended around neck; one handle missing; some fill on neck and shoulder. Dulled, pitted surface; many pinprick and elongated bubbles.

Compare Neuburg 1946, pl. XXI/76; von Saldern 1974, 211 no. 599; Matheson 1980, 127-8 no. 343; *Shining Vessels* 1991, 78 no. 142 (a very similar but smaller vessel); Kunina 1997, 333 no. 401 (with refs)

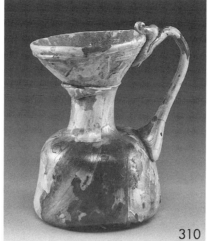
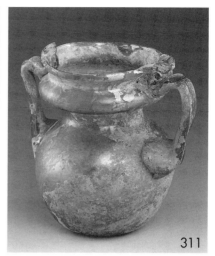

309 A1961.991 Flask with ornate handles

Blue-green
Fourth to fifth century AD
Bought from Amie, Lady Noble (of Ardkinglos)
H 11.9, D (rim) 4.6, W (max.) 6.6

- Rim folded out, over and in; flaring mouth; cylindrical, slightly conical neck; squat body; kick in bottom with traces of pontil around centre; two handles applied as large pads to shoulder drawn up vertically and turned in horizontally to neck, then drawn out again and up, folded under rim and up onto top edge.
- Horizontal trail on neck; another spiral trail applied at top of neck and wound round and up to outer edge of rim; five irregular indents in body giving the vessel a five-sided shape.
- Intact, but part of trail missing. Limy weathering around undercurve of rim; elsewhere dulling and faint iridescence; pinprick and larger bubbles.

310 A1927.87 Small handled jug

Blue-green
Late fourth to fifth century AD; Syro-Palestinian
H (rim) 6.9, D (rim) 4.45-4.35, D (body) 4.95

- Rounded rim; broad, funnel mouth; short, cylindrical neck; bell-shaped body; deep, pushed-in bottom with kick and pontil scar; rod handle applied to top of body in thick pad, drawn up and out, angled in and trailed under and over rim.

- Trail applied around top of neck from left to right, starting in a large pad; another trail wound three times around neck under rim.
- Intact. Thick creamy enamel-like weathering, flaking off to leave brilliant iridescence, dulling and pitting; some pinprick bubbles.

Compare Matheson 1980, 89 no. 241; Fleming 1997a, 28 fig. 7 (UPM 29-105-705, from the north cemetery at Bet Shean, Israel)

311 A1899.307 Two-handled jar

Blue-green
Fourth to fifth century AD; from Hebron, Palestine
Bought from G. F. Lawrence
H (to rim) 10.3, D (rim) 7.9-7.2, D (base) 7.5

- Everted, rounded and thickened rim; bulging hollow fold around neck; sloping shoulder; squat bulbous body; pushed-in bottom with pontil scar; two rod handles applied in a large pad on shoulder, drawn up and dropped onto fold and rim, trailed off above.
- Intact. Some soil encrustation; creamy weathering, flaking off to leave iridescence, dulling and surface pitting; some elongated bubbles.

For other vessels with bulging fold below rim, see Welker 1987, 46-7 nos 58-60.

Compare Herbert 1964, 186 no. 981 (from Cyprus); von Saldern 1980, 107 no. 106; Hayes 1975, 95 nos 328-30, 105 nos 385-6; Whitehouse 1997, 169-70 nos 297-8; Arveiller-Dulong and Nenna 2005, 422 no. 1173

312 **A1966.59 Jar**

Pale blue-green
Fourth to fifth century AD
Bequeathed by Mrs A. W. Acworth; formerly
in the Acworth Collection
H 7.3, D (rim) 5.8, D (base) 7.75

- Rounded, slightly inverted rim; vertical band
  below rim, with horizontal bulge at bottom; deep
  concave neck; bulbous body; slightly concave
  bottom with pontil mark at centre.
- Eight pre-moulded ribs around body, extending
  from neck to bottom, slanting slightly from top
  right to bottom left (ribs form bulge on interior
  and exterior of wall).
- Intact. Patchy fine enamel weathering and
  iridescence; some dulling of surfaces.

313 **A1937.522 Jar**

Yellow-green
Fourth to fifth century AD; Syro-Palestinian
H 7.55, D (rim) 6.2-6.0, D (body) 8.1

- Rounded, vertical rim; shallow, out-turned fold
  below; narrow, concave neck; bulbous body;
  pushed-in bottom with central pontil scar.
- Fine trail applied around centre of body in slightly
  more than two turns.

- Intact. Exterior dulling; soil-encrusted weathering
  and iridescence on interior; many pinprick
  bubbles.

Compare *Shining Vessels* 1991, 80 no. 146

314 **A1903.146   Jar**

Colourless with deep blue-green trail
Fourth century AD; found at Mount Carmel
H 7.7, D (rim) 7.0, D (base) 7.4

- Slightly thickened, rounded rim; flaring mouth;
  below, tubular fold, turned out and down; angular
  concave neck; squat bulbous body; pushed-in
  bottom with pontil scar.
- Trail applied on bottom and drawn up in a spiral
  to shoulder.
- Intact, apart from part of trail. One patch of thick
  limy weathering; some dulling and faint iridescence;
  pinprick and very large bubbles.

Compare Kunina 1997, 333 no. 406

315 **A1899.308   Two-handled jar**

Blue-green with deep blue-green trails and handles
Fourth century AD; found at Mount Carmel
Bought from G. F. Lawrence
H (max.) 8.1, D (rim) 6.45-6.2, D (max.) 7.75

315

316

317

- Rounded, slightly thickened, vertical rim; below, concave collar with ridge at bottom; short neck, tapering downwards and pushed into shoulder; globular body; pushed-in bottom with central pontil scar; handles applied as thick trails over decoration at top of body, drawn up and out, turned in horizontally and trailed up collar, nipt off on top edge of rim.
- Zigzag trail applied around body from right to left with 14 upward points and 15 downward ones in an angular pattern.
- Intact. Brownish red opaque streaks in handles. Fine iridescent weathering and dulling; some pinprick and large bubbles; some soil encrustation on surfaces.

Compare Herbert 1964, 186 no. 984 (from Cyprus); *Kofler* 1985, 24 lots 30-1; Arveiller-Dulong and Nenna 2005, 422 no. 1174

316 A1903.262 Lentoid flask

Blue-green with deep blue-green trails
Fourth to fifth century AD; found at Hebron, Palestine
H (max.) 8.5, D (rim) 3.0, L (body) 4.8, W (body) 2.3

- Rounded, vertical rim; flaring neck; globular and lentoid body; round bottom with pontil scar; two handles dropped onto shoulder and drawn up, turned in and trailed onto top of neck and rim, with ends nipt off above rim.
- Single trail in same colour glass applied below rim, wound round once horizontally, then trailed

down in spiral to base of neck and wound round twice; another trail in darker glass wound three times round body and then formed into a zigzag pattern below.
- Intact. Faint iridescence and slight dulling; some soil encrustation; pinprick and elongated bubbles.

Compare Hayes 1975, 96 nos 334-5

317 A1903.261 Small amphora

Blue-green with deep blue-green trail and handles
Fourth to fifth century AD; found at Hebron, Palestine
H 13.8, D (rim) 2.9, D (max.) 5.05-4.95, D (base) 1.45

- Rounded, slightly thickened, vertical rim; cylindrical neck, tapering downwards; curving shoulder; straight sides to body, tapering towards small rounded bottom; attached base knob with pontil scar; rod handles, applied over decoration, dropped onto shoulder drawn up vertically, turned in at right angle to edge of rim.
- Trail applied at base of neck and wound in spiral upwards around neck nine times; another trail in deeper blue-green glass wound two and a half times round upper body with zigzag below, forming nine downward points and eight upward ones.
- Intact. Some purple streaks in handles. Iridescent weathering and dulling; some pinprick and large bubbles.

Compare *Kofler* 1985, 24 lot 32

318 A1961.989   One-handled jug

Greenish with dark blue-green trails and deep brown,
almost opaque, handle and trails; fourth to fifth century AD
Bought from Amie, Lady Noble (of Ardkinglos)
H 9.4, D (rim) 4.3-4.2, D (base) 6.5

- Rounded rim and flaring mouth; slightly conical
  neck; squat, bulbous body; pushed-in bottom with
  pontil scar; rod handle dropped onto shoulder,
  drawn up vertically and turned in, then trailed
  onto outer edge of rim; handle applied after trail
  decoration.
- Brown trail wound one and a half times around
  underside of rim; another brown trail wound once
  round neck; on body, fine blue-green trail wound
  round one and a half times and then formed into
  thicker zigzag trail below with ten downward
  points and nine upwards points, forming angular
  but slightly irregular shapes.
- Intact. Brown impurity streak in neck. Some
  iridescent weathering on exterior; patch of staining and weathering on interior; pinprick bubbles.

Compare *Verres* 1985, nos 415 and 417; Arveiller-Dulong and
Nenna 2005, 381 no. 1017

319 A1966.53   Two-handled jar (amphora)

Pale green with bluish tinge; dark blue base-ring, handles and trail
Fourth to fifth century AD
Bequeathed by Mrs A. W. Acworth; formerly in the Acworth Collection
H (max.) 12.1, H (rim) 11.7, D (rim) 9.2-8.95, D (body) 11.3,
D (base) 4.9-4.45

- Tubular rim, folded out, over and in; concave
  neck; sloping shoulder; globular body; applied
  solid, oval base-ring; round bottom; two handles
  applied in broad pad to shoulder, drawn up and
  trailed off onto outer edge of rim; in middle of
  each handle a horizontal tooled fold.
- Trail below rim, applied from right to left in just
  over one turn.
- Intact. Patches of creamy enamel-like weathering;
  iridescence, dulling and surface pitting; many
  pinprick and some very large bubbles.

Compare Hayes 1975, 105 no. 384

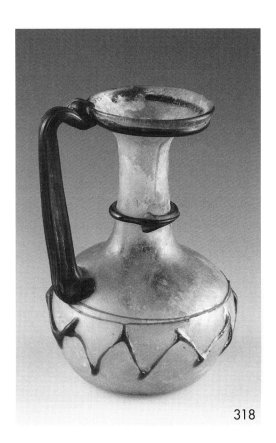

318

320 A1895.281   Indented jar with openwork zigzag trail around neck

Green
Fourth to fifth century AD; from a tomb at Mount Carmel
H 7.45-7.35, D (rim) 6.1-5.7, D (max.) 7.55

- Oval, tubular, broad rim, folded over and in with
  uneven flattened collar on inside of mouth; concave
  neck; bulbous sides to body; pushed-in bottom
  with pontil scar.
- Decoration of nine irregularly shaped indents in
  sides; zigzag trail in same colour glass dropped
  onto shoulder and trailed up to outer edge of rim,
  wound round nine times with eight downward
  points on shoulder.
- Cracked around body; broken and repaired on
  rim with one piece of glass added from another
  vessel. Fine enamel weathering with iridescent
  surface; some dulling; pinprick and larger bubbles.

Such jars are commonly found in the Near East and
Egypt; see Harden 1936, 175 (with refs).

Compare Hayes 1975, 115 no. 443; Platz-Horster 1976, 58 no. 106;
Fitzwilliam 1978, 53 no. 106 (from Cumae, Italy); Arveiller-Dulong
and Nenna 2005, 424 nos 1181-3 (all from sites in Syria)

321

323

321 A1881.2.1 Jar with openwork zigzag trail around neck

Blue-green
Fourth to fifth century AD; from Tyre, Lebanon; found in a tomb in 1876
H 8.4, D (rim) 7.1-6.7, D (bottom) 8.4

- Rounded, everted rim; irregularly shaped, flaring mouth; deep concave neck; sloping shoulder; bulbous body, curving in to bottom; concave bottom with small central pontil scar.
- One trail wound once horizontally round under-curve of mouth; another applied in large pad to shoulder and formed into wavy zigzag pattern with twelve matching upward and downward points; trail knocked off at end.
- Intact, except for one hole in shoulder. Iridescence and dulling on exterior; some brown staining and weathering on interior; very bubbly.

Similar to no. 320

322 Unused

323 A1971.31 Jar with openwork zigzag trail around neck

Dull yellowish-green
Fourth to fifth century AD; Egyptian
H 11.1-10.1, D (rim) 8.4, D (base) 9.4

- Everted rim, folded over and in, tooled into sides of mouth; concave neck; bulbous body; pushed-in bottom.
- Thick trail wound twice round outer edge of rim and trailing off on neck; thick zigzag applied over this, dropped onto shoulder and applied from right to left between trail on rim and shoulder, six times pointing upwards on rim and five times down-wards on shoulder, with trail ending on top of first upward trail.
- Intact, except for two cracks in body. Many large bubbles; black impurities.

For discussion, see Harden 1936, 174-5 (Class VIII.A.I).

Compare Harden 1936, 179 no. 493

324 A1971.30 Large jar with openwork zigzag trail around neck

Pale green with blue tinge
Fourth to fifth century AD; probably Egyptian
Purchased from the executors of Dr James S. Richardson, Edinburgh
H 15.6, D (rim) 13.7-13.3, D (body) 12.6, D (base) 8.9-8.3

- Horizontal, everted rim, folded over and in, forming rounded outer lip; broad, flaring mouth; neck curving in to shoulder; shoulder sloping outwards; rounded sides to body; deep kick in bottom with central pontil scar; integral, high, splayed base-ring with slanting tooling marks around outer edge.
- Single trail applied horizontally from left to right (anti-clockwise) around neck; thick trail dropped onto shoulder and drawn up to underside of rim in an irregular zigzag pattern, comprising nine upwards and nine downward chevrons, with tooling marks and indents in the angles, trailed off on outer edge of rim.
- Intact. Little weathering; many black impurities in rim, mouth, neck and trail decoration; blowing striations; many bubbles.

324

325

325 A1971.32 Jar

Deep amber brown with dull yellowish-green trail
Fourth to fifth century AD; Egyptian
H 7.8, D (rim) 8.6-8.1, D (base) 4.7

- Rim folded in and pressed into flaring mouth as a broad collar; neck curving in sharply and joining shoulder at acute angle; sides of body curving gently in towards bottom; applied pad base with tooling marks on upper surface and pontil scar at centre of bottom.
- Trail applied to shoulder and wound from right to left with twelve upward points and eleven downward ones of irregular length and shape; tooling impressions in angles of trail.
- Intact. Many bubbles and gritty white inclusions.

For discussion, see Harden 1936, 174-5 (Class VIII.A.II.1).

Cf. Harden 1936, 180 nos 494-6; *Winfield Smith* 1957, 161 no. 330

326 A1936.436 Tall flask

Green with yellow tinge
Third to fourth century AD
H 25.45, D (rim) 3.4, D (body) 8.0, D (base) 5.3-5.1

- Rounded, slightly inverted rim; funnel mouth; tall, cylindrical neck; spherical body; solid, vertical pedestal; base-ring with conical upper surface; bottom concealed by wooded base.
- Single trail wound around neck from right to left.
- Broken around body and mended; some plaster fill. Limy encrustation; iridescence and faint dulling; a few black impurities; large, elongated bubbles in neck; pinprick bubbles in body.

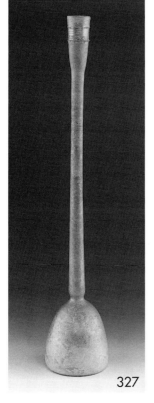

327

330

327 A1924.1 Tall flask

Pale blue-green
Fourth to sixth century AD
Given by Mr James Curle, Priorwood, Melrose
In ink on bottom: 'S12507 OVM' (or OKM?)
H 36.0, D (rim) 2.5, D (max.) 6.8

- Rounded, vertical rim; deep, flaring mouth; tall, slender, slightly conical neck, with deep tooled indent around base; bell-shaped body; concave bottom.
- Trail around top of neck, thicker at top and bottom with fine spiral in eight turns between.
- Intact. Creamy weathering and iridescence on interior of neck; dulling, pitting and iridescence on exterior; blowing striations and some bubbles.

Compare BM GR1913.5-22.108 (from Syria; see Tait 1991, illus. 125); UPM no. MS 5023 (see Fleming 1997a, 36 and fig. 26); Neuburg 1949, pl. XXVI/85a-c (Rockefeller Museum, Jerusalem); Ferrari 1998, 176 (no. 1967.115.790)

328 A1981.418 Jar

Pale green with bluish tinge
Fourth century AD
H 6.3, D (rim) 5.1, D (body) 5.2

- Rounded, slightly thickened rim; neck tapering downwards, with indent around base; globular body; flattish bottom with slight kick at centre.
- Intact, except for internal crack in rim. Creamy weathering, partially flaked off to leave dulling and iridescence; some pinprick and larger bubbles.

329 A1937.526 Bottle

Pale green
Third to fourth century AD
H 9.3, D (rim) 3.7, D (body) 5.8

- Everted rim, folded over and in; flaring mouth; neck expanding downwards; squat, globular body; concave bottom with slight pontil scar at centre.
- Intact. Soil encrustation and creamy weathering on interior; dulling and iridescence on exterior; many bubbles.

Compare Oliver 1980, 112 nos 183-4; Lightfoot 1992, 121 no. 68; Barkóczi 1996, 86 no. 262

330 A1937.525 Flask

Colourless with yellow-green tinge
Third to fourth century AD
H 9.7, D (rim) 3.6-3.5, D (body) 5.9

- Everted rim, folded round and in; flaring mouth; slightly conical neck; bulbous body; shallow, pushed-in bottom with traces of pontil mark.
- Intact. Whitish enamel-like weathering, flaking off to leave iridescence and dulling; blowing striations; pinprick bubbles.

Compare Herbert 1964, 185 no. 972 (from Tyre, Lebanon); Spartz 1967, no. 122 (from Olbia)

331 A1921.126 Small flask

Pale blue-green
Third to fourth century AD; found in Cyprus
H 8.4, D (rim) 5.4, D (body) 7.1

- Rounded, slightly thickened rim; flaring mouth; narrow, concave neck; bulbous body; concave bottom with small kick.
- Intact. Patches of weathering, dulling, pitting and iridescence.

332 A1937.523 Small flask

Colour uncertain
Probably fourth century AD
H 9.1, D (rim) 4.2, D (body) 5.4

- Rounded, slightly thickened rim; tall, flaring mouth; concave neck; slightly bulbous body; concave bottom.
- Intact. Creamy brown weathering, partially flaked off to leave brilliant iridescence; some pitting of surface bubbles; blowing striations; many pinprick bubbles.

333 A1927.611 Small flask

Blue-green
Probably fourth century AD
H. 9.3, D. (rim) 4.4, D. (body) 6.8

- Rounded, vertical rim; neck tapering downwards, then curving out to join squat, globular body; small bottom with slightly concave centre.
- Intact. Some creamy brown weathering on interior; patches of dulling, pitting and iridescence on exterior.

334 A1937.516 Flask

Yellow-green
Fourth to fifth century AD
H 11.1, D (rim) 6.9, D (body) 9.4

- Rounded, vertical rim, partially thickened; flaring neck; globular body with small flattened patch on one side; concave bottom.
- Intact. Thick, creamy weathering flaking off to leave dulling and iridescence; many bubbles.

335 A1966.52 Flask with trail decoration

Pale green
Fourth to fifth century AD
Bequeathed by Mrs A. W. Acworth; formerly in the Acworth Collection
H 18.2, D (rim) 6.8, D (body) 7.3

- Rounded, thickened rim; broad, flaring mouth, oval in section; cylindrical neck, with tooling indents; sloping shoulder; tall, conical body; rounded bottom draw out to point.
- Trail applied on undercurve of mouth in just over one circle.
- Intact. Creamy weathering, pitting, dulling and brilliant iridescence; pinprick and larger bubbles.

Compare Auth 1976, 126 no. 156

336 A1937.509 Flask

Colourless with pale green tinge
Fourth to fifth century AD
H 14.2, D (rim) 4.8, D (body) 8.7

- Rounded, vertical, thickened rim; cylindrical neck, tapering downwards and tooled around base; sloping shoulder; globular body; deep concave bottom.
- Intact. Creamy weathering, mostly flaked off to leave dulling and iridescence; a few pinprick bubbles.

Compare Arveiller-Dulong and Nenna 2005, 389 no. 1047 (from Sidon, Lebanon)

337

339

337 A1895.282 Flask

Light green
Fourth to fifth century AD; from a tomb at Mount Carmel
H 13.0-12.3, D (rim) 6.85-6.65, D (max.) 10.2

- Rim folded over and in, tooled to form mouth with thick outer lip; broad funnel neck; bulbous body; shallow concave bottom.
- Pre-moulded decoration.
- Faint iridescent weathering and dulling; a few pinprick bubbles; some black impurities in rim. Stands aslant on base.

338 A1966.54 Flask

Pale blue-green
Fourth century AD
Bequeathed by Mrs A. W. Acworth; formerly in the Acworth Collection
H 14.6, D (rim) 4.2, D (body) 7.5

- Rounded, vertical rim; flaring mouth; slender neck, expanding downwards with slight indent around base; gentle downward curve to shoulder; acute curve below, turning in to small, concave bottom. Rim aslant to body and body aslant to bottom.
- Intact. Thick, creamy weathering, flaking off to leave pitting and iridescence; many pinprick bubbles.

339 A1966.55 Flask with nipt decoration

Yellow green
Fourth to fifth century AD
Bequeathed by Mrs A. W. Acworth; formerly in the Acworth Collection
H 13.5, D (rim) 2.8, D (body) 6.5

- Vertical, slightly thickened, rounded rim; flaring mouth; tall, conical neck, with tooled indent around base bulbous body; concave bottom.
- Six nipt protrusions on upper part of body.
- Intact. Black enamel weathering, flaking off to leave dulling and iridescence; pinprick bubbles.

340

341

340 A1955.11 Flask

Turquoise blue-green
Fourth to fifth century AD
H 15.2, D (rim) 5.9, D (body) 6.6

- Rounded rim, slightly thickened; flaring, broad
  mouth, with outward bulge below; neck expanding downwards and joining imperceptibly with
  globular/bulbous body; deep, pushed-in bottom
  with pontil scab on top of central kick.
- Pre-moulded, vertical ribs around neck and over
  bulge, becoming numerous, fine, parallel lines on
  body.
- Intact. Several glassy inclusions, forming little
  knobs on surface of vessel.

341 A1937.511 Flask

Pale olive green
Fourth century AD
H 12.8, D (rim) 3.2-3.1, D (max.) 6.65

- Rim folded over and in, smoothed into sides of
  neck; flaring mouth; cylindrical neck with tooling
  around its base; curved, conical body; pushed-in
  bottom with pontil scar at centre.
- Pre-moulded ribs on body, tightly spaced and
  slanting from top right to bottom left; ribbing
  continues on bottom in spiral towards centre.
- Faint iridescent weathering; some soil encrustation;
  pinprick and elongated bubbles.

For other vessels with similar decoration, see Oliver 1980, 122-3
nos 213-15

342 A1937.506   Flask

Blue-green
Third to fourth century AD; eastern Mediterranean
H 16.7, D (rim) 3.9, D (base) 13.9

- Thickened, everted rim, folded in and tooled into mouth forming angular inner lip; cylindrical neck, slightly funnel-shaped at top, tooled in at bottom; horizontal shoulder; broad globular body; small concave bottom.
- Intact. Black enamel-like weathering, mostly flaked off leaving iridescence and dulling; pitting of surface bubbles and striations.

Isings Form 101
Compare Matheson 1980, 78 no. 204

343 A1966.63   Lentoid flask

Blue-green
Second to third century AD
Bequeathed by Mrs A. W. Acworth; formerly in the Acworth Collection
H 8.0, D (rim) 2.2, L (body) 4.4, W (body) 1.7

- Everted rim, folded over and in; neck flaring up-wards; flattened, disk-shaped body; round bottom.
- Intact. Creamy enamel-like weathering, brilliant iridescence, dulling and pitting.

Compare Thomas 1976, 28 nos 111-12

344 A1981.423   Lentoid flask

Pale green
Second to third century AD
H 9.8, D (rim) 3.5-3.4, L (body) 5.0, W (body) 1.5

- Broad, tubular rim, folded over and in, flattened into sides of flaring mouth; concave neck; flattened, disk-shaped body; thick-walled bottom with small pontil scar forming pad at lower edge.
- Intact, but some cracks in rim. Thick white enamel-like weathering, mostly flaked off leaving faint iridescence; some soil encrustation around mouth; few pinprick bubbles.

Compare Canav 1985, 62 no. 89

345 A1927.91   Small jar

Colourless(?)
Possibly first to second century AD
H 6.9, D (rim) 2.7, D (body) 2.6

- Everted rim, folded over and in, smoothed into flaring mouth; short, neck curving inwards at bottom; rounded shoulder; elongated ovoid body, with sides to body tapering in to round bottom.
- Intact, except for internal cracks. Patches of brown enamel-like weathering; brilliant iridescence and pitting; many pinprick bubbles.

Compare Vessberg 1956, 160 fig. 48.44; Sternini 1997, 71 no. V21

346

346 A1921.196 Miniature bottle

Pale blue-green
Second to fourth century AD; found in Cyprus
H 3.6, D (rim) 1.8, D (body) 2.9

- Everted rim, folded over and in, flattened on top; cylindrical neck; squat, bulbous body, irregularly shaped with bulge on one side; slightly uneven, concave bottom.
- Intact, except for internal crack running down neck from rim. Whitish enamel-like weathering, iridescence and dulling; blowing striations.

347 A1937.515 Flask

Pale green
Second to fourth century AD
H 13.3, D (rim) 4.0, D (body) 4.1

- Rim partially folded over and with thick outward lip on one side; flaring mouth; short, funnel neck; tall, slender body, tapering upwards; pushed-in bottom with central kick and pontil scar.
- Intact. Dulling and iridescence on exterior; some soil encrustation and whitish enamel-like weathering on interior; pinprick and some larger bubbles.

348 A1966.58 Nipt jar

Uncertain colour
Fourth to fifth century AD
Bequeathed by Mrs A. W. Acworth; formerly in the Acworth Collection
H 6.7, D (rim) 3.4, D (body) 5.8

- Rounded, thickened rim, with outer lip folded over and in; neck tapering downwards; small, horizontal shoulder on one side, but curving out from neck to body on other; squat, bulbous body; deep, pushed-in bottom with pointed kick. Seven horizontal pinched folds around body.
- Intact, except for two holes in body. Black weathering and iridescence on interior; dulling and iridescence on exterior; deep pitting of exterior surface.

Similar to no. 294

Compare Matheson 1980, 111 no.289 (with refs); but also see *Shining Vessels* 1991, 58 no. 99 (Islamic, dated to the ninth to eleventh centuries AD)

349 A1966.65 Miniature jar

Blue
Possibly third to fourth century AD
Bequeathed by Mrs A. W. Acworth; formerly in the Acworth Collection
H 3.5, D (rim) 3.1, D (body) 3.2

- Everted, folded rim; short, concave neck; squat, globular body; rounded bottom with pontil scar.
- Intact. White and brown weathering, flaking off to leave patches of dulling and iridescence.

Compare Matheson 1980, 100 no. 267

350 A1955.18 Jar

Yellow-green
Fourth to fifth century AD
H 4.9, D (rim) 3.8, D (body) 5.2

- Everted rim, folded over and in, with ridged outer lip; neck tapering downwards, aslant to body; almost horizontal, narrow shoulder; squat, bulbous body; rounded bottom with small kick at centre.
- Vertical pre-moulded ribs around neck.
- Intact. Black weathering and iridescence on interior; dulling and iridescence on exterior; deep pitting of exterior surface.

Compare Platz-Horster 1976, 94 no. 191 (early Islamic?);
Auth 1976, 220 no. 460

351

351 A1966.62 Jar

Colour uncertain
Fourth to fifth century AD; acquired in Cairo, Egypt
Bequeathed by Mrs A. W. Acworth; formerly in the Acworth Collection
H 6.4, D (rim) 3.4, D (body) 5.7

- Rounded rim, folded out, over and in, with tooling marks around and below vertical edge; neck tapering downwards; squat, bulbous body; deep kick in bottom with trace of pontil scar.
- Twenty-one pre-moulded ribs running from rim to shoulder, mostly aslant.
- Intact. Black weathering on interior; dulling, pitting and brilliant iridescence on exterior; many pinprick and some larger bubbles.

Similar to no. 350

352 A1927.89 Jar

Yellow-green
Possibly fourth to fifth century AD
H 5.1, D (rim) 2.6, D (body) 4.6

- Vertical rim with flat top and bevelled outer edge, with bulge on one side; cylindrical neck, expanding and curving out at base to narrow sloping shoulder; body curving in to round bottom.
- Pre-moulded ribs around body below shoulder.
- Intact. Patches of creamy brown weathering; elsewhere brilliant iridescence and pitting of surface bubbles.

Compare Platz-Horster 1976, 95 no. 192 (early Islamic?);
Auth 1976, 232, nos 537-8

Notes

1 See Stern 1999a, 469 and no. 160. For discussion of pottery unguentaria in the Hellenistic and early Roman periods, see Anderson-Stojanovic 1987.

2 For lids, see Isings Form 66; for other funnels, see Whitehouse 1997, 203 no. 354 (with discussion); Kunina 1997, 329 nos 384-5 (from Panticapaeum and Kertch); for stoppers, see Ferrari 1998, 182 (no. 1967.115.816, with refs).

3 For discussion of closed vessels shaped like a bird, see Whitehouse 1997, 120-1 no. 187. While most of these are western pieces, two other examples in blue glass and shaped as ducks are known from Alexandria in Egypt; see Empereur 1995, 23 and fig. 36. Spherical examples are also known; for discussion, see Isings Form 10, with an additional example in Kunina 1997, 324 no. 356 (from the Panticapaeum necropolis). For other references, see Stern 1999a, 467 no. 145. For examples of spherical and bird-shaped vessels, depicted with other 'toilet' articles made of glass, see Follmann-Schulz 1992, 91-5 nos 49-55.

4 *ILS* 1224b; see Stern 1999a, 471.

5 See Vessberg 1956, 170 fig. 51:1-2 and fig. 62:4-5; Spartz 1967, no. 124; Kunina 1997, 329 nos 379-81 (all from the Panticapaeum necropolis).

6 See Isings Form 99; Kunina 1997, 327-9 nos 377-8 (from Panticapaeum and Kertch). Kunina described these two vessels as 'bird gutti' and 'vessels in form of stylised figure of bird (duck?) [*sic*]'. However, their shape more closely resembles that of a breast with a teat.

7 See Isings Form 76, 79. For discussion on spoons, see Whitehouse 1997, 204-5 no. 357 and 234-5 no. 398.

8 For discussion on the use of glass containers for cremated remains, see Fleming 1997b, 55-8.

9 See, for example, Foy and Nenna 2001, 129-30 no. 163, 138-9 no. 168, 206-9 nos 371-6 (all from southern France); *La fragilitat* 2005, 71 no. 68 (from Tarragona, Spain).

10 Information kindly supplied by Dr Sally-Anne Coupar, Curator of Archaeology.

11 Price 1985a, 88, 92 nos 77-8, fig. 6:11; Weinberg 1992, 121-2 no. 91; Lightfoot 2003a, 342, 345 no. 1, fig. 1,1.

Roman Perfume Bottles

The vast majority of glass vessels to have survived from Roman times belongs to a type known as unguentaria or perfume bottles.[1] Although they must have served in a variety of ways in daily life as general purpose storage vessels, it is as receptacles for perfumes and unguents either used or donated at funerary rites that they are most commonly known. Such use is well attested in the ancient literary sources.[2] Early archaeologists, however, regarded these plain bottles as lacrimatories in the sentimental belief that they were intended to hold the tears of the mourners. In some cases bottles have survived with their contents still sealed inside, and scientific analysis of the remaining liquids has shown conclusively that the bottles contained oil-based perfumes and unguents, not tears.[3]

Bottles come in a multitude of shapes and sizes, making it very difficult in most cases both to date them accurately and to assign them to specific workshops. Unprovenanced examples in museum collections can thus be given only a general attribution. A more precise identification of such vessels is also limited by two other factors. First, despite the fact that perfume bottles have been found in great quantities throughout the Roman Empire, relatively few tomb groups have been recorded and published from the East, so that there is little comparative material available from dated contexts.[4] Second, the bottles were mass-produced, probably in numerous local glasshouses or even by itinerant glassmakers. Speed and ease of manufacture were more important in most cases than uniformity or a distinguishing shape. Some producers did take the time and trouble to identify their wares with a mould stamp on the bottom (see no. 384), but these are very much the exception to the rule. In other cases a distinctive shape has allowed scholars to attribute certain vessels to a specific area or even to a particular workshop.[5] But most perfume bottles were non-descript and defy all but a general classification.

Nonetheless, perfume bottles do have certain characteristics that are fairly standard. These were dictated by their function and practicality. So, for example, most have a relatively narrow mouth and neck, features that allowed for a carefully regulated dispensing of the contents. Long necks may also have aided this operation, but their principal advantage was that they inhibited the contents from evaporating. Although there are numerous exceptions, most perfume bottles were also shaped so that they had a low centre of gravity and a broad base; these are known by the generic term 'candlestick unguentarium' (see nos 435-6, 439-45, and 447-50).[6] These features gave the vessels great stability and allowed them to be set down on any flat surfaces without fear that they would overturn and spill their contents. While some examples are made of thick glass and would thus seem to have been intended for fairly rough handling, others are extremely fragile and cannot have been made for daily use. It may be assumed that many were in fact made specifically as funerary gifts or, more correctly, containers for grave offerings. This is shown most clearly in the case of bottles that have 'false bottoms'; that is, they have deeply pushed in bottoms that greatly reduced the volume of the contents they held.[7] So, whereas these bottles would appear large and generous in volume, they in fact allowed mourners to make a much smaller, almost token, offering.

Many of the present examples come from Cyprus, where glass vessels, particularly perfume bottles of the 'candlestick' type, have been found in great profusion.[8] A number of tomb-groups have been published, indicating that the majority of the candlestick-type bottles belongs to the Antonine and Severan periods.[9] Sadly, it has not been possible to reconstruct any such groups from amongst the vessels in National Museums Scotland since the surviving records do not provide details of their discovery. But the fact that several are quite similar and are attributed to the same site, notably Amathus, suggests that they were found, if not in the same tomb, at least in contemporary and closely related burials. It may be noted that tombs could, and often did, contain a sizeable number of objects; for example, one tomb at Limassol, excavated by the Cypriot Department of Antiquities in 1948, produced no fewer than 70 intact glass vessels.[10]

Early Imperial
Perfume Bottles

353

353 A1966.71 Miniature bottle

Deep turquoise blue
First century AD
Bequeathed by Mrs A. W. Acworth;
formerly in the Acworth Collection
H 2.6, D (rim) 1.1, D (body) 1.2

- Thick, rounded rim, folded out, over and in,
  pressed into sides of mouth; cylindrical neck, with
  tooled indent at base; rounded body; thick, slightly
  concave bottom.
- Intact. Dulling and whitish weathering on most
  of exterior surface.

354

354 A1966.70 Miniature bottle

Turquoise blue with opaque white speckles
First century AD
Bequeathed by Mrs A. W. Acworth;
formerly in the Acworth Collection
H 2.7, D (rim) 1.6, D (body) 1.1

- Thick rim with bevelled, uneven edges; cylindrical
  neck, with tooled indent at base; slightly bulbous
  body; flattened bottom.
- Intact. A few brown, gritty inclusions; whitish
  weathering on most of exterior surface.

For discussion of early Roman vessels decorated with glass
fragments, see Whitehouse 1997, 207

355 A1921.189 Small bottle

Pale blue-green
First century AD; found in Cyprus
H 3.9, D (rim) 1.7, D (body) 3.1

- Everted rim, folded over and in, flattened unevenly on top; cylindrical neck with tooled indent around base; double bulge in sides to body; slightly convex bottom.
- Intact. Patches of creamy enamel-like weathering; faint iridescence and dulling; soil encrustation on interior; blowing striations; pinprick bubbles.

Compare Vessberg 1956, 157 (type A.ɪɪɪ.γ.1) fig. 48:36; Whitehouse 1997, 130 no. 208 and 147 no. 248

356 A1895.238.76 Small bottle

Colourless with blue-green tinge
First century AD; found at Amathus, Cyprus; transferred from the BM
H 5.4, D (rim) 1.7, D (bottom) 2.8

- Everted rim, folded over and in, flattened aslant on top; cylindrical neck with tooled indent around base; double bulge to body; small, flat bottom.
- Intact, except for internal cracks in rim, top of neck and down across body. Whitish iridescent weathering; some dulling; blowing striations.

Compare Arveiller-Dulong and Nenna 2005, 279 no. 838 (from Samothrace)

357 A1889.498 Bottle

Purple and colourless with blue-green tinge
First century AD
H 5.9, D (rim) 1.9, D (body) 3.6

- Everted, folded rim; cylindrical neck with tooling marks and indents at base; piriform body with more tooling indents lower down, forming double bulge in sides; slightly concave bottom.
- Glass poorly prepared, half decolourised, half remaining coloured.
- Intact. Patches of iridescent weathering and slight surface pitting; few bubbles.

358 A1921.187 Small bottle with trefoil mouth

Pale blue-green
First century AD; found in Cyprus
H 4.3, D (body) 3.4

- Everted rim, folded out, down and round, then partially tooled away to form trefoil mouth; short, flaring neck with tooled indent around base; bulge on upper body with tooling lines below; rounded, bulbous sides to body; broad, flat bottom.
- Intact. Creamy enamel-like weathering, mostly flaked off leaving iridescence, dulling and pitting of surface bubbles.

Similar to no. 356
Compare Lubsen-Admiraal 2004, 347 no. 753

359

359 A1880.18.66 Carinated bottle

Blue
First century AD; probably eastern Mediterranean;
formerly Piot Collection
H 6.8, D (rim) 2.0, D (body) 4.9

- Everted, rounded, horizontal rim; short, cylindrical neck, tooled around base; narrow, horizontal shoulder with vertical band below; conical upper segment of body, then curving in gently to slightly concave bottom.
- Intact. Patches of thick, creamy brown weathering, dulling and iridescence; few bubbles.

There are similar examples in the Ashmolean Museum, Oxford (1931.4), the BM (GR1856.12-26.1200, GR1856.12-26.1201, GR1856.12-26.1264, GR1868.1-10.459, GR1878.12-30.79, GR1878.12-30.80, GR1839.10-2.15 and GR TB305 from Aegina), and the MMA (81.10.265, 81.10.289, 91.1.1354, 91.1.1355 and 17.194.164)

For the latter group, see Lightfoot 2003a, 342, 345-6 nos 2-6, fig. 1.2-6

Another example, now in the Eskişehir Archaeological Museum, was found in the Kocakızlar Tumulus, near ancient Dorylaeum (Turkey); see Atasoy 1981, 12 illus

Compare also Matheson 1980, 22 no. 57 (with refs); for other examples from the West (possibly made at Aquileia), see Bonomi 1996, 57 nos 84-5 (from tombs in the Canalbianco necropolis at Adria); Dilly 1997, 104 no. 245; Newby 1999, 40 no. 35; Arveiller-Dulong and Nenna 2005, 30, 94 nos 173 and 175

Compare the cast examples above, nos 43-4

360 A1880.18.67 Carinated bottle

Blue
First century AD; formerly Piot Collection
H 5.1, D (rim) 1.5, D (body) 3.3

- Everted, horizontal rim with rounded outer lip; short, cylindrical neck with tooled indent around base; rounded, bulbous shoulder; conical, slightly concave sides to body; small, slightly concave bottom.
- Intact. Creamy enamel-like weathering, mostly flaked off leaving faint iridescence and dulling; pinprick bubbles.

Smaller version of no. 359

361 A1955.15 Bottle with trefoil mouth

Deep purple
First century AD
H 7.9, D (body) 5.2

- Folded rim, tooled into trefoil-shaped mouth; neck expanding downwards; piriform body; small, flat bottom.
- Intact. Creamy weathering around interior of mouth; faint dulling and iridescence on exterior.

362 A1921.182 Small perfume bottle

Pale blue-green
Possibly first century AD; found in Cyprus
H 4.4, D (rim) 1.6, D (body) 2.3

- Everted rim, folded over and in, flattened unevenly on top; cylindrical neck, with tooled indent at base; piriform body; small, flat bottom.
- Intact. Creamy weathering, iridescence and pitting.

361

362

363

364

363 A1921.181 Small bottle

Pale yellow-green
Possibly first century AD; found in Cyprus
H 4.8, D (rim) 1.5, D (body) 2.2

- Uneven folded rim; neck tapering downwards to slight indent at base; tall, piriform body; small, slightly concave bottom.
- Intact. Creamy weathering on interior; dulling and faint iridescence on exterior; blowing striations; pinprick bubbles.

Similar to no. 362

364 A1880.18.62 Bottle

Deep blue
First century AD; formerly Piot Collection
H 5.7, D (rim) 2.1, D (body) 5.5

- Everted, horizontal and tooled rim, with thickened outer edge; short, cylindrical neck, with tooling marks around base; large, globular body; small, flat bottom.
- Intact. Patches of whitish weathering; dulling and iridescence; blowing striations; pinprick bubbles.

Isings Form 26a
Compare Whitehouse 1997, 125-6 nos 196-8

365 A1880.18.63 Small bottle

Blue
First century AD; formerly Piot Collection
H 6.0, D (rim) 2.0, D (body) 5.6

- Everted rim, rounded but slightly uneven; cylindrical neck, tapering slightly upwards; broad, sloping shoulder; curving sides to squat, bulbous body; bottom concave at centre.
- Intact. Creamy brown enamel-like weathering, almost entirely flaked off leaving dulling and faint iridescence; some elongated bubbles in neck.

366 A1880.18.69 Bottle

Pale amber yellow
First century AD; formerly Piot Collection
H 7.2, D (rim) 1.1, D (body) 6.0

- Rounded and thickened rim; flaring mouth; conical neck flaring downwards; squat body, expanding outwards to acute curve and then tapering in to small, slightly concave bottom.
- Part of rim missing. Patches of iridescence, pitting and surface dulling; some pinprick bubbles.

Similar to no. 365

367 A1880.18.65 Globular bottle

Blue
First century AD; formerly Piot Collection
H 7.1, D (rim) 2.3, D (body) 6.2

- Everted, horizontal, tooled rim; cylindrical neck, with tooling indent at base; bulbous body with conical upper section and gentle undercurve; small, flat bottom.
- Intact. Glossy exterior surface with blowing striations; trail-like protrusions from blowing on interior of neck.

365

368 A1880.18.68 Bottle

Amber brown
First century AD; formerly Piot Collection
H 7.4, D (rim) 2.3, D (body) 5.8

- Horizontal, tooled rim with thickened outer lip; cylindrical neck, with slight tooling around base; broad, piriform body; flat bottom.
- Intact. Patches of deep pitting and brilliant iridescence; elsewhere slight pitting and dulling of surface pinprick bubbles.

Compare *Solid Liquid* 1999, 59 no. 90 and 61 no. 97

371

369 A1921.148   Bottle

Colourless with greenish tinge
First century AD; found in Cyprus
H 9.1, D (rim) 2.1, D (body) 6.1

- Everted rim, flattened on top and aslant to neck,
  forming inner lip to mouth; neck expanding
  downwards, with tooling around base; squat
  piriform body, curving in to flat bottom.
  Horizontal wheel-cut bands around body(?).
- Intact. Some soil encrustation and iridescent
  weathering on interior; iridescence and dulling
  on exterior; blowing striations; usage scratches.

Compare Matheson 1980, 30-1 nos 85-6 (no. 85 from Kurcoğlu,
Syria; no. 86 with wheel-cut line around body); Barkóczi 1996, 84
no. 254-5 (no. 255 from Cyprus); see also Oliver 1992, 102

370 A1921.195   Small bottle

Pale blue-green
Mid-first century AD; found in Cyprus
H 4.2, D (rim) 1.7, D (body) 2.9

- Everted rim, folded over and in, aslant to neck;
  cylindrical neck, with tooled indent at base;
  globular body; slightly concave bottom.
- Intact, but crack in rim. Black streaky impurities
  in rim and neck; some encrusted soil on interior
  of neck; dulling and iridescence on exterior;
  pinprick bubbles.

Compare Hayes 1975, 69 no. 217; Sternini 1998, 77 no. V44

371 A1981.424   Small bottle

Pale blue-green
First century AD
H 6.5, D (rim) 2.2, D (body) 2.8

- Flaring rim with uneven, flame-rounded outer lip;
  cylindrical neck with tooled indent at base; squat,
  piriform body; slightly concave bottom.
- Intact. Enamel-like weathering, iridescence and
  pitting on one side; dulling and encrusted staining
  film on other; many bubbles, some large and
  elongated.

372 A1887.375   Small bottle

Blue
Possibly first century AD
H (as extant) 6.5, D (body) 2.3

- Cylindrical neck, aslant to body, with irregular
  tooled indents at base; piriform body; small, flat
  bottom.
- Broken around neck; rim is modern fill. Dulling
  and slight pitting on exterior; some creamy
  iridescent weathering on interior.

373

374

375

376

377

373 A1966.67 Bottle

Blue
First century AD; bequeathed by Mrs A. W. Acworth;
formerly in the Acworth Collection
H 7.6, D (rim) 1.8, D (body) 3.8

- Flaring rim with uneven, fire-rounded outer lip;
  slender neck, flaring downwards to join piriform
  body; small, slightly concave bottom.
- Intact. Black enamel-like weathering almost
  entirely flaked off exterior surfaces, leaving
  iridescence, dulling and pitting; some weathering
  on neck, rim and inside mouth.

374 A1937.527 Bottle

Blue
Possibly first century AD
H 7.9, D (rim) 4.2, D (body) 6.0

- Everted, tubular rim, folded over and into flaring
  mouth; concave neck; globular body; flat but
  uneven bottom with a ridge around the edge
  (probably caused during manufacture by the
  flattening of the bottom).
- Intact. Weathering, iridescence and dulling on
  one side; some glassy impurities in body; some
  large and many pinprick bubbles.

Compare Matheson 1980, 79 no. 206

375 A1880.18.64 Bottle

Blue
Possibly first century AD; formerly Piot Collection
H 8.4, D (rim) 2.8-2.7, D (max.) 7.1

- Everted, horizontal rim with tooled lip; short,
  cylindrical neck; large, globular body; small,
  slightly concave bottom.
- Intact. Patches of iridescent weathering; dulling
  and surface pitting; blowing striations; pinprick
  bubbles.

Compare Lightfoot 1992, 41 no. 8

376 A1880.18.57 Trailed bottle

Deep purple with trail in opaque white
First century AD; formerly Piot Collection
H 12.2, D (rim) 2.6-2.5, D (max.) 6.8

- Rim folded out, over and in, unevenly tooled;
  conical cylindrical neck, curving out to join
  piriform body; flat bottom.
- Feather-trail decoration on body.
- Intact. Iridescent weathering and dulling;
  many bubbles.

Compare Platz-Horster 1976, 34 no. 44

377 A1880.18.56 Trailed bottle

Purple with trail in opaque white
First century AD; formerly Piot Collection
H 11.6, L (rim) 2.5, D (max.) 6.2

- Rounded rim; trefoil mouth; cylindrical neck,
  expanding downwards; globular body; round
  bottom.
- Trail applied as fine line in relief on neck and
  wound round and down in spiral, becoming
  thicker and marvered into body of vessel, ending
  on bottom.
- Intact, except for part of trefoil mouth. Small
  patches of iridescent weathering and pitting;
  pinprick bubbles.

Compare Dusenbery 1967, 41 nos 16-17 (from Samothrace);
Auth 1976, 90 no. 95, 203 nos 355-8; Oliver 1992, 103 and
115, no. T.340/26 (from Amathus, Cyprus); Kunina 1997, 294
no. 198; Sternini 1998, 90 no. V72

378 A1880.18.55 Trailed perfume bottle

Purple with trails in opaque white
First century AD; formerly Piot Collection
H 9.1, D (rim) 2.45, D (body) 3.2

- Fire-rounded rim; flaring funnel mouth; elongated piriform body; round bottom.
- Three trails applied around bottom and trailed up body to edge of rim; trails marvered but still forming thicker ridges on body.
- Intact. Weathering of trails; iridescence and dulling.

Compare Higashi 1991, 48 no. 8; Weinberg 1992, 116-17 no. 82

379 A1889.499 Trailed perfume bottle

Amber yellow with opaque white
First to second century AD; possibly Egyptian
H 19.2, D (rim) 4.15-4.0, D (max.) 7.05

- Broad rim, folded down, round and in, pressed flat on top; tall, cylindrical neck; conical body; shallow concave bottom with pontil scar at centre.
- Marvered trails in opaque white running from rim to bottom down vessel in wavy lines.
- Intact. Dulled, slight iridescent surface; a few black impurities; some bubbles.

Decoration in imitation of the semi-precious stone onyx; compare Matheson 1980, 30 no. 84 (with refs)

Same shape as no. 401

Compare Neuburg 1949, pl. xviii/60; *Kofler* 1985, 51 lot 80 (said to be from Egypt); Arveiller-Dulong and Nenna 2005, 79 no. 100

380 A1921.156 Tall pointed bottle

Colourless with streaks of manganese purple
First century AD; found in Cyprus
H 25.0, D (rim) 2.5, D (body) 3.2

- Thickened, rounded, vertical rim with short, flaring mouth below; tall, cylindrical neck joining imperceptibly with slender, globular body, drawn out to a pointed end.
- Part of rim missing. Creamy enamel weathering on interior; some dulling and iridescent weathering on exterior; many pinprick bubbles.

Compare McFadden 1946, 486 no. 114, pl. xlv (from tomb 8 at Kourion, Cyprus); Vessberg 1956, 155 figs 50:30 and 62:2 (H 18.0 cm); Auth 1976, 116 no. 140 (with refs); Weinberg 1992, 115-16 no. 80 (from Amorgos, Greece); *Solid Liquid* 1999, 58 nos 84-7; Arveiller-Dulong and Nenna 2005, 95 nos 177-8

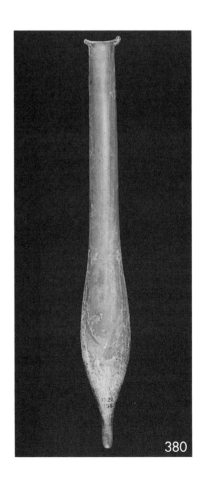

381 A1921.154 Bottle

Pale amber yellow with trail in opaque white
First century AD
H 9.1, D (rim) 2.5-2.4, D (bottom) 6.2

- Rim partially folded over and into flaring mouth; conical neck; globular body; rounded bottom.
- Unmarvered spiral trail applied around shoulder as fine line, wound down round body down becoming thicker towards bottom.
- Broken and mended. Thick white enamel weathering, iridescence and dulling.

Similar to no. 377

382 A1879.34.27 Small bottle

Pale blue-green
First century AD; formerly Northesk Collection
H 6.9, D (rim) 1.8, D (body) 2.7

- Flame-rounded rim; flaring mouth; short, cylindrical neck with slight tooling around base; elongated piriform body; round bottom with small flat pad at centre. Stands unstably on base.
- Intact. Patches of thick creamy enamel-like weathering, pitting and iridescence; pinprick bubbles.

Compare Arveiller-Dulong and Nenna 2005, 116 no. 265

382

383 A1921.179 Bottle

Pale blue-green
Probably late first to second century AD; found in Cyprus
H 6.9, D (rim) 1.8, D (body) 4.5

- Everted rim, folded over and in, with bevelled upper lip; cylindrical neck, expanding towards base; globular body; concave bottom. Slightly ridged band around upper part of body, possibly intended as a simple form of decoration.
- Intact. Some dulling; limy encrustation in small patches.

Mid-Imperial
Perfume Bottles

384

384

384 A1892.500 Bottle

Blue-green

Second century AD; found in a grave at La Puebla de Guzman, Huelva, Spain

H 10.4, D (rim) 3.0, D (body) 3.8

- Flame-rounded rim; flaring mouth; tall neck, flaring slightly at bottom; squat, thick-walled body; broad, pad bottom.
- Moulded stamp off-centre on bottom; ivy leaf and stem facing outwards above and below letters with serifs; AVG.
- Intact. Soil encrustation on bottom and interior; no weathering on exterior; blowing striations; elongated bubbles.

This bottle probably came from one of the cemeteries associated with the Roman mines at Rio Tinto, where silver (and to a lesser extent copper) was extracted on a large scale between the late first and late second centuries AD. Many similar bottles, both stamped and plain examples, have been found in this area of south-west Spain. Rare examples have also been found in Portugal and North Africa, but not elsewhere. The concentration of such vessels in the Huelva region strongly suggests that they were made locally. It has been argued that it indicates some form of imperial interest in either the production of the vessels themselves or in their contents. In her study of these bottles, Price preferred to see the stamp as referring to the contents rather than glass manufacturer. It remains, however, uncertain what the stamp represents; see Price 1977, and esp. fig. 7.

Published: Price 2006, 294 no. E-UNG.006

385 A1892.499 Bottle

Blue-green

Second century AD; from a grave at La Puebla de Guzman, Huelva, Spain; acquired from J. Kerr of Glasgow, 1892

H 12.9, D (rim) 3.7, D (body) 7.9

- Everted rim with bevelled upper edge; cylindrical neck, tooled around base; squat, bulbous body; flat bottom. Stands aslant.
- Intact, except for chip in rim. Some creamy weathering and iridescence on interior; few bubbles.

386 A1921.194 Small, squat bottle

Pale yellow-green

Second to third century AD; found in Cyprus

H 3.8, D (rim) 1.8, D (body) 3.1

- Everted rim, folded over and in with bevelled upper edge; cylindrical neck; globular body; small, slightly concave bottom.
- Intact, except for internal cracks running from rim to body. Iridescent weathering and dulling; pinprick bubbles.

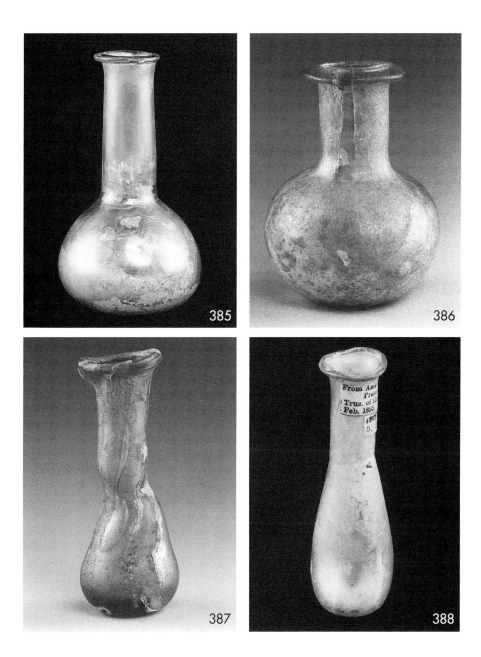

385

386

387

388

387 A1914.103 Small perfume bottle

Pale yellow-green
Second to third century AD; found in Cyprus
H 4.6, D (rim) 1.6, D (body) 1.8

- Uneven, everted, tubular rim with protrusion on lower edge of one side; cylindrical neck with indent at base; poorly-formed conical or piriform body; small concave bottom.
- Intact, but internal cracks around bottom. Some patches of iridescent weathering; dulling and fine pitting of exterior; blowing striations; some very large bubbles.

388 A1895.238.74 Small perfume bottle

Pale yellow-green
Second to third century AD; found at Amathus, Cyprus; transferred from the BM
H 5.9, D (rim) 1.5, D (bottom) 2.0

- Partially tubular and poorly-fashioned rim, folded over and in; flaring mouth; cylindrical neck, slightly tapering towards bottom, with tooled indents around base; slender, elongated piriform body; round bottom, slightly concave at centre.
- Intact. Faint iridescent weathering on exterior; whitish enamel-like weathering on interior; blowing striations; pinprick and small elongated bubbles.

390

391

392

393

394

389 Unnumbered Small perfume bottle

Pale yellowish green
Second to third century AD; found in Cyprus
H 6.1, D (rim) 1.9, D (body) 3.4

- Uneven, everted, folded rim; cylindrical neck with slight tooled indent at base; elongated piriform body; rounded bottom, slightly concave at centre.
- Broken around top of body with crack running down to hole in side; one loose fragment. Faint iridescent weathering and dulling; some pinprick bubbles.

390 A1914.98 Small bottle

Pale blue
Second to third century AD; found in Cyprus
H 6.2, D (rim) 1.9, D (body) 5.3

- Knocked-off, uneven, vertical rim, with outward fold below; cylindrical neck, with slight indent around base; double bulge to bulbous body, with horizontal tooled indent between two sections; concave bottom.
- Intact, except for crack across bottom. Dark brown enamel weathering and iridescence on most of interior surfaces; dulled and pitted on exterior; many pinprick bubbles in neck.

391 A1921.190 Small bottle

Dark blue-green
Second to third century AD; found in Cyprus
H 5.0, D (rim) 1.9, D (body) 3.6

- Everted rim, folded over and in; neck tapering downwards; conical body; flat bottom.
- Intact. Iridescence and dulling; blowing striations; deep pitting of exterior surface.

392 A1921.175 Spindle-shaped bottle

Pale green
Second to third century AD; found in Cyprus
H 5.0, D (rim) 4.7, D (body) 4.4

- Rounded rim; broad flaring mouth; slightly conical neck; short body, expanding downwards in a gentle curve; bottom concave at centre with pontil scar.
- Intact. Remains of black enamel-like weathering on interior; dulled, iridescent surfaces on exterior; blowing striations with pinprick and larger bubbles.

393 A1966.60 Spindle-shaped bottle

Colourless with light green tinge
Second to third century AD
Bequeathed by Mrs A. W. Acworth;
formerly in the Acworth Collection
H 6.1, D (rim) 4.6, D (body) 4.2

- Everted, horizontal, rounded rim; slightly concave neck; squat body, curving out to bottom; flat bottom with off-centre concavity.
- Intact, except for small chip in rim and crack in bottom. Brown enamel-like weathering and iridescence on interior; dulling and pitting on exterior; many bubbles.

394 A1904.134.55 Squat bottle

Dark blue-green
Second to third century AD; excavated at el-Bahnasa (Oxyrhynchus), Egypt
H 6.0, D (rim) 3.4, D (base) 4.7

- Everted rim with bevelled outer edge; cylindrical neck, slightly tooled in around the middle and with tooled groove at base; squat, bulbous body; flattened bottom with traces of pontil mark.
- Intact, except for small chip in outer edge of rim. Some surface dulling and scratches; gritty impurities; many bubbles.

Compare *Verres* 1985, nos 317-23

395   396   397

395   A1881.2.7   Squat bottle

Dark blue-green

Second to third century AD; from Tyre, Lebanon; found in a tomb in 1876

H 7.9, D (rim) 3.5-3.4, D (body) 3.5

- Broad rim, folded out, over and in, pressed into top of mouth with bevelled upper lip; cylindrical neck expanding outwards at bottom and joining imperceptibly with conical body; slightly concave sides to body; flat bottom with pontil scar at centre. Thick-walled vessel.
- Intact. Dulling and pitting of surface bubbles; blowing striations.

396   A1898.28   Squat bottle

Dark blue-green

Second to third century AD; from Tyre, Lebanon; formerly in the Edinburgh Museum of Science and Art, exhibited as 'Industrial Art'

H 8.7, D rim 3.2-3.1, D (body) 3.8

- Thick-walled vessel; everted, rounded and thickened rim, unevenly tooled around outer lip; tall, cylindrical neck expanding outwards at bottom and joining imperceptibly with short, conical body; flat bottom with indented pontil scar at centre.
- Intact, except for chip on lower edge of rim. Patches of black enamel-like weathering and deep pitting; elsewhere, creamy brown iridescent weathering; soil encrustation on interior.

397   A1921.170   Spindle perfume bottle

Blue-green

Second to third century AD; found in Cyprus

H 6.3, D (rim) 3.9, D (body) 3.8

- Broad, horizontal rim, with rounded outer lip; cylindrical neck, with uneven tooling indent at base; small, pad-like body; flat, broad bottom, with trace of sharp pontil scar. Thick-walled body and bottom.
- Part of rim missing. Creamy weathering on interior; iridescence and pitting on exterior; some large, elongated bubbles.

Karanis Type C; possibly Egyptian

Compare Harden 1936, 275 no. 818; Vessberg 1956, 165 and figs 50:14-16; Canav 1985, 57 no. 78

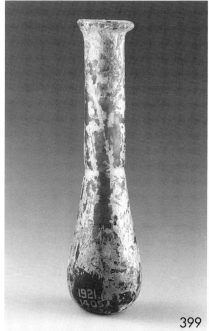

398

399

400

398 A1903.331.17 Bottle

Dark blue-green

Second to third century AD; excavated in 1902/3 at el-Bahnasa (Oxyrhynchus), Egypt

H 9.1, D (rim) 3.2, D (body) 3.5

- Everted rim, tooled flat on top with bevelled outer edge and lip at bottom; neck expanding outwards at bottom and joining with squat body; thick, flat bottom with off-centre pontil scar.
- Intact, except for chips on lower edge of rim. Some slight iridescent weathering and pitting; black impurities in rim; many bubbles.

399 A1921.1405 Bottle

Dark green

Late first to early third century AD; found in Cyprus in 1882; transferred from the V&A

H 11.0, D (rim) 2.3-2.1, D (body) 2.9

- Everted, oval rim, folded over and in, flattened on top; tall, cylindrical neck with tooled-in groove at base; tall, conical body; flat pad base with pontil scar on bottom. Thick-walled vessel.

- Intact. Patches of iridescent weathering, flaking off to leave dulling; pinprick and elongated bubbles. Cork in mouth.

Compare Oliver 1992, 102 and 114, no. T.295/31 (from Amathus, Cyprus)

400 A1936.517 Bottle

Dark blue-green

Late first to early third century AD

H 13.3, D (rim) 2.4, D (body) 3.9

- Everted rim, folded up and in, with bevelled edge on top forming slight constriction to mouth; tall, slightly conical neck with tooled indent around base; piriform body; flattened bottom with jagged, off-centre pontil scar.
- Stands aslant and unstable. Thick-walled, heavy vessel.
- Intact, except for chip in rim. Faint iridescence and surface pitting; many bubbles.

401 A1882.28.1   Large bottle

Green with blue tinge
Late first to early third century AD; possibly Egyptian
H 18.2, D (rim) 4.2-4.1, D (body) 7.1-6.95

- Tubular, everted rim, folded down, round and in, flattened on top, aslant to neck; tall, cylindrical neck, with tooling marks around base; conical body; shallow, pushed-in bottom with off-centre pontil mark.
- Intact. Faint iridescence and dulling; a few black and gritty impurities; many bubbles, some elongated.

Isings Form 28b; Karanis Type A.I.
Same shape as no. 379
Cf. Harden 1936, 271 no. 797; Oliver 1980, 82 no. 102; Canav 1985, 49-50 nos 54-7 (with refs); Kunina 1997, 325 no. 362 (from tomb group found at Panticapaeum); Whitehouse 1997, 135 no. 219 (acquired in Luxor, Egypt); Arveiller-Dulong and Nenna 2005, 268 no. 809

402 A1921.186   Small bottle

Pale blue-green; first to early third century AD; found in Cyprus
H 4.9, D (rim) 1.7, D (body) 3.2

- Everted, folded rim, unevenly formed; short, cylindrical neck with pinched indent at base; angled shoulder to globular body; small bottom, slightly concave at centre.
- Intact. Creamy weathering, flaking off to leave iridescence, dulling and pitting; pinprick bubbles.

Compare Matheson 1980, 31-2 nos 89-90; Lightfoot 1992, 79 no. 35; Sternini 1998, 77-8 no. V45

403 A1914.99   Small bottle

Pale green with yellow tinge
Late first to early third century AD; found in Cyprus
H 6.4, D (rim) 1.9, D (body) 3.3

- Everted rim, folded over and in; cylindrical neck, slightly bulbous towards bottom, with tooled indent at base; spherical body; round bottom with small, central flattened pad.

- Intact, except for internal crack in body. Thick creamy enamel-like weathering, mostly flaked off leaving faint iridescence and dulling on exterior; soil encrustation on interior; blowing striations; many pinprick bubbles.

404 A1914.97   Small bottle

Pale blue-green
Late first to early third century AD; found in Cyprus
H 6.9, D (rim) 1.9, D (body) 4.3

- Everted rim, folded over and into mouth, flattened on top edge; cylindrical neck; conical body; flat bottom. Horizontal, probably tooled, groove around body, 2.8 cm above bottom.
- Intact. Weathering on interior; some pitting, dulling and faint iridescence on exterior; some pinprick bubbles.

405 A1879.34.28   Small bottle

Pale blue-green
Late first to early third century AD; formerly Northesk Collection
H 6.9, D (rim) 1.6, D (max.) 2.4

- Flaring rim with partially folded, tubular rim; tall, slender neck, flaring at base and joining squat, conical body; slightly pushed-in bottom.
- Intact. Thick enamel-like weathering, mostly flaked off leaving faint iridescence and dulling; blowing striations; some very large and many elongated bubbles.

406 A1921.176   Small bottle

Colourless with purple streaks
Late first to early third century AD; found in Cyprus
H 7.0, D (rim) 2.0, D (body) 5.1

- Everted rim, folded over and in; cylindrical neck, with tooling marks at top and bottom, and slight indent at base; globular body; concave bottom.
- Intact, except for internal cracks in body. Pitting and brilliant iridescence on one side, dulling on the other; blowing striations; pinprick bubbles.

401

403

404

406

407 A1921.158 Small bottle

Very pale blue-green
Late first to early third century AD; found in Cyprus
H 7.2, D (rim) 1.9, D (body) 1.7

- Horizontal, tubular rim, folded over and in;
  cylindrical neck tapering downwards to slight
  tooled indent at base; slender, elongated piriform
  body; round bottom with small flat pad at centre.
- Intact. Dulling and faint iridescence on exterior;
  enamel-like weathering on interior; very many
  bubbles.

408 A1921.146 Small bottle

Colourless with yellowish tinge
Late first to early third century AD; found in Cyprus
H 7.4, D (rim) 2.9, D (body) 5.9

- Everted, tubular, horizontal rim, folded over
  and in; neck expanding slightly downwards;
  squat, conical body; slightly concave bottom.
- Intact. Some brown enamel-like weathering on
  interior and bottom; dulling and faint iridescence
  elsewhere on exterior; some large, elongated and
  pinprick bubbles.

409 A1921.159 Bottle

Colourless with green tinge
Late first to early third century AD; found in Cyprus
H 7.8, D (rim) 1.7, D (body) 2.5

- Everted rim, folded over and in; cylindrical
  neck with tooled indent around base; slender,
  piriform body; round but slightly flattened bottom.
- Intact. Iridescence and pitting on exterior; some
  soil encrustation and white enamel-like weathering
  on interior; many bubbles.

410 A1921.178 Bottle

Pale blue-green
Late first to early third century AD; found in Cyprus
H 7.9, D (rim) 1.7, D (body) 4.1

- Everted, folded rim; cylindrical neck with
  tooled indent at base; piriform body, curving
  in to flattened bottom.
- Intact. Patches of iridescence and dulling; many
  pinprick bubbles; horizontal lines visible around
  neck and body, possibly wear marks.

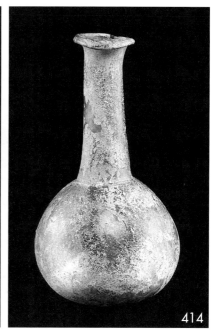

411 A1921.149 Bottle

Light blue with greenish tinge
Late first to early third century AD; found in Cyprus
H 8.4, D (rim) 2.0, D (body) 6.0

- Everted, rounded rim with thickened outer lip; slender neck with slight bulge near centre and tooling marks around base; bulbous body; slightly convex bottom.
- Intact. Some iridescence and surface pitting; black streaky impurities in rim and a few glassy impurities in body; pinprick bubbles.

412 A1881.2.5 Small bottle

Yellow-green
Late first to early third century AD; from Tyre, Lebanon; found in a tomb in 1876
H 8.7, D (rim) 2.8, D (body) 4.3

- Tubular, everted rim; cylindrical neck; squat, bulbous body; deep pushed-in bottom.
- Intact. Patches of iridescent weathering on interior; dulling and faint iridescence on exterior; many bubbles.

413 A1914.96 Bottle

Pale yellow
Late first to early third century AD; found in Cyprus
H 10.1, D (rim) 2.6, D (body) 6.3

- Everted rim, folded over and in, flattened on top to form uneven mouth to vessel; cylindrical neck, with slight indent around base; broad, piriform body; flat bottom. Pinched mark on underside of rim from tooling during manufacture.
- Intact, except for crack around body and one tiny hole. Creamy weathering, mostly flaked off leaving dulling and faint iridescence; blowing striations; pinprick bubbles.

414 A1921.135 Bottle

Colourless with green tinge
Late first to early third century AD; found in Cyprus
H 12.0, D (rim) 2.9, D (body) 6.9

- Everted rim, folded unevenly up and over, forming raised lip on top of flaring mouth; conical neck, with tooling marks around base; broad, piriform body; flat bottom.
- Intact. Patches of fine weathering and iridescence; some pitting and dulling; pinprick bubbles.

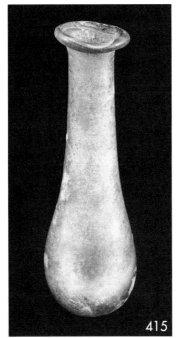
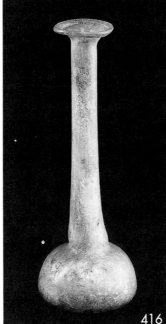
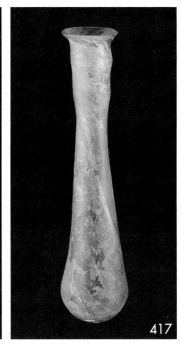

415 A1921.163 Bottle

Colourless with greenish tinge
Late first to early third century AD; found in Cyprus
H 12.0, D (rim) 2.5, D (body) 4.5

- Uneven folded rim, aslant to neck; neck flaring downwards to join with piriform body; round bottom with small flattened pad at centre.
- Intact, except for crack in rim. Patches of iridescent weathering and pitting; few bubbles.

416 A1981.422 Bottle

Pale blue-green
Late first to early third century AD
H 12.0, D (rim) 2.5 D (body) 4.5

- Rim folded over and in, pressed into outer edge of flaring mouth; tall neck, flaring downwards with tooled indent at base; squat body with sides curving out and down; concave bottom.
- Intact. Faint iridescence, dulling and pitting; blowing striations; many bubbles.

Compare Arveiller-Dulong and Nenna 2005, 238 nos 706-7

417 A1964.5 Bottle

Pale blue-green
Late first to early third century AD
Given by Mrs Lilian Shaw of Tordarroch
H 10.4, D (rim) 2.0-1.8, D (body) 2.6

- Everted, oval rim with bevelled lip; cylindrical neck with two horizontal convex bulges, joining imperceptibly with tall, conical body; thick, round bottom, slightly flattened at centre.
- Intact. Dull enamel-like weathering covering most of body; faint iridescent film, flaking off; blowing striations; many elongated bubbles.

418 A1916.10 Bottle

Pale blue-green; late first to early third century AD

Excavated from a grave in Cyprus by General Cesnola and presented by him to the Rev. Joseph Owen DD on a visit to the island in 1869

Given by Mrs A. R. Wilson of Hopewell, Aberdeenshire

H 8.45, D (rim) 2.2-2.0, D (body) 2.2

- Tubular rim, folded out, over and in; tall, cylindrical neck, tapering slightly downwards with slight groove around base; short, conical body; slightly concave bottom.
- Intact. Thick black enamel-like weathering, mostly flaked off leaving brilliant iridescence, pitting and dulling; many pinprick and elongated bubbles.

For other objects dating to the Bronze and Iron Ages in Cyprus, with the same attribution, see Goring 1988, 57 no. 42 and 79 no. 97

For a brief account of Cesnola's activities in Cyprus, see also Goring 1988, 10-13

419 A1921.144 Bottle

Pale blue-green

Late first to early third century AD; found in Cyprus

H 9.6, D (rim) 2.3, D (body) 5.8

- Everted rim, folded over and in, flattened on top, making an irregular shape around mouth; cylindrical neck with slight indent around base; conical body, curving gently in at bottom; uneven bottom, partly concave, partly convex.
- Intact. Brownish enamel-like weathering, flaking off to leave dulling, pitting and brilliant iridescence; very many pinprick bubbles.

420 Unnumbered Bottle

Pale blue-green; late first to early third century AD

H 9.8, D (rim) 2.1-1.9, D (body) 2.3

- Knocked-off, uneven rim; short, flaring mouth; cylindrical neck with tooled-in groove around base; tall, conical body; round bottom with central flat pad.

419

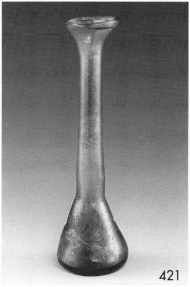

421

- Stands aslant and unstable.
- Intact. Dulling and slight pitting on exterior; thick creamy enamel-like weathering and brilliant iridescence on interior; blowing striations; many pinprick and elongated bubbles.

421 A1964.4 Bottle

Green with bluish tinge

Late first to early third century AD

Given by Mrs Lilian Shaw of Tordarroch

H 10.4, D (rim) 2.6, D (max.) 3.2

- Partially folded rim, flattened into flaring mouth; tall, cylindrical neck with slight tooling indent at base; conical body; flat but slightly uneven bottom.
- Intact. Dulling and iridescence, some patches of creamy enamel-like weathering; blowing striations; many elongated bubbles.

 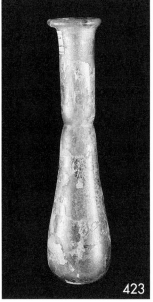 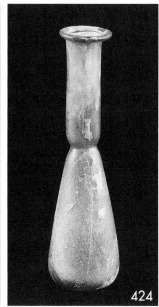 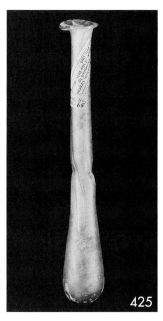

422 A1879.34.33 Bottle

Pale blue-green
Late first to early third century AD; formerly Northesk Collection
H 11.7, D (rim) 2.5, D (max.) 3.6

- Rounded rim; flaring mouth; tall, slender neck with slight tooling indent at base; conical body with slightly concave sides; flat bottom.
- Intact. Encrusted staining and faint iridescent weathering; few bubbles.

423 A1895.238.64 Bottle

Blue-green
Late first to early third century AD; found at Amathus, Cyprus; transferred from the BM
H 12.0, D (rim) 2.5-2.4, D (body) 3.2

- Everted rim, folded over and in, flattened on top; cylindrical neck with tooled indent at base; tall, conical body; small, concave bottom with large circular pontil mark.
- Intact. Some patches of weathering and dulling and pitting on exterior; pinprick and elongated bubbles.

424 A1914.100 Bottle

Pale yellow-green
Late first to early third century AD; found in Cyprus
H 10.3, D (rim) 2.0, D (body) 2.9

- Everted, tubular rim, folded over and in; cylindrical neck with deeply tooled indent at base; conical body; flat bottom.
- Intact. Thick creamy enamel-like weathering, almost entirely flaked off leaving iridescence and dulling; blowing striations and trail on interior of neck; some elongated and pinprick bubbles.

425 A1895.238.65 Bottle

Pale green with yellow tinge
Late first to early third century AD; found at Amathus, Cyprus; transferred from the BM
H 12.5, D (rim) 1.7-1.6, D (body) 2.0

- Roughly shaped folded rim, with irregular wavy outer lip; tall, slender neck with tooled indent at base; conical body with slightly concave sides; small, round bottom with jagged pontil scar.
- Intact. Slight iridescent weathering, dulling and pitting on exterior; soil encrustation on interior; three very large bubbles forming elongated raised ribs in side to body.
- The vessel shows obvious signs of poor and hasty workmanship.

426 A1887.378 Bottle

Light blue
Late first to early third century AD
H 13.1, D (rim) 2.5-2.3, D (body) 2.8

- Flaring, uneven rim, rounded in the flame; tall, cylindrical neck, tapering downwards, with slight tooled indent around base; conical body, curving in to rounded bottom.
- Intact. Some dulling and surface pitting on exterior; thick enamel-like weathering and brilliant iridescence on interior; blowing striations; pinprick bubbles.

427 A1964.3 Bottle

Blue-green
Late first to early third century AD
Given by Mrs Lilian Shaw of Tordarroch
H 13.2, D (rim) 2.6, D (body) 4.1

- Flame-rounded rim; flaring mouth; slender neck, expanding downwards with tooling indents at base; conical body with slightly concave sides; shallow concave bottom.
- Intact. Dulling and faint iridescence on exterior; patches of creamy enamel-like weathering on interior; blowing striations in relief on surface; pitting of surface bubbles.

428 A1887.380 Bottle

Colourless with blue-green tinge
Second century AD
H 15.4, D (rim) 3.0-2.9, D (body) 6.6

- Everted, tubular rim, folded over and in; short, flaring mouth; tall, conical neck with band of irregular tooling indents around base; conical body; flattish bottom with pushed-in centre and circular pontil mark. Irregular, slanting bulge at bottom of neck.

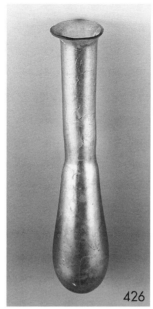
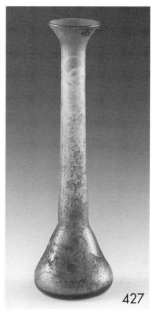

426   427

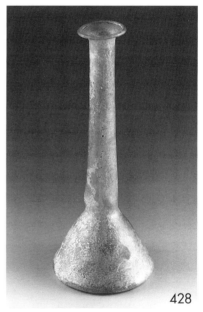

428

- Intact. Soil-encrusted weathering on interior; faint iridescence and dulling on exterior; pinprick bubbles.

Isings Form 82A(2)
For similar vessels from the Bosphoran kingdom on the north coast of the Black Sea, see Kunina 1997, 325 no. 365
Compare Matheson 1980, 63-4 no. 156; Lightfoot 1992, 87 no. 43; Whitehouse 1997, 153 no. 261 and 154 no. 263 (both acquired in Egypt); Arveiller-Dulong and Nenna 2005, 301 nos 896-8 (all from Panticapaeum)

429 A1927.86 Bottle

Colourless
Late first to early third century AD
Paper label 'H3/424. 20/-/-. 50/Cy/-.'
H 13.3, D (rim) 3.1, D (body) 6.9

• Everted rim, folded over and flattened on top,
  forming uneven lip to mouth; slightly conical
  neck, with tooling marks around base; globular
  body.
• Intact. White enamel weathering on interior;
  brilliant iridescent weathering on all of exterior;
  pitting of bubbles and blowing striations.

430 A1937.513 Bottle

Pale green
Late first to early third century AD
H 13.5, D (rim) 2.9, D (body) 7.2

• Everted rim, folded over and in, forming uneven
  mouth; tall, conical neck with deep, tooled indent
  around base; globular body; slightly concave
  bottom.
• Intact. Thick, creamy weathering, mostly flaked
  off leaving deep pitting and brilliant iridescence;
  many pinprick and some larger bubbles.

431 A1921.138 Bottle

Pale blue-green with yellow streak
Late first to early third century AD; found in Cyprus
H 13.6, D (rim) 3.1, D (body) 6.4

• Everted, tubular rim, flattened and forming ring
  around mouth; neck expanding downwards;
  squat, piriform body; flat bottom. Pinched tooling
  mark in side of body.
• Intact, except for one crack in body. Black
  inclusions in rim; blowing striations; some
  large and pinprick bubbles.

432 A1914.94 Bottle

Yellow-green
Late first to early third century AD; found in Cyprus
H 13.6, D (rim) 3.2, D (body) 6.4

• Everted rim, folded over and in, then pressed flat
  on top; cylindrical neck, with tooled indent around
  base; piriform body; slightly concave bottom.
• Intact. Thick white weathering, flaking off to
  leave dulling and patches of brilliant iridescence;
  blowing striations; pinprick bubbles.

432   434   435   436

433 A1981.421 Bottle

Light blue-green
Late first to early third century AD
H 14.3, D (rim) 2.4, D (body) 3.5

- Everted, partially tubular rim, folded over and in, flattened on top; tall, cylindrical neck with tooling indent at base; double bulge in sides to body; shallow concave, thick bottom.
- Intact. Dulling and pitting with some patches of iridescent weathering; blowing striations; some pinprick bubbles.

Compare Vessberg 1956, 165 fig. 50:26; Matheson 1980, 66 no. 169; *Joukowsky* 1985, 122 no. 103; Higashi 1991, 54 no. 17; Barkóczi 1996, 70-1 nos 192, 193 and 195; Kunina 1997, 325 nos 366-7 (both from graves in the Crimea); Arveiller-Dulong and Nenna 2005, 217 nos 627 and 629 (from Phoenicia and Jerusalem respectively), 285 nos 861-2 (from Elaious, Thracian Chersonesus)

434 A1914.93 Bottle

Pale blue-green
Late first to early third century AD; found in Cyprus
H 14.8, D (rim) 3.0, D (body) 8.3

- Everted, tubular rim, folded in to form inner, rounded lip to mouth; tall, conical neck, with broad indent around base; squat, globular/piriform body; flat bottom.
- Intact. Soil encrustation with some surface staining; patches of iridescent weathering; elongated and pinprick bubbles.

435 A1921.1397 Candlestick bottle

Colourless with a yellowish tinge
Late first to early third century AD; found in Cyprus in 1882; transferred from the V&A
H 15.7, D (rim) 3.7, D (body) 9.4

- Everted and partially tubular rim, folded over and in, pressed flat but left uneven and aslant; conical neck, with indent around base; sloping, broad body; slightly concave bottom.
- Intact. Patches of dulling and pitting; some black impurities and bubbles in rim; pinprick and larger bubbles in body.

436 A1895.238.70 Candlestick bottle

Colourless with yellow-green tinge
Late first to early third century AD; found at Amathus, Cyprus; transferred from the BM
H 15.0, D (rim) 3.3, D (body) 8.0

- Rounded rim, folded over and in to flaring mouth; tall, conical neck, with slight indent at base; low, conical body; pushed-in bottom with circular pontil scar at centre.
- Intact. Black impurity streaks in rim; one glassy impurity in body; faint weathering and iridescence.

437 A1921.1400 Bottle

Colourless with yellow green tinge
Mid-second to early third century AD; found in Cyprus in 1882;
transferred from the V&A; previously marked as '555/114-'83'
H 15.0, D (rim) 3.5, D (body) 6.85

- Tubular rim, partially pressed flat into mouth;
  tall, conical neck, tooled in at base; curving sides
  to conical body; shallow, concave bottom.
- Intact. Dulling on exterior; thick brown enamel-
  like weathering and brilliant iridescence on
  interior; many bubbles.

Compare McFadden 1946, 475 no. 35 and 485 nos 98-101
(all from Tomb 8 at Ayios Ermoyenis, Kourion, Cyprus); Oliver 1980,
81 nos 96-8; Matheson 1980, 66 no. 168; Nielsen 1992, 103-4 nos
228-63; Sternini 1998, 82 no. V59

438 A1880.18.85 Bottle

Colourless
Mid-second to early third century AD; formerly Piot Collection
H 13.5, D (rim) 2.8, D (body) 8.2

- Everted rim, folded over and in, flattened on top
  and with a slightly pointed outer lip; cylindrical
  neck, tapering downwards; piriform body; slightly
  concave bottom. Horizontal tooling ribs around
  lower part of neck and around its base.
- Intact. Thick, creamy brown weathering on
  interior; most of weathering on exterior flaked
  off leaving brilliant iridescence covering the whole
  surface; blowing striations; many pinprick bubbles.

Similar to 437 (A1921.1400)

439 A1880.18.86 Candlestick bottle

Colourless with blue tinge
Mid-second to early third century AD; formerly Piot Collection
H 17.5, D (rim) 4.3-4.1, D (body) 9.0

- Irregular, folded rim, flattened on top and forming
  lip around mouth; cylindrical neck, slightly tooled-
  in around base; squat, bulbous body; flat bottom.

437   440

- Intact. Patches of brown limy weathering, flaking
  off to leave brilliant iridescence and pitting; many
  bubbles.

Compare Nielsen 1992, 90 nos 86-90; Barkóczi 1996, 80 no. 234
(from Cyprus)

440 A1937.512 Candlestick bottle

Blue-green
Late first to early third century AD
H 15.3, D (rim) 4.1, D (body) 6.5

- Tubular rim, folded out, down, round and in,
  forming a thick, outer lip to mouth; tall, conical
  neck; slightly uneven but flat bottom.
- Tooled indents around body in two circles as
  decoration.
- Intact. Patches of thick, creamy and brown
  weathering on interior and exterior; elsewhere
  weathering flaked off leaving dulling, iridescence
  and some pitting of surface bubbles; blowing
  striations.

Compare Nielsen 1992, 92 nos 94-107; Barkóczi 1996, 78 no. 226

442   443

441 A1914.88 Candlestick bottle

Pale green
Late first to early third century AD; found in Cyprus
H 15.4, D (rim) 4.0, D (body) 7.9

- Rounded rim; flaring mouth; tall, concave, cylindrical neck, with broad indent at base, making flat band around shoulder; conical body; concave bottom.
- Intact. Soil-encrusted weathering and iridescence on interior; dulling and pitting on exterior; large and elongated bubbles; many black impurities.

442 A1921.1390 Candlestick bottle

Colourless with blue-green tinge
Late first to early third century AD; found in Cyprus in 1882; transferred from the V&A
H 16.6, D (rim) 4.0, D (body) 9.2

- Rounded, everted rim, folded over and in to flaring mouth; conical neck, with tooled indent around base; conical body; pushed-in, off-centre bottom with trace of pontil mark.
- Intact. Small patches of creamy weathering and soil encrustation; iridescence; some pinprick bubbles.

443 A1921.1389 Candlestick bottle

Blue-green
Late first to early third century AD; found in Cyprus in 1882; transferred from the V&A
H 17.2, D (rim) 4.5, D (body) 9.7

- Everted, rounded rim, folded over and pressed flat into flaring mouth; tall, conical neck, with indent around base; broad, conical body; pushed-in bottom.
- Intact, except for internal crack in rim. Soil-encrusted surface; two small patches of brilliant iridescent weathering; faint dulling; a few glassy inclusions; pinprick bubbles.

444 A1914.92 Candlestick bottle

Pale blue-green
Found in Cyprus
H 15.7, D (rim) 4.0, D (body) 8.9

- Everted, tubular rim, folded over and in, with bevelled upper edge and rounded inner lip to mouth; cylindrical neck, with indent around base; globular body; flat bottom.
- Part of rim missing. Creamy weathering and iridescence on interior; dulling on exterior; blowing striations; a few pinprick bubbles.

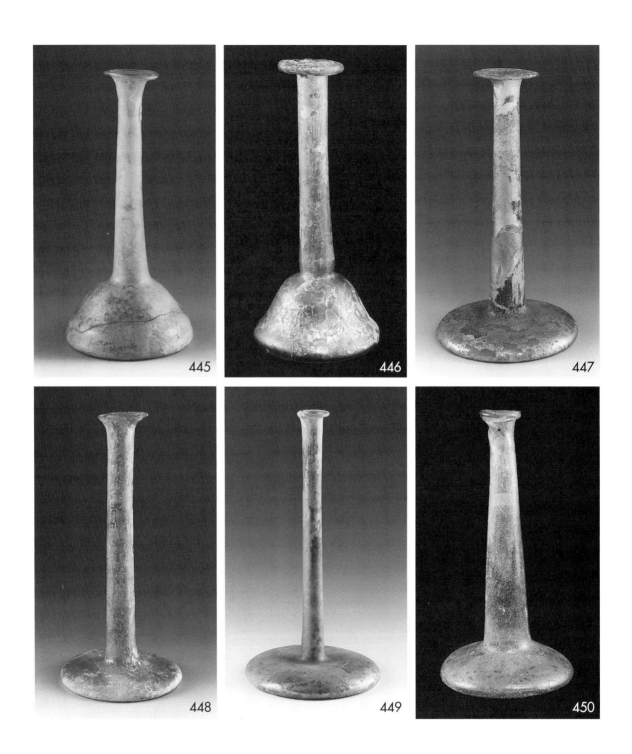

445

446

447

448

449

450

445 A1895.238.68 Candlestick perfume bottle

Pale green
Second to third century AD; found at Amathus, Cyprus; transferred from the BM
H 15.2, D (rim) 3.2, D (body) 7.5

- Everted, rounded rim, folded over and pressed into mouth; tall, slightly curving, cylindrical neck, with uneven tooling mark near top; bell-shaped body; slightly concave bottom.
- Cracked around body, with one hole near bottom. Creamy white weathering on bottom; elsewhere on exterior dulling and faint iridescence; pinprick bubbles in rim.

446 A1921.86 Bell-shaped bottle

Pale green
Second to third century AD; found in Cyprus
H 16.0, D (rim) 3.8, D (body) 7.6

- Thick, rounded rim, folded down, round and in, forming thick outer lip; cylindrical neck, with slight indent around base; bell-shaped body; pushed-in, even bottom
- Intact. Black enamel weathering on bottom; elsewhere weathering flaking off to leave pitting, iridescence and dulling. Few pinprick bubbles.

447 A1880.18.83 Candlestick bottle

Colourless
Second to third century AD; formerly Piot Collection
H 16.7, D (rim) 4.2-4.0, D (max.) 9.45

- Broad, everted rim, folded out, down and round, flattened into mouth at top; tall, slightly conical neck, with tooling marks around base; very shallow body with convex sides; pushed-in bottom.
- Intact. Thick, enamel-like weathering, partially flaked off leaving brilliant iridescence, dulling and pitting; soil encrustation on interior of neck.

Possibly Syro-Palestinian
Compare Auth 1976, 115 no. 138; Kunina 1997, 327 nos 372-4; Sternini 1998, 82 no. V60

448 A1914.86 Candlestick bottle

Colourless with green tinge
Mid-second to early third century AD; found in Cyprus
H 16.6, D (rim) 3.3-3.05, D (body) 8.05

- Uneven, rounded rim; flaring mouth; tall, cylindrical neck; flat body with uneven sides; concave bottom with small kick at centre.
- Intact. Soil encrustation on interior; faint weathering, iridescence and dulling on exterior.

Similar to no. 447
Compare Vessberg 1953, 167 and pl. 58 (from Limassol Oasis Tomb I, Cyprus); Hayes 1975, 75 no. 264; Nielsen 1992, 96-8 nos 134-92; see also Oliver 1992, 104-5

449 A1914.89 Candlestick bottle

Pale green
Mid-second to early third century AD; found in Cyprus
H 14.9, D (rim) 1.8, D (body) 8.1

- Everted rim, folded over and in, with projecting lip on one side; tall, slender neck, concave at base; lentoid, flat body; concave bottom with pontil scar at centre.
- Intact. Soil encrustation and iridescent weathering on interior; black weathering, flaking off to leave dulling on exterior.

Compare Arveiller-Dulong and Nenna 2005, 303 no. 902 (from Panticapaeum)

450 A1895.238.71 Candlestick bottle

Colourless
Mid-second to early third century AD; found at Amathus, Cyprus; transferred from the BM
H 18.0, D (rim) 2.8, D (body) 9.7

- Rim folded over and in, then pressed into sides of mouth; tall, conical neck with slight oval shape in section; broad, flat body; pushed-in bottom with central kick.
- Intact. Uneven ridges around base of neck where compressed during manufacture. Black inclusions in rim and top of neck; faint weathering; patches of internal staining. Usage scratches on surface.

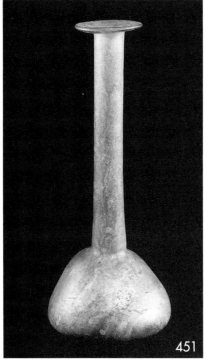

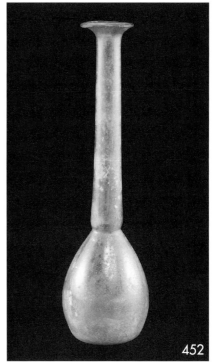

451 A1921.84 Tall bottle

Colourless
Second to early third century AD; found in Cyprus
H 19.1, D (rim) 4.4, D (body) 8.4

- Everted, tubular, horizontal rim, pressed into mouth at top; tall neck, with slight indent around base; irregular shape to body, bell-shaped on one side, conical on the other; slightly pushed-in bottom.
- Intact. Thick, black weathering on interior; dulling and faint iridescence on exterior; elongated bubbles in neck; pinprick and larger bubbles in rim and body.

452 A1968.903 Tall bottle

Colourless with greenish tinge
Second to early third century AD
H 20.1, D (rim) 3.4, D (body) 5.9

- Everted, thickened and folded rim, smoothed into short, flaring mouth; tall, slightly conical neck, with tooled indent at base; globular piriform body; deep, pushed-in bottom with kick surrounded by a pontil scar.
- Intact. Patches of dulling and slight weathering with iridescence; elongated and round bubbles.

Late Roman
Perfume Bottles

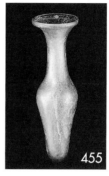

453 A1921.134 Bottle

Colourless with pale yellow tinge
Third to fourth century AD; found in Cyprus
H 9.85, D (rim) 3.2, D (body) 6.8

- Rounded rim with slanting uneven, outward and downward fold; slightly concave neck; bulbous body; deep kick in bottom with small pontil scar at centre.
- Intact. Black enamel-like weathering, mostly flaked off leaving iridescence, dulling and surface pitting; some pinprick and elongated bubbles.

Compare Matheson 1980, 79 no. 205; Lightfoot 1992, 178 no. 113

454 A1981.420 Fusiform bottle

Blue-green
Fourth century AD
Given by Mrs J. Forbes
H 26.5, D (rim) 2.6, D (max.) 4.4

- Everted rim, folded over and in, pressed unevenly into mouth; tall, cylindrical neck; globular bulge to centre of body, drawn out in long, slightly concave projection to rounded, thick bottom with pontil scar slightly to one side.
- Intact. Creamy weathering, mostly flaked off leaving brilliant iridescence in patches; dulling elsewhere; blowing striations; some large, elongated bubbles.

Isings Form 105
Compare Fleming 1997a, 40 fig. 31 (from Tomb 295 at Scythopolis/Bet Shean, Israel, with coins of Constantius II, c. AD 350. UPM no. 32-15-83); Spartz 1967, no. 139 (from Mainz); Hayes 1975, no. 461; Welker 1987, 31 no. 30 (right); Sternini 1998, 83-4 no. V63; *Sangiorgi* 1999, 78 no. 197; Foy and Nenna 2001, 218 no. 387 (from Arles, France); Arveiller-Dulong and Nenna 2005, 459 no. 1288

455 A1961.992 Small bottle

Blue-green
Fourth century AD
Bought from Amie, Lady Noble (of Ardkinglos)
H 9.8, D (rim) 3.1, D (body) 2.8

- Rim folded over and into flaring mouth; cylindrical neck, tapering slightly upwards; short curving shoulder; slightly concave sides to body, tapering to small, round bottom.
- Intact. Dulling on exterior; creamy enamel-like weathering and brilliant iridescence on interior; sandy impurities and blowing striations; elongated bubbles in neck.

Compare *Sangiorgi* 1999, 74 no. 182

Tomb Group
from Egypt

456 A1911.210.4.M Bottle

Colourless

Early second century AD; excavated by Sir Flinders Petrie at Hawara, Egypt; found on a girl's mummy with other items, including five other glass vessels (listed below)

H 4.6, D (max.) 4.8

- Rounded rim; flaring mouth to short neck; small, squat ovoid body; rounded bottom.
- Cut decoration comprising a band of tiny leaf-sprays on neck and shoulder, numerous fine vertical ribs on body, and a four-petalled rosette on bottom.
- Intact. Faint weathering.

Published: Walker 1997, 84 no. 73 (described as 'mould-made'); see also *Memphis* IV, 20 and pl. XIV

A1911.210.4.H Perfume bottle

Green
Found with A1911.210.4.M
H 9.0, D (bottom) 3.1

- Broad, flat rim; tall, cylindrical neck; squat body.

Published: Walker 1997, 84 no. 68

A1911.210.4.I Perfume bottle

Green
Found with A1911.210.4.M
H 5.0, D (bottom) 2.5

- Broad, flat rim; tall, cylindrical neck; squat body.

Published: Walker 1997, 84 no. 69

A1911.210.4.J Bottle

Green
Found with A1911.210.4.M
H 6.5, D (bottom) 2.5

- Flat rim; cylindrical neck; ovoid body.

Published: Walker 1997, 84 no. 70

456 M

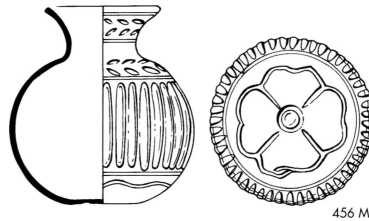

456 M

A1911.210.4.K Perfume bottle

Brownish
Found with A1911.210.4.M
H (as extant) 3.6, D (bottom) 2.6

- Short, cylindrical neck; rounded, conical body.
- Broken, with rim missing.

Published: Walker 1997, 84 no. 71

A1911.210.4.L Bottle

Brownish
Found with A1911.210.4.M
H 4.5, D (max.) 3.2

- Broad, horizontal rim; short, cylindrical neck; rounded body with broad shoulder, sides tapering downwards.
- Six vertical indents in sides.
- Most of rim missing.

Published: Walker 1997, 84 no. 72

Notes

1. For discussion of the perfume industry in antiquity, see Daygi-Mendels 1989, 90-112. In addition to the 109 vessels recorded here, the collection contains fragments of three further perfume bottles (A1879.34.16.1-3), the first of which comprises the deformed rim and neck. All three come from the Northesk Collection and so were probably acquired in Italy.
2. For references, see Ferrari 1998, 173. For additional references to the use of perfumes and spices in funerary rites, see Daygi-Mendels 1989, 126-33.
3. See Barag 1972; Basch 1972; Lightfoot 1991, 107; Stern 1999a, 467 n. 145.
4. Notable exceptions include Harden 1958, Carington Smith 1982, Oliver 1983, Nicolaou 1984, Hadjisavvas 1987 and Oliver 1992. For a list of finds from Turkey, see Lightfoot 1989, 13-4 n. 10. An additional problem is that many tombs in the East were reused by successive generations, whereas in the western provinces single-period burials are probably more common; see, for example, Tytgat 1990 (tombs at Amathus). For a general discussion of dated tombs in Cyprus, see Vessberg 1956, 213-16.
5. See, for example, Lightfoot 1991.
6. It has also been suggested that the design of these bottles was deliberately intended to provide space on the bottom for an inscription; see Stern 1999a, 469 and n. 158.
7. See, for example, Lightfoot 1992, 180-1 nos 115-16.
8. For comments on the glass and cosmetic industries in Cyprus, Seefried 1986, 148-9.
9. See, for example, Vessberg 1956, 213-16.
10. Vessberg 1953, 167 and pl. 58. Note also Tomb 61 at Curium Site E, reported to have contained 33 perfume bottles (of which only three were kept and are now in the BM), two cups and two jars; see Bailey 1988, 292.

Roman Glass Objects

457

457   A1979.129
Stirring or dipping rod, with bird finial

Colourless with pale blue tinge
Second century AD; probably from the Eastern Mediterranean
L 19.5

- Thick, tubular spiral rod with loop handle at top end drawn out from rod and worked into bird finial at other end.
- Intact, except for head of bird which has been broken and repaired. Patches of brown weathering with limy encrustation.

Isings Form 79

Compare *Winfield Smith* 1957, 149 no. 298; Auth 1976, 158 no. 213 (from Syria); Thomas 1976, 24 no. 83; von Saldern 1980, 112 no. 112 (with refs); *Luzern* 1981, 102 nos 396 and 397D; Kunina 1997, 263 nos 79-80 (one from the Panticapaeum necropolis); Newby 1999, 64 no. 55; Whitehouse 2003, 52-3 nos 972-3
Published: *Constable-Maxwell* 1979, 117 lot 202

458   A1907.330   Stirring or dipping rod

Yellow-green
Second century AD; found in Egypt
L 10.7, (max.) D (of rod) 0.9, D (of ring loop) 1.8

- In three pieces: (1) rod fragment with loop handle at one end; (2) central section of rod with, at one end, a tubular disk or stopper, pierced at centre by rod (used for holding the rod upright in a bottle); and (3) bottom end of rod with applied trail finial, shaped as a bird.
- Rod decorated with a spiral, tapering downwards from the loop handle, with twists becoming tighter towards finial.
- Broken into three pieces; head of bird at end of fragment (3) missing. Faint white weathering; iridescence and slight pitting; many bubbles in disk in fragment (2).

Similar to no. 457

459   A1879.34.15   Rod fragment

Pale blue
Second century AD; formerly Northesk Collection
L 5.6, D (max.) (of rod) 0.85

- Lower end of rod with small, flattened pad at end.
- Slight weathering and faint iridescence; dulling; a few, slender, elongated bubbles.

Compare Akat 1984, 55-6 nos 103-10; Lightfoot 1992, 219-20 nos 147-9; Kunina 1997, 263-5 nos 81-3 (found in the Crimea)

460 A1966.61A Rod applicator or spatula

Blue
Probably first to second century AD
L 13.9, D 0.27

- Rod, circular in section; bent over at one end to form hook.
- Intact, except for one chip in side (tooling scar?). Patches of flaking iridescent weathering.

In shape this tool resembles a class of hooked, bronze surgical instruments known as 'retractors'; see, for example, Bliquez 1994, 40-2 and 124-8 nos 60-81

Compare other delicate glass instruments such as the 'needle' or 'hair-pin' from the Panticapaeum necropolis; see Kunina 1997, 265 no. 84; see also *Winfield Smith* 1957, 149 no. 300; Chavane 1990, 86 no. 700; Lightfoot 2003b

See above no. 264

460

461 A1987.356 Spoon

Pale blue
Third to fourth century AD; from Beth Gibrin, Palestine; formerly in the collection of G. F. Lawrence; labelled 'Lwrnc Nov. 1898'; and the Pitt-Rivers Museum, Dorset
L 18.3, W (max.) 4.2

- Tubular oval bowl, made by blowing; handle drawn up from bowl in 'S' shape as a tubular rod, twisted with four ribs.
- Broken and repaired. Patches of limy encrusted weathering on exterior; whitish iridescence on inside of bowl.

Compare Auth 1976, 156 no. 210 (with refs); Kunina 1997, 265 no. 85 (from Syria); Whitehouse 1997, 204-5 no. 357; Bernheimer 2002, 290 no. GR-17a-c. An example in the MMA (74.51.313) is said to come from Idalion, Cyprus
Published: *Ancient Glass* 1987, 52 lot 121; Whitehouse 1997, 205

461

462 A1880.18.88 Oval plaque

Purple with colourless streaks; cast
First century AD; formerly Piot Collection
H 4.1, W 3.0, Th 0.6

- Uneven back with tooling marks; edge rounded on one side, chipped off on the other.
- Within frame, male bust in relief facing right, curly locks falling to nape of neck; garment on shoulder and chest. The bust may tentatively be identified as representing the god Dionysus, and the object may have been used as a medallion or pendant.
- Broken and mended. Patches of brilliant iridescent weathering; dulling and pitting elsewhere.

463

464

463 A1880.18.87 Appliqué

Opaque blue-grey
First century AD; formerly Piot Collection
D 4.44

- Circular disk with rounded edge and almost flat back. Decoration in deep relief, depicting a female head with hair falling in long curls to sides of face, made be pressing circular mould into a round mould of soft glass.
- Broken; large chip missing from upper right above head. Patches of whitish weathering, flaking off to leave dulling and iridescence.

Compare Whitehouse 2001a, 229-30 no. 803 (Medusa?), 223 no. 813 (actor's mask); La fragilitat 2005, 84 no. 130 (found at Ampurias, northern-east Spain)

For objects made in a similar opaque light blue glass but used as decorative plaques or inlays on furniture, see Whitehouse 1997, 19 no. 5, 21 no. 9, 22 no. 12 and 23 no. 15

For jugs decorated with appliqués attached to the base of the handle, see von Saldern 1980, 55; Harden 1987, 118-19 nos 50-1; Follmann-Schulz 1992, 21-2 no. 10; Whitehouse 2001a, 225-7 nos 797-8

There is also the fine two-handled jar in the BM, from Santelpidio in Campania, Italy; see Harden 1968, 60 no. 75

464 A1873.54.53 Appliqué from vessel

Deep opaque turquoise and colourless
Fourth century AD
L 2.1, H 3.0, Th 1.7

- Circular appliqué in relief in opaque turquoise, applied to body of vessel in colourless glass. Theatrical mask with stylised hair arranged in radiating curls.
- Faint weathering and iridescence.

This appliqué may have been made to decorate the base of the handle on the vessel to which it was once attached. Alternatively, it may have been added either singly or as one of a group of stamped bosses on the body of the vessel; see, for example, von Saldern 1968, no. 55; Isings 1964, *passim*; Harden 1968, 85 no. 112; Harden 1987, 204-5 no. 113. In either case the appliqués belong securely in the fourth century AD and have recently been attributed to an Egyptian workshop; see Arveiller-Dulong and Nenna 2005, 429.

Compare von Saldern 1974, 193-4 nos 529-31 (with refs); Auth 1976, 107 no. 123; Welker 1987, 17 no. 10 (left, inv. no. 87.61); *Sangiorgi* 1999, 66 nos 153-4 and 157; Arveiller-Dulong and Nenna 2005, 440-1 nos 1227-34

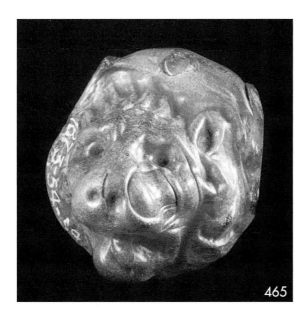

465

465   A1873.54.54   Appliqué from vessel

Pale green with yellow tinge
Fourth century AD
L 2.9, H 3.3, Th 2.0

- Appliqué in relief applied to vessel. Head of a lion
  with gaping mouth.
- Ground down at edges where broken off side of
  vessel.

Similar to no. 464, but also compare von Saldern 1974, 194 no.
532; Welker 1987, 17 no. 10 (right, inv. no. 87.60); Arveiller-Dulong
and Nenna 2005, 438-9 nos 1221-6

466   A1879.34.14   Bracelet fragment

Blue
First to fourth century AD, or later; formerly Northesk Collection
Estimated D (exterior) 4.6, W (of band) 0.8

- Round in section, thicker at one end.
- Very slight weathering and dulling.

Undecorated monochrome bracelets with a circular
section were popular throughout the Roman period,
although they have antecedents dating back well
into classical times.[1] What is remarkable is that
some of the earliest datable glass bracelets are

incomplete hoops, decorated with gold finials;
see, for example, a pair of cobalt blue bracelets in
the so-called 'Lydian Treasure'.[2] These bracelets not
only show the high social standing that glass could
achieve as jewellery, but also demonstrate that the
producers and wearers alike were prepared to
sacrifice the greater strength of a solid hoop in
order to add rich and impressive gold decoration
to the glass.

See Spaer 1988, 54 (Type A.1)
Compare Lightfoot 1992, 222-3 nos 152-5

467   A1957.525   Small bracelet

Blue
First to fourth century AD, or later
Given by Dr G. G. Allan
D 4.3

- Penannular section. Uneven circle. No visible join.
- Intact. Brilliant iridescence and pitting.

The small size of the band indicates that it was worn
by a child.

See Spaer 1988, 54 (Type A.2a)
Compare Duval 1989, 30 nos 34 and 36

468   A1957.524   Bracelet

Green
Possibly third to fourth century AD
D 8.2, W (of band) 1.3

- Penannular section, with sixteen tooled, diagonal
  ribs on outer face.
- Intact. Small patches of creamy brown weathering;
  dulling and faint iridescence; many elongated
  bubbles.

See Spaer 1988, 56-7 (Type B.3b), quoting dated examples

469 A1927.95 Bracelet

Dark purplish brown
Possibly sixth to seventh century AD
D 8.2, max. W (of band) 1.3

- Broad band, slightly convex in section, decorated on exterior with five horizontal tooled ribs. Tooled in at one point to a width of 1.0.
- Broken and mended. Brilliant iridescence and deep pitting.

See Spaer 1988, 57 (Type B.4a), quoting dated examples
Compare also Duval 1989, 30 no. 32

470 A1966.66 Bracelet

Uncertain colour
Possibly sixth to seventh century AD
Bequeathed by Mrs A. W. Acworth; formerly in the Acworth Collection
D 8.4, W (of band) 2.0

- Broad band, slightly convex in section, decorated on exterior with six horizontal tooled ribs. Ends of band pressed together with slanting join in a broader but slightly flatter segment.
- Intact. Thick black enamel-like weathering, flaking off in places to leave brilliant iridescence and deep pitting.

Similar to no. 469

471 A1982.600 Circular button

Light green
First century AD, or later
D 2.8, Th 0.7

- Circular; flat bottom; round edge; conical, ridged upper surface; central hole.
- Intact, except for small chip in edge. Faint iridescent weathering and slight dulling.

A similar object was found in a Neronian context (AD 54-68) during excavations at the Unexplored Mansion at Knossos, Crete; see Price 1992, 456-7 no. 317 (with discussion). As well as their possible use as dress ornaments and buttons, such objects are sometimes found attached to pins and stirring rods; see, for example, a stirring rod from Cyprus in the MMA (74.51.153) and no. 458 (A1907.330) above. They have also been regarded as spindle whorls; see Thomas 1976, 24 no. 82, together with an example in the BM (M&LA 1878.10-12.2, from Egypt, dating from the third to fourth century AD).

Compare Canav 1985, 35 nos 12-14; Chavane 1990, 85-6 nos 695-9 (from tombs at Amathus, Cyprus)

472 A1982.602 Circular button

Pale green
First century AD, or later
D 2.1, Th 0.9

- Circular; flat bottom; round edge; conical upper surface, with spiral, indented ridge; central hole.
- Intact. Deep pitting inside hole; iridescence and slight dulling elsewhere.

Similar to no. 471

473 A1902.559 Group of four counters

First to third century AD
(1) Opaque white (D 2.3)
(2) Opaque dull pale blue (D 1.5)
(3) Opaque green (D 1.3)
(4) Opaque pale blue (D 1.4)

- Flat bottom, except for (d) which has an uneven bottom; convex upper surface.
- All intact.

These objects are generally described as counters or gaming pieces. Individual counters have been found on sites throughout the Roman world (for example, 39 were recovered from the Roman city of Knossos on Crete), while some have also been found in tombs in sets of gaming pieces; see Price 1992, 454-5 (with refs). However, they could also find several other uses, as is shown by two terracotta architectural relief plaques from south Italy in the MMA (GR 1998.210.1-2, possibly Tarentine and dated to the late fourth century BC), which are decorated with small glass inlays of exactly the same shape as a counter.[3] Alternatively, it has been suggested that such objects, when made of transparent colourless glass, could have been used as magnifiers or lens pieces, especially by craftsmen when carrying out very detailed miniature work. A recent study has, however, argued against the use of magnifying lenses in antiquity; see Plantzos 1997, 455-9

474 A1902.161-3   Three counters

Dark purple brown, appearing black, and opaque blue-grey
First to third century AD
(a) D (max.) 1.9, D (upper surface) 1.3
(b) D (max.) 1.8, D (upper surface) 1.4
(c) D (max.) 2.1, D (upper surface) 1.6-1.5

• Faint weathering and pitting.
• Flat circular disk; conical in section. The lighter coloured glass is cast on top of the darker in imitation of layered sardonyx.
• Intact.

475 A1902.316   Disk

Dark purple appearing black, with opaque white trails
Uncertain date
Th 1.2

• Circular, thick disk, with round edges and flat top and bottom, decorated with white feather trails. Tooled indent on bottom.
• Intact. Dulling and slight pitting.

The purpose of this object is uncertain; it may have been a gaming piece or, possibly, a decorative inlay.

476 A1957.527   Pendant miniature vase

Light blue
Fourth to fifth century AD; probably Palestinian
H 1.9, W (max.) 1.8

• Cylindrical body. Two horizontal bands around body with zigzag trail between them, then trailed up to rim as handle. Piece of fine gold wire, twisted into loop, attached to handle.
• Broken at top. Thick creamy brown weathering, partially flaked off leaving dulling and iridescence.

For discussion of the type, see Weinberg 1988, 230 no. 22 (with refs); Newby 1999, 98 no. 94
Compare Neuburg 1949, pl. XXXI no. 104 (said to have been found in Palestine); Platz-Horster 1976, 33 no. 41; Thomas 1976, 36 no. 171; *Kofler* 1985, 110 lot 204 (top left)

477 A1921.212   Pendant miniature amphora

Purple
Probably first to third century AD
H 1.6, W 0.8-1.0

• Rounded, bulging rim; ovoid body; pointed bottom, with trail curled over to one side; two trail handles drawn up from shoulder to rim.
• Intact. Thick creamy brown weathering, partially flaked off leaving dulling and iridescence.

Compare Platz-Horster 1976, 33 no. 41 (five different examples, all 3 cm or less in height); *Kofler* 1985, 110 lot 204 (16 pieces); *Holy Land* 1998, 32 illus. (from the site of Castra, near 'En Hashofet, Israel); *Sangiorgi* 1999, 57 lot 125

478 A1904.134.60   Pendant miniature kylix

Opaque yellow
Probably first to third century AD
H 2.0, W 1.9

• Broken at one end. Some surface weathering.

Glass Beads

479 A1880.18.93 Compound eye-bead

Dark blue, with opaque white and yellow
Probably fourth to third century BC; Phoenician or Punic; formerly Piot Collection
L. 3.1, D 3.2

- Cylindrical, with applied decoration of fused-on beads; at top and bottom, plain white and yellow blobs in two rows; at centre, six larger stratified eyes, each comprising six beads, fused on top of each other, alternately blue and opaque white and getting progressively smaller.
- Intact. Encrusted weathering on interior; patches of weathering on exterior.

For a general discussion of 'eye beads' see Hævernick 1981, 233-44; Venclová 1983 (esp. p. 13 and figs 2:2 and 4:1). They are closely related to the head or face beads; see, for example, Goldstein 1979, 111-12 no. 224 (with refs); *Wolf* 1994, 192-3 no. 37.

Compare Tatton-Brown 1981, 155 no. 451; Uberti 1993, 103-4 nos 107-8 (from the necropolis at Olbia, Sardinia); *Wolf* 1994, 195 no. 39 (with discussion); *Sangiorgi* 1999, 16 lot 23 and 20 lot 35 (at centre); Schlick-Nolte 2002b, 213 no. P-54

480 A1880.18.91 Bead

Dark blue, with opaque white and yellow
Probably fourth to third century BC; formerly Piot Collection
L. 2.5, D 2.2

- Intact. Encrusted weathering on interior; grey enamel-like weathering on exterior.

Similar to no. 479

481 A1890.971 Bead

Deep blue, with opaque white
Uncertain date
D 1.1, Th 0.9

- Decorated with white spiral trail
- Intact.

482 A1890.972 Bead

Deep purple, appearing black, with amber brown, opaque white and yellow
Uncertain date
D 1.8, Th 1.7

- Marbled swirl decoration in white and brown trails, with yellow dots, all marvered into surface.
- Intact. Slight dulling and patches of deep pitting.

483 A1890.974 Three beads

Translucent pale reddish brown, with opaque white and pink
Uncertain date
D (all three) 1.7, Th 1.3 (two) and 1.2 (one)

- Flattened on top and bottom around hole. Decorated with spiral trail wound round three times and tooled into a feather pattern in three places. On one bead the white trail continues one more turn round side.
- All intact. Deep pitting around hole on one side.

484 A1921.999 Bead

Blue, red and opaque white
Probably modern
L 5.7, D 2.1-3.5

- Long cylindrical shape, at the tapering ends; pierced lengthwise with central hole. Chevron-like pattern with central elongated blue lozenges and red bands, flanking zigzags in white, with an additional white zigzag trail around mouth of hole at both ends.
- Intact. Faint dulling and pitting.

Probably belonging to the type known as 'Aggry-beads'; see Neuburg 1949, 53-4 pl. XXIII nos 114(a), (b) and (e). Similar examples on display in the CMG are divided between beads with 'old-type chevrons', made in Venice, Italy before the 19th century and those with 'new-type chevrons' that are Venetian or Czech, dating to the 19th century.

485 A1921.1000 Bead

Blue, red and opaque white
Probably modern
L 3.8, D 1.7-2.6

- Intact. Irregular deep tooling indents. Dulling and some pitting.

Similar to no. 484, but shorter and more rounded in shape

National Museums Scotland also possesses a large number of beads strung into necklaces; these have been left unrecorded and only a summary list is appended here.[4]

A1880.18.94	100 beads
A1880.18.95	86 beads
A1880.18.96	79 beads
A1880.18.97	88 beads
A1880.18.98	105 beads
A1880.18.99	32 beads
A1880.18.100	52 beads
A1880.18.101	64 beads
A1880.18.102	27 beads
A1880.18.103	69 beads
A1880.18.104	103 beads
A1880.18.105	33 beads
A1880.18.106	33 beads
A1904.135.57	13 and 38 beads on two separate strings[5]

Notes

1 It has been argued that the fashion for wearing glass bracelets in the East only arose in the third century AD, but this view is quite misleading and should not be taken seriously; *pace* Spaer 1988, 51.

2 See Özgen 1996, 161 no. 111. For other examples, see Deppert-Lippitz 1996, 53 and 129 no. 30 (from Etruria, Italy) and a pair in the MMA (57.11.8-9).

3 The Ionic capitals of the north porch of the Erechtheium at Athens were also decorated with coloured glass inlays; see Stern 1999b, 37 and fig. 16.

4 In addition, a number of individual beads have not been fully recorded. They include the following examples: A1882.28.5 (in opaque yellow, with guilloche pattern in green and blue; recorded as from West Africa), A1904.135.56 (excavated at el-Bahnasa, Egypt); A1921.207-208 (in blue; found in Cyprus), A1921.210-213 (also found in Cyprus). Three other beads (A1880.18.91-93), together with three pendant amulets (A1880.18.89 in the form of a man's head, A1880.18.90 in the form of a monkey eating, and A1880.18.92) have been published elsewhere; see Culican 1966, 93, illus. 103; Seefried 1982, 102 no. 20, fig. 33; 143 no. 12; 149-50 no. 41.

5 Excavated at el-Bahnasa (Oxyrhyncus), Egypt.

Glass of Ancient Egypt

The most important pieces of Egyptian glass in the collection are undoubtedly the fragments of vessels belonging to the Late Bronze Age in the second half of the second millennium BC (nos 486-490), but there are also several minor objects, including a number of rod-formed penannular earrings, also dating to the 18th-19th Dynasty of the New Kingdom. Five of these, all slightly different, were seen on display in the Egyptian gallery but could not be recorded in detail.[1]

486 A1964.457 Body fragment of an unguent bottle (krateriskos)

Opaque medium blue with threads in opaque yellow and white; core-formed

New Kingdom, Eighteenth Dynasty, first half of the fourteenth century BC

L. 5.2, H 3.9, Th 0.4-0.25

- Part of neck, rounded shoulder and upper body, with ends of one loop handle, applied after the thread decoration on the body had been completed.
- Thick iridescent weathering on interior.

Compare Grose 1989, 60-1 no. 7; *Wolf* 1994, 130 no. 5.2; Schlick-Nolte 2002a, 47-9 nos V-1, V-2 and V-3a-c[2]

487 A1965.254 Rim fragment of an unguent bottle (krateriskos)

Dark blue with threads in opaque yellow, white and light blue; core-formed.

New Kingdom, Eighteenth Dynasty, first half of the fourteenth century BC

L 2.3, H 2.4, Th (rim) 0.5-0.8

- Rounded, everted rim, flat on top; part of tall cylindrical neck.
- Iridescent weathering on interior.

Compare Goldstein 1979, 67 no. 44; Grose 1989, 62-3 no. 12

488 A1965.253 Rim fragment of an unguent bottle (krateriskos)

Dark blue, decorated with opaque yellow, blue white threads; core-formed

New Kingdom, Eighteenth Dynasty, first half of the fourteenth century BC

L 3.7, H 1.3, Th (rim) 0.2-0.6

- Applied coil of dark blue and yellow spiral threads on outer edge of rim; short horizontal rim, uneven and sloping slightly outward; cylindrical

neck decorated with opaque white and pale blue threads, tooled into an irregular wavy pattern.
- Slight dulling on exterior; iridescent weathering on interior.

Compare Grose 1989, 61 no. 8

489 A1965.250 Neck and shoulder fragment of an unguent bottle (krateriskos)

Dark blue, decorated with opaque yellow, dull orange brown, light blue and white threads; core-formed

New Kingdom, Eighteenth Dynasty, first half of the fourteenth century BC

L. 4.35, H 3.0, Th 0.4-0.35

- Dense zigzag pattern on neck; threads on body tooled up onto shoulder in tall festoon pattern. Rotary grinding marks on neck.
- Pitting of surface bubbles. Iridescent weathering on exterior; thick, limy weathering on interior.

Compare *Wolf* 1994, 130 no. 5

490 A1965.248 Rim and neck fragment of bottle

Greyish blue, with opaque yellow, white and turquoise threads; core-formed.[3]

New Kingdom, Eighteenth Dynasty, first half of the fourteenth century BC

H 5.4, W. 3.3, Th 0.45-0.25

- Thickened, rounded rim, with outer lip tapering downwards; cylindrical neck with convex sides; threads extending from rim to body in tooled wavy pattern.
- Dulling and faint weathering.

Compare Goldstein 1979, 68 nos 50-51

492   493

491   A1965.247   Miniature flask

Bright blue, with opaque yellow, white, cherry red
and dark blue; core-formed

New Kingdom, Eighteenth Dynasty, first half
of the fourteenth century BC

Donated by Dr C. T. Trechmann

H 3.0, W 2.2, D 1.6

- Applied coil on top edge of mouth, forming
  rounded, outward rim; cylindrical neck; lentoid
  body; rounded bottom; three rod handles, one
  in red, the other two in bright blue, applied to
  shoulder in a pad and drawn up in a loop to neck.
- Decoration of marvered trails and blobs on body,
  applied before the handles.
- Intact. Very little weathering.

Published: Nolte 1968, 113 and pl. XVI, 5

492   A1911.286   Floral inlay fragment

Light blue, yellow, white and red

Ptolemaic, third to first century BC

H 8.6, W 4.6, Th 0.5

- Fragment, broken on three sides; uneven edge to
  left of vertical floral design comprising flowers,
  buds and leaves.

For discussion of these plaques, see Grose 1989,
355; *Wolf* 1995, 404-5.

Compare Dumbarton Oaks, no. 57.6; Goldstein 1979, 254-7 nos
758-76; *Kofler* 1985, 114-15 lots 221-22 (reputedly to be from el-
Bahnasa, Egypt); Grose 1989, 365-7 nos 646-53; Nenna 1993b,
46-7 and fig. 1a (from the Chatby necropolis at Alexandria); *Wolf*
1995, 406-7 no. 147; *Sangiorgi* 1999, 38 no. 95; *Ancient Glass* 2001,
118-9 and 202 no. 118; Schlick-Nolte 2002a, 81-2 no. V-36a-c

493 A1911.285 Floral inlay fragment

Light blue, yellow, white and red
Ptolemaic, third to first century BC
H (max.) 9.4, W (max.) 4.5, Th 0.6

- Fragment, broken on three sides; rounded edge to right of vertical floral design comprising flowers, buds and leaves; bowed in section. Polished front surface.

Similar to no. 492

494 A1887.365 Scarab

Cobalt blue. Cast and cut.[4]
Probably Ptolemaic, third to first century BC
L. 2.4, W 1.7, Th (max.) 1.2

- Remains of iron pin in hole pierced through scarab from front to back. Flat underside, carved in intaglio with figure of Nike, standing facing left, holding a large wreath in both hands, surrounded by an incised line forming an oval around the edge; the edge itself is notched.
- Intact. Dulling and iridescence; patches of milky weathering in details of carving.

For other glass scarabs, compare Goldstein 1979, 160-2 nos 369-81; *Wolf* 1994, 366-7 nos 120-21 (with discussion)

Notes

1 All in dark blue glass; two are plain, but the other three are decorated along the outer edge with spirally twisted threads in blue and opaque white, while two are further provided with vertical hoops in opaque yellow. Compare *Fitzwilliam* 1978, 13 no. 5a; Goldstein 1979, 80-1 nos 129-31; Wolkenberg 1991, lot 162; Tait 1991, illus. 36 (top right); *Sangiorgi* 1999, 18 no. 29; Bianchi and Schlick-Nolte 2002, 127 no. EG-5a-b.

2 For another group of New Kingdom vessel fragments, see von Saldern 1974, 22-6 nos 11-23.

3 Four other core-formed fragments – A1965.251 (with end of handle on body below shoulder), A1965.252, A1965.257 and A1965.256 – are probably also examples of Egyptian glassware dating to the Late Bronze Age.

4 The NMS collection also includes another blue glass scarab (A1887.366), recorded as having been found at Bari, southern Italy, in the same tomb as an iron sword and arrowhead (A1887.345-346). The register suggests that these objects may be 'Late Roman', but a date in the Hellenistic period seems more likely.

Post-Roman Glass

Merovingian Glass

495 A1922.175 Jar

Yellow-green
Probably late fifth or sixth century AD; label 'Marchélepot, Somme, 1886'
H 7.0, D (rim) 8.35-8.25, D (base) 9.6

- Everted, rounded and thickened rim; short concave neck; bulbous body; push-in bottom with pontil scar. Thin-walled vessel.
- Numerous pre-moulded shallow vertical ribs around undercurve of body.
- Intact, but repair on rim and one small internal (impact) crack in body. Thick creamy brown weathering, mostly flaked off, leaving fine brilliant iridescence and dulling; pinprick and some large bubbles.

496 A1922.178 Bell beaker

Light green with opaque white trails and base blob
Late fifth to early sixth century AD
H 9.4, D (rim) 6.4-6.25

- Everted, rounded, thickened rim; sides to body curving in gently and then tapering to point at bottom; knob base surrounded by pontil ring; pointed indent made by tool on interior of bottom.
- Band of fine trails, 0.55-0.9 below rim; another band of thicker, marvered trails around body, drawn down and out into six rounded, knob-like protrusions; blob on knob base.
- Intact, but one knob missing. Patches of faint enamel weathering; many pinprick bubbles.

This beaker belongs to a type that appears to have been common only in northern France; for discussion, and two similar examples in the MMA (17.191.350 and 17.191.356), see Edison 2000, 271 and figs 223-4.

Compare Hayes 1975, 155 no. 645; Harden 1978, 308 no. 15 (from Herpes, France). A fragment in the CMG may also be from the base of a bell beaker; see Whitehouse 2003, 171 no. 1192

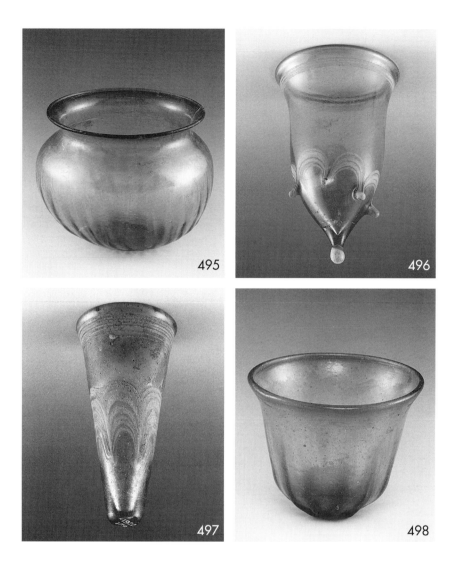

495

496

497

498

497 A1922.179 Cone beaker

Pale blue-green with opaque greenish white trails
Sixth century AD
H 9.7, D (rim) 4.9, D (bottom) 1.5

- Rounded, thickened rim with slightly everted lip; straight sides to conical body; small flattened bottom.
- Spiral trail in six(?) turns below rim from bottom to top; another trail marvered into sides and tooled down into a feather pattern.
- Intact. Some black impurities; dulling and slight iridescence; many pinprick bubbles.

Compare Vanderhoeven 1958, 63-4 no. 66 (found at Souverain-Wandre, Belgium)

498 A1922.180 Palm cup

Green with yellow tinge
Late sixth or seventh century AD
H 6.6, D (rim) 9.0-8.55

- Rounded, thickened rim; slightly flaring neck; tapering sides to body; round bottom with central pontil scar, partially obscuring decoration.
- Pre-moulded decoration comprising a four-arm cross in an almost flat disk, surrounded by twelve radiating ribs, extending from bottom up sides; ribs thickened on interior and exterior.
- Intact. Some black impurities; slight dulling; many pinprick and larger bubbles.

Compare Vanderhoeven 1958, 65-6 nos 69-70; *Fitzwilliam* 1978, 57 no. 117; *JGS* 20 (1978), 121 no. 12 (Toledo Museum of Art); Merseyside 1979, 29 no. B3 (a pair of cups found in Kingston, grave 146); plus two other examples, one in the CMG (54.1.94), the other in the MMA (17.193.339)

Byzantine Glass

499

499 1960.4 Architectural revetment plaque in sandwich-gold glass

Purplish brown and colourless; cast
Eleventh to twelfth century AD; probably from the monastery church at Maarat el Nuaaman near Aleppo, Syria
L. 9.0, W. 8.7, Th 0.8.

- Square plaque, with jagged, chipped edges; thick base layer in purplish brown with gold leaf applied to its upper surface; thinner colourless upper layer
- Intact. Thick weathering on back, flaking off to leave iridescence and pitting; areas of upper layer missing from front, leaving iridescent weathering.

Presumably used as part of the decoration on the interior wall of a large building. All of the known tiles apparently have the same pattern of cut-out triangles in gold leaf, sandwiched between two layers of glass. This uniformity of design would seem to reinforce the claim that they all came from the same site, usually described as a monastery church in Syria. For general discussion of the tiles and identification of their provenance, see Philippe 1975, *passim*. For a small fragment of sandwich-gold glass, found in Egypt and regarded as 'probably Roman', see Grose 1989, 35 fig. 16. Similar in basic production technique are the small gold-glass mosaic tesserae that were used to decorate Byzantine churches such as Hagia Sophia in Istanbul or the recently excavated church at Amorium (Turkey); see Witte-Orr 2003, esp. 146, pls X/37, 39.[1]

Compare Winfield Smith 1957, 221 no. 446 (CMG 54.1.82); Auth 1976, 235 (inv. no. 72.138); Oliver 1980, 150 no. 268 (with discussion listing other examples); *Kofler* 1985, 9 lots 1 and 2; Wolkenberg 1991, lot 37; *Benzian* 1994, 18 lot 11; Sotheby's, London, December 8, 1994, Evans and Wixom 1997, 386 no. 256; lot 28; *Sangiorgi* 1999, 87 lot. 224

Published: Philippe 1975, 98 fig. 3

Islamic Glass

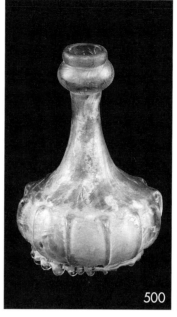

500   501

500   A1956.455   Squat flask

Colourless.[2]

Eleventh to twelfth century AD, possibly later

H 9.0, D (rim) 1.9, D (body) 6.45; D (base) 5.0-4.8

- Vertical rounded rim; bulge at top of neck, forming collar below rim; cylindrical neck, flaring out and joining curve of shoulder; squat body; applied base ring of pinched feet; deep pushed-in bottom with pontil scar at centre.
- Twelve tooled, almost vertical ribs on body, tapering downwards and extending on to bottom.
- Intact. Dulled and slight iridescent weathering swirls; some pinprick bubbles.

The vessel is unusual, and no clear parallel has been found. The bulge on the neck seems to resemble those found on Islamic vessels of various shapes, dating to the eleventh to twelfth century, but the possibility cannot be discounted that it is of relatively recent manufacture.

501   A1955.9   Kohl bottle

Dark blue-green with opaque pale green trail

Possibly Mamluk, fourteenth to fifteenth century AD

H 13.8, D (rim) 1.4, D (body) 3.4

- Uneven (knocked-off or cut) rim; slender, cylindrical neck; elongated ovoid body; tooled knob base, squared off at sides and rounded at bottom.

- Trail applied to neck below rim and wound body from left to right, tooled and marvered.
- Intact. Iridescence, dulling and pitting; many bubbles.

Compare Wolkenberg 1991, lot no. 64 (dated first to second century AD). For Islamic vessels with similar marvered trails, see Winfield Smith 1957, 253-4 nos 509, 511-13; Luzern 1981, 121 nos 488-92; Whitcomb 1983, 103 and fig. 2: cc-ee, mm-pp. Marvered bottles have been given various dates, ranging from the 7th-8th century to Ottoman times, but finds from excavations appear to suggest that they belong principally in the 14th-15th century; see Shindo 1993, esp. 302-3 and fig. 7.

502   A1887.741   Bracelet

Dark translucent glass and opaque pale yellow

Islamic (Mamluk or later)

D 6.7-7.0, W 0.7

- Semicircular section, comprising a band in translucent glass, circular in section, attached to outer side of a flat band in opaque yellow, with 21 yellow blobs applied to outer edge. No visible join.
- Cracked and chipped. Thick, white weathering covering most of surfaces.

For Islamic bracelets, see Spaer 1992, *passim*

Glass of
Uncertain Date

503 A1928.284 Cylindrical bottle

Pale green with bluish tinge
Possibly third to fourth century AD, or post-Roman
H 6.3, D (rim) 2.5, D (body) 2.9; D (base) 4.2

- Everted, almost horizontal rim; flaring mouth; short neck narrow shoulder, curving out to cylindrical body; deep kick in bottom, surrounded by pontil scar.
- Intact, except for small chip in rim. Faint iridescence; white, gritty inclusion in side; pinprick and small, elongated bubbles.

Despite its resemblance to Roman cylindrical bottles, there is some doubt about the antiquity of this vessel, and it may well be a medicinal bottle of relatively modern date.

Isings Form 102a
Compare Spartz 1967, no. 123 (with refs); Auth 1976, 234 no. 552; Matheson 1980, 82-3 nos 221-3

504 UC.631 Bowl

Dark opaque glass, appearing black
Possibly early Byzantine, sixth century AD
H 5.2, D (bottom) 6.4

- Rounded rim, folded in and down, with curved upper lip; vertical sides tapering downwards; deep pushed-in bottom with central pontil mark.
- Fifteen slender vertical, pre-moulded ribs on body.
- Broken and mended; several holes. Dulling and iridescence; blowing striations.

The vessel bears some resemblance to cylindrical jars of Isings Form 130.

505 A1911.210.14 Miniature jar

Green
Possibly late Islamic; probably from Egypt
H 3.5, D (rim) 3.1, D (body) 3.2

- Rounded, thickened, vertical rim; neck tapering downwards, tooled around base; squat, bulbous body; kick in bottom, covered by pontil mark.
- Intact. No weathering; a few large and pinprick bubbles.

Compare Auth 1976, 233 no. 545

506 A1937.518 Flask

Pale purple
Possibly post-Roman
H 13.4, D (body) 6.1

- Cylindrical neck, with tooled indent around base; sloping shoulder; body curving downwards to small bottom with pontil scar at centre covering kick.
- Intact body and neck, but made-up rim. Weathering flaking off on interior; dulling and iridescence on exterior; blowing striations.

507 A1937.425 Large flask

Deep blue-green
Probably post-Roman, possibly Islamic
H 26.9, D (rim) 3.9, D (body) 6.9

- Fire-rounded, vertical rim, partially flattened and bevelled on upper edge; flaring neck, tooled around base; rounded shoulder; tall, tapering sides to body; small bottom with kick and pontil scar.
- Intact. Soil encrustation on interior; some gritty and many glassy inclusions; a few very large bubbles.

Compare Auth 1976, 231 no. 534

Notes

1   Some coloured glass mosaic tesserae (A1879.34.18.1-18) are also registered amongst the objects in NMS from the Northesk Collection.
2   Ten Abbasid glass weights (A1903.266-275), found at Ramleh in Palestine, have not been included in the catalogue.

Concordance

Register No.	Cat. No.	Register No.	Cat. No.	Register No.	Cat. No.
UC.631	504	A1879.34.4.2	114	A1879.34.7.2	62
A168.267A	168	A1879.34.4.8	115	A1879.34.7.3	61
A1857.157.2	253	A1879.34.4.10	117	A1879.34.7.4	69
A1857.157.3	179	A1879.34.4.11	112	A1879.34.7.5	73
A1873.54.53	464	A1879.34.4.12	113	A1879.34.7.6	60
A1873.54.54	465	A1879.34.4.16	116	A1879.34.7.9	63
A1879.34.1.1	118	A1879.34.5.1	77	A1879.34.7.10	64
A1879.34.1.4	38	A1879.34.5.4	75	A1879.34.7.12	71
A1879.34.1.58	119	A1879.34.5.6	132	A1879.34.7.15	74
A1879.34.1.70-79	120	A1879.34.5.8	76	A1879.34.7.16	72
A1879.34.1.80	105	A1879.34.5.9	80	A1879.34.7.18	68
A1879.34.1.81-93	120	A1879.34.5.11	131	A1879.34.7.19	66
A1879.34.1.94	107	A1879.34.5.12	79	A1879.34.7.21	67
A1879.34.1.95-104	120	A1879.34.5.14	81	A1879.34.7.24	91
A1879.34.1.105	110	A1879.34.5.16	104	A1879.34.7.25	70
A1879.34.1.106-9	120	A1879.34.5.17	98	A1879.34.7.30	56
A1879.34.1.110	106	A1879.34.6.1	85	A1879.34.7.31	59
A1879.34.1.111-14	120	A1879.34.6.2	89	A1879.34.7.32	55
A1879.34.1.115	111	A1879.34.6.3	93	A1879.34.7.33	57
A1879.34.1.116-27	120	A1879.34.6.4	90	A1879.34.7.34	58
A1879.34.1.128	78	A1879.34.6.6	100	A1879.34.7.35	54
A1879.34.1.129	108	A1879.34.6.7	101	A1879.34.14	466
A1879.34.1.130-6	120	A1879.34.6.8	97	A1879.34.15	459
A1879.34.1.137	109	A1879.34.6.9	99	A1879.34.19	49
A1879.34.1.138	120	A1879.34.6.12	87	A1879.34.27	382
A1879.34.2.1-11	121	A1879.34.6.13	129	A1879.34.28	405
A1879.34.2.12	123	A1879.34.6.17	102	A1879.34.33	422
A1879.34.2.13	52	A1879.34.6.18	83	A1880.18.2	34
A1879.34.2.14-17	123	A1879.34.6.19	88	A1880.18.4	35
A1879.34.2.19	136	A1879.34.6.21	126	A1880.18.5	36
A1879.34.2.26	124	A1879.34.6.22	84	A1880.18.6	32
A1879.34.2.28-32	122	A1879.34.6.24	130	A1880.18.7	139
A1879.34.2.33	53	A1879.34.6.26	128	A1880.18.8	138
A1879.34.2.34-39	122	A1879.34.6.27	82	A1880.18.10	33
A1879.34.2.40	134	A1879.34.6.28	103	A1880.18.11	45
A1879.34.2.58	133	A1879.34.6.29	125	A1880.18.12	30
A1879.34.2.65	94	A1879.34.6.31	92	A1880.18.12A	31
A1879.34.2.68	96	A1879.34.6.33	86	A1880.18.13	137
A1879.34.2.76	95	A1879.34.6.36	127	A1880.18.14	207
A1879.34.3.3	135	A1879.34.7.1	65	A1880.18.15	152

Register No.	Cat. No.	Register No.	Cat. No.	Register No.	Cat. No.
A1880.18.16	44	A1880.18.68	368	A1887.378	426
A1880.18.17	222	A1880.18.69	366	A1887.380	428
A1880.18.18	221	A1880.18.70	196	A1887.741	502
A1880.18.19	163	A1880.18.71	156	A1888.378	246
A1880.18.20	150	A1880.18.72	274	A1889.497	146
A1880.18.21	172	A1880.18.73	143	A1889.498	357
A1880.18.22	148	A1880.18.75	166	A1889.499	379
A1880.18.23	147	A1880.18.76	50	A1890.971	481
A1880.18.24	240	A1880.18.77	254	A1890.972	482
A1880.18.25	234	A1880.18.78	270	A1890.974	483
A1880.18.26	235	A1880.18.80	178	A1890.1040	160
A1880.18.27	233	A1880.18.81	190	A1892.499	385
A1880.18.28	239	A1880.18.82	154	A1892.500	384
A1880.18.30	236	A1880.18.83	447	A1895.238.64	423
A1880.18.32	47	A1880.18.85	438	A1895.238.65	425
A1880.18.33	48	A1880.18.86	439	A1895.238.68	445
A1880.18.34	28	A1880.18.87	463	A1895.238.70	436
A1880.18.35	27	A1880.18.88	462	A1895.238.71	450
A1880.18.36	26	A1880.18.91	480	A1895.238.73	202
A1880.18.37	21	A1880.18.93	479	A1895.238.74	388
A1880.18.38	12	A1881.2.1	321	A1895.238.76	356
A1880.18.39	10	A1881.2.2	255	A1895.276	296
A1880.18.40	11	A1881.2.3	297	A1895.277	157
A1880.18.41	7	A1881.2.4	208	A1895.278	261
A1880.18.42	15	A1881.2.5	412	A1895.280	191
A1880.18.43	16	A1881.2.7	395	A1895.281	320
A1880.18.44	9	A1881.32	247	A1895.282	337
A1880.18.46	14	A1881.32A	248	A1895.283	289
A1880.18.47	4	A1882.28.1	401	A1895.284	218
A1880.18.48	2	A1882.28.2	283	A1895.286	282
A1880.18.49	3	A1882.28.3	242	A1898.28	396
A1880.18.50	1	A1883.22.1	40	A1899.302	258
A1880.18.53	8	A1883.22.2	41	A1899.303	256
A1880.18.55	378	A1883.22.4	37	A1899.304	302
A1880.18.56	377	A1887.365	494	A1899.305	230
A1880.18.57	376	A1887.367	13	A1899.306	229
A1880.18.60	267	A1887.370	23	A1899.307	311
A1880.18.61	271	A1887.371	249	A1899.308	315
A1880.18.62	364	A1887.371A	250	A1899.309	259
A1880.18.63	365	A1887.372	184	A1899.310	257
A1880.18.64	375	A1887.373	185	A1899.311	305
A1880.18.65	367	A1887.374	158	A1901.547.9	199
A1880.18.66	359	A1887.375	372	A1902.161-3	474
A1880.18.67	360	A1887.376	272	A1902.316	475

Register No.	Cat. No.	Register No.	Cat. No.	Register No.	Cat. No.
A1902.559	473	A1921.108	162	A1921.190	391
A1903.146	314	A1921.112	204	A1921.194	386
A1903.261	317	A1921.113	206	A1921.195	370
A1903.262	316	A1921.114	183	A1921.196	346
A1903.263	231	A1921.115	291	A1921.202	39
A1903.264	307	A1921.116	174	A1921.212	477
A1903.265	243	A1921.117	188	A1921.999	484
A1903.331.17	398	A1921.119	285	A1921.1000	485
A1903.374	220	A1921.121	286	A1921.1389	443
A1904.134.55	394	A1921.123	241	A1921.1390	442
A1904.134.60	478	A1921.124	189	A1921.1397	435
A1906.353	18	A1921.125	181	A1921.1400	437
A1907.297	151	A1921.126	331	A1921.1405	399
A1907.330	458	A1921.127	273	A1922.175	495
A1911.210.4.M	456	A1921.128	225	A1922.176	219
A1911.210.14	505	A1921.130	187	A1922.177	201
A1911.285	493	A1921.131	176	A1922.178	496
A1911.286	492	A1921.132	175	A1922.179	497
A1914.86	448	A1921.134	453	A1922.180	498
A1914.88	441	A1921.135	414	A1922.541	308
A1914.89	449	A1921.138	431	A1923.353	290
A1914.92	444	A1921.144	419	A1924.1	327
A1914.93	434	A1921.146	408	A1926.284	200
A1914.94	432	A1921.147	284	A1927.83	214
A1914.96	413	A1921.148	369	A1927.84	193
A1914.97	404	A1921.149	411	A1927.85	281
A1914.98	390	A1921.150	140	A1927.86	429
A1914.99	403	A1921.151	195	A1927.87	310
A1914.100	424	A1921.154	381	A1927.89	352
A1914.103	387	A1921.156	380	A1927.90	25
A1914.107	276	A1921.158	407	A1927.91	345
A1914.107A	277	A1921.159	409	A1927.95	469
A1914.108	278	A1921.163	415	A1927.610	269
A1914.108A	279	A1921.164	144	A1927.611	333
A1916.10	418	A1921.170	397	A1928.284	503
A1921.84	451	A1921.175	392	A1936.435	17
A1921.86	446	A1921.176	406	A1936.436	326
A1921.94	275	A1921.178	410	A1936.438	182
A1921.100	205	A1921.179	383	A1936.517	400
A1921.101	203	A1921.181	363	A1937.425	507
A1921.104	159	A1921.182	362	A1937.506	342
A1921.105	165	A1921.186	402	A1937.507	224
A1921.106	153	A1921.187	358	A1937.508	303
A1921.107	164	A1921.189	355	A1937.509	336

Register No.	Cat. No.	Register No.	Cat. No.	Register No.	Cat. No.
A1937.510	300	A1957.13	186	A1966.63	343
A1937.511	341	A1957.369	244	A1966.64	141
A1937.512	440	A1957.519	198	A1966.65	349
A1937.513	430	A1957.520	223	A1966.66	470
A1937.514	287	A1957.521	301	A1966.67	373
A1937.515	347	A1957.522	217	A1966.68	280
A1937.516	334	A1957.524	468	A1966.69	294
A1937.517	171	A1957.525	467	A1966.70	354
A1937.518	506	A1957.527	476	A1966.71	353
A1937.519	215	A1958.95	262	A1966.358	46
A1937.520	212	A1960.4	499	A1968.903	452
A1937.521	161	A1961.952	211	A1970.907	169
A1937.522	313	A1961.953	265	A1970.908	304
A1937.523	332	A1961.987	228	A1971.30	324
A1937.524	293	A1961.988	213	A1971.31	323
A1937.525	330	A1961.989	318	A1971.32	325
A1937.526	329	A1961.990	209	A1979.30	237
A1937.527	374	A1961.991	309	A1979.127	142
A1937.528	306	A1961.992	455	A1979.128	238
A1937.642	173	A1964.3	427	A1979.129	457
A1937.643	226	A1964.4	421	A1979.130	210
A1942.16	177	A1964.5	417	A1979.131	170
A1944.1	268	A1964.457	486	A1979.132	227
A1948.407	232	A1965.247	491	A1979.133	216
A1950.39	5	A1965.248	490	A1981.415	197
A1950.41	22	A1965.249	29	A1981.416	155
A1950.42	6	A1965.250	489	A1981.417	167
A1950.43	260	A1965.253	488	A1981.418	328
A1950.44	263	A1965.254	487	A1981.419	295
A1954.53	149	A1965.258	20	A1981.420	454
A1954.54	266	A1965.259	24	A1981.421	433
A1955.9	501	A1966.51	180	A1981.422	416
A1955.11	340	A1966.52	335	A1981.423	344
A1955.12	145	A1966.53	319	A1981.424	371
A1955.13	245	A1966.54	338	A1982.600	471
A1955.14	194	A1966.55	339	A1982.602	472
A1955.15	361	A1966.56	299	A1983.61	51
A1955.16	292	A1966.57	298	A1983.1104	42
A1955.17	288	A1966.58	348	A1987.355	43
A1955.18	350	A1966.59	312	A1987.356	461
A1956.450	251	A1966.60	393	Unnumbered	192
A1956.450A	252	A1966.61	264	Unnumbered	389
A1956.455	500	A1966.61A	460	Unnumbered	420
A1956.516	19	A1966.62	351		

List of Sources[*]

Provenance List

Amathus, Cyprus: 202, 356, 388, 423, 425, 436, 445, 45

Amiens, France: 201

Beth Gibrin, Palestine: 61

Cairo, Egypt: 351

Crete: 30-1

Cyprus: 39, 153, 159, 164-6, 174-6, 181, 183, 187-9, 203-6, 225, 241, 275, 284-6, 291, 331, 346, 355, 358, 362-3, 369-70, 380, 383, 386-7, 389-92, 397, 399, 402-4, 406-11, 413-15, 418-19, 424, 431-2, 434-5, 437, 441-4, 446, 448-9, 451, 453

Egypt: 458

el-Bahnasa, Egypt: 394, 398

Grecian Archipelago: 190, 274

Hawara, Egypt: 456

Hebron, Palestine: 257, 311, 316-17

Huainan Province, China: 200

Kôm Ushîm, Fayyum, Egypt: 199

La Puebla de Guzman, Huelva, Spain: 384-5

Libarna, Italy: 247-8

Maarat el Nuaaman, nr. Aleppo, Syria: 499

Marchélepot, Somme, France: 495

Mount Carmel, Israel: 157, 231, 243, 256, 258, 261, 296, 302, 307, 314-15, 320, 337

Nazareth, Palestine: 230

Puteoli, Italy: 249-50

Sidon, Lebanon: 259, 305

Syria: 182, 198

Tharros, Sardinia: 179, 253

Tyre, Lebanon: 208, 218, 229, 255, 282, 289, 297, 321, 395-6, 412

Former Collections

Acworth Collection: 141, 180, 264, 280, 294, 298-9, 312, 319, 335, 338-9, 343, 348-9, 351, 353-4, 373, 393, 460, 470

Barbetti Sale: 179, 253

Cesnola Collection: 418

Constable-Maxwell Collection: 51, 142, 170, 210, 227, 238, 457

G. F. Lawrence Collection: 229-30, 256-9, 302, 305, 311, 315, 461

Northesk Collection: 38, 52-136, 382, 405, 422, 459, 466

Piot Collection: 1-4, 7-12, 14-16, 21, 26-8, 30-6, 44-5, 47-8, 50, 137-9, 143, 147-8, 150, 152, 154, 156, 163, 166, 172, 178, 190, 196, 207, 221-2, 233-6, 239-40, 254, 267, 270-1, 274, 359-60, 364-8, 375-8, 438-9, 447, 462-3, 479-80

BM, London: 202, 356, 388, 423, 425, 436, 445, 450

Museum of Science and Art, Edinburgh: 396

Pitt-Rivers Museum, Dorset: 462

V&A, London: 182, 399, 435, 442-3

Donor List

Allan, Dr G. G.: 198, 467

Callender, Mrs D.: 22

Curle, Mr James: 327

Forbes, Mrs J.: 454

Hume-Campbell, Sir Hugh: 23

Ramsay, Sir William: 177

Shaw, Mrs Lilian: 417, 421, 427

Wilson, Mrs A. R.: 418

* The numbers used throughout this list refer to this catalogue.

Bibliography

Abbreviations:

AIHV	Association Internationale pour l'Histoire du Verre
AJA	American Journal of Archaeology
ArchJ	Archaeological Journal
BAR	British Archaeological Reports
IEJ	Israel Exploration Journal
JGS	Journal of Glass Studies
JRA	Journal of Roman Archaeology
JRS	Journal of Roman Studies
PSAS	Proceedings of the Society of Antiquaries of Scotland
RDAC	Report of the Department of Antiquities, Cyprus

(Abdul Hak 1965) S. Abdul Hak: 'Contribution d'une découverte archéologique récente à l'étude de la verrerie syrienne à l'époque romaine', in *JGS* 7, 26-34 (1965).

(Akat, *et al.* 1984) Y. Akat, N. Fıratlı and H. Kocabaş: *Hüseyin Kocabaş Koleksiyonu Cam Eserler Kataloğu. Catalogue of Glass in the Hüseyin Kocabaş collection* (İstanbul 1984).

(*Ancient Glass* 1987) *Ancient Glass* (London 20 November 1987), Sotheby's sale catalogue.

(*Ancient Glass* 2001) *Ancient Glass* (Miho Museum 2001), exhibition catalogue.

(Anderson-Stojanovic 1987) V. R. Anderson-Stojanovic: 'The Chronology and Function of Ceramic Unguentaria', in *AJA* 91, 105-22 (1987).

(Arveiller 2006) V. Arveiller: 'Les vases signés', in Foy and Nenna 2006, 65-9 (2006).

(Arveiller-Dulong, *et al.* 2005) V. Arveiller-Dulong and M.-D. Nenna: *Les Verres Antiques du Musée du Louvre, II. Vaisselle et contenants du Ier siècle au début du VIIe siècle après J.-C* (Paris 2005).

(Atasoy 1981) S. Atasoy: 'Eskişehir – Alpu Kocakızlar tümülüsü', in *Arkeoloji ve Sanat Dergisi* 3/11, 7-13 (1981).

(Atık 1998) Ş. Atık: 'İstanbul Arkeoloji Müzeleri'inde bulunan İ.Ö. II-I. Bin Yıllarına ait Mezopotamya Cam Eserleri', XXXIV, in *Uluslararası Assiriyoloji Kongresi. 6-10/VII/1987 – İstanbul*, 365-76. (Ankara 1998).

(Auth 1976) S. Auth: *Ancient Glass at the Newark Museum* (Newark 1976).

(Ayabakan 1991) C. Ayabakan: 'Maşattepe tümülüsü kurtarma kazısı', in *I. Müze Kurtarma Kazıları Semineri. 19-20 Nisan 1990*, 49-62 (Ankara 1991).

(Bailey 1965) D. M. Bailey: 'Lamps in the Victoria and Albert Museum', in *Opuscula Atheniensia* 6, 1-83 (1965).

(Bailey 1988) D. M. Bailey: *A Catalogue of the Lamps in the British Museum. III. Roman Provincial Lamps* (London 1988).

(Baldoni 1987) D. Baldoni: 'Una lucerna romana con raffigurazione di officina vetraria: Alcune considerazioni sulla lavorazione del vetro soffiato nell' antichità', in *JGS* 29, 22-9 (1987).

(Barag 1970) D. Barag: 'Syro-Palestinian Flasks within Flasks', in *Atiqot* 6 (Hebrew series), 74-5 (1970).

(Barag 1972) D. Barag: 'Two Roman Glass Bottles with Remnants of Oil', in *IEJ* 22, 24-6 (1972).

(Barag 1985) D. Barag: *Catalogue of Western Asiatic glass in the British Museum* (London/Jerusalem 1985), vol. 1.

(Barag 1987) D. Barag: 'Recent Important Epigraphic Discoveries Related to the History of Glass-making in the Roman Period', in *Annales du 10e Congrès de l'AIHV (Madrid-Segovie, Sept. 23-28, 1985)*, 109-16 (Amsterdam 1987).

(Barag 2005) D. Barag: 'Alexandrian and Judaean Glass in the Price Edict of Diocletian', in *JGS* 47, 184-6 (2005).

(Barkóczi 1996) L. Barkóczi: *Antike Gläser* (Rome 1996).

(Başak, *et al.* 2005) A. Başak, A. B. Knapp and J. M. Webb: *The Collection of Cypriote Antiquities in the Hunterian Museum University of Glasgow*, Corpus of Cypriote Antiquities 26 (Sävedalen 2005).

(Basch 1972) A. Basch: 'Analyses of Oil from Two Roman Glass Bottles', in *IEJ* 22, 27-32 (1972).

(Bass 1984) G. F. Bass: 'The nature of the Serçe Limanı glass', in *JGS* 26, 64-9 (1984).

(Bass 1986) G. F. Bass: 'A Bronze Age shipwreck at Ulu Burun (Kaş): 1984 season', in *AJA* 90, 269-96 (1986).

(Bayburtluoğlu 2003) C. Bayburtluoğlu: *Yüksek Kayalığın Yanındaki Yer Arykanda* (Istanbul 2003).

(*Benzian* 1994) *The Benzian Collection of Ancient and Islamic Glass* (London 7 July 1994), Sotheby's sale catalogue.

(Bernheimer 2002) G. M. Bernheimer: 'Catalogue of Classical Glass Objects', in R. S. Bianchi (ed.), *Reflections on Ancient Glass from the Borowski Collection*, 282-303 (Mainz 2002).

(Bianchi 2002) R. S. Bianchi (ed.): *Reflections on Ancient Glass from the Borowski Collection* (Mainz 2002).

(Bianchi, *et al.* 2002) R. S. Bianchi and B. Schlick-Nolte: 'Catalogue of Ancient Egyptian Glass Objects', in Bianchi 2002, 123-56 (2002).

(Bliquez 1994) L. J. Bliquez: *Roman Surgical Instruments and Other Minor Objects in the National Archaeological Museum of Naples* (Mainz 1994).

(Bonomi 1996) S. Bonomi: *Vetri antichi del Museo Archelogico Nazionale di Adria* (Venice 1996).

(Boosen 1984) M. Boosen: *Antike Gläser*, Kataloge der Staatlichen Kunstsammlungen Kassel 11 (Kassel 1984).

(Braat 1966) W. C. Braat: 'Two Near Eastern Glasses Recently Acquired by the Rijksmuseum van Oudheden at Leiden', in *JGS* 8, 62-4 (1966).

(Breeze 1996) D. J. Breeze: *Roman Scotland: Frontier Country* (London 1996).

(Brill 1967) R. H. Brill: 'A Great Glass Slab from Ancient Galilee', in *Archaeology* 20, 88-95 (1967).

(Brill 1988) R. H. Brill and N. D. Cahill: 'A Red Opaque Glass from Sardis and Some Thoughts on Red Opaques in General', in *JGS* 30, 16-27 (1988).

(*British Rail* 1997) *Important Ancient Glass from the Collection formed by the British Rail Pension Fund* (London 24 November 1997), Sotheby's sale catalogue.

(Buckton 1984) D. Buckton (ed.): *The Treasury of San Marco Venice* (Milan 1984).

(Bucovala 1968) M. Bucovala: *Vase antice de Sticla la Tomis* (Constanza 1968).

(Calvi 1968) M. Calvi: *I vetri romani del Museo di Aquileia. Aquileia*, Publicazioni dell'Associazone Nazionale per Aquileia 7 (1968).

(Cameron 1996) A. Cameron: 'Orfitus and Constantius: A Note on Roman Gold-glass', in *JRA* 9, 295-301 (1996).

(Canav 1985) Ü. Canav: *Türkiye Şişe ve Cam Fabrikaları A.Ş. Cam Eserler Koleksiyonu. Ancient Glass Collection* (İstanbul 1985).

(Carington Smith 1982) J. Carington Smith: 'A Roman Chamber Tomb on Monasteriaki Kephala', in *BSA* 77, 255-91 (1982).

(Catalogue 1892) *Catalogue of the Royal Museum of Scotland* (Edinburgh 1892).

(Charlesworth 1966) D. Charlesworth: 'Roman Square Bottles', in *JGS* 8, 26-40 (1966).

(Chavane 1990) M.-L. Chavane: *La Nécropole d'Amathonte, Tombes 113-367. IV. Les Petits Objets* (Nicosia 1990).

(Clarke, *et al.* 1980) D. V. Clarke, D. J. Breeze, and G. Mackay: *The Romans in Scotland: An Introduction to the Collections of the National Museum of Antiquities of Scotland* (Edinburgh 1980).

(Cohen 1997) E. Cohen: 'Roman, Byzantine and Umayyad Glass', in Y. Hirschfeld *et al.*, in *The Roman Baths of Hammat Gader*, 396-431 (Jerusalem 1997).

(*Constable-Maxwell* 1979) *The Constable-Maxwell Collection of Ancient Glass* (London 4-5 June 1979), Sotheby Parke Bernet sale catalogue.

(Cool 1996) H. E. M. Cool: 'The Boudican Uprising and the Glass Vessels from Colchester', in Fleming 1996a (1996).

(Cool 2003) H. Cool: 'Sex and the Cemetery: Glass Vessels in Romano-British Graves', in *Current Archaeology* 186, 247-8 (2003).

(Crawford 1987) M. H. Crawford: 'Tableware for Trimalchio', in *Art and Production in the World of the Caesars*, 37-46 (Milan 1987).

(Culican 1966) W. Culican: *The First Merchant Venturers* (London 1966).

(Curle 1911) J. Curle: *A Roman Frontier Post and its People. The Fort at Newstead in the Parish of Melrose* (Glasgow 1911).

(Curle 1931-2) J. Curle: 'An Inventory of Objects of Roman and Provincial Roman Origin found on Sites in Scotland not definitely associated with Roman Constructions', in *PSAS* 66, 277-397 (1931-2).

(Curtis, *et al.* 2005) J. E. Curtis and N. Tallis (eds): *Forgotten Empire: The World of Ancient Persia* (London 2005).

(Czurda-Ruth 1989) B. Czurda-Ruth: 'Zu den römischen Gläsern aus den Hanghäusern von Ephesus', KölnerJb 22, 129-40 (1989).

(Davidson 1885-6) J. Davidson: 'Notice of a Small Cup-shaped Glass Vessel, found in a Stone Cist at the Public School, Airlie, and now presented to the Museum by the School Board of Airlie', in *PSAS* 20, 136-41 (1885-6).

(Dayagi-Mendels 1989) M. Dayagi-Mendels: *Perfumes and Cosmetics in the Ancient World* (Jerusalem 1989).

(De Franciscis 1963) A. de Franciscis: 'Vetri antichi scoperati ad Ercolano', in *JGS* 5, 137-9 (1963).

(Deppert-Lippitz 1996) B. Deppert-Lippitz: *Ancient Gold Jewelry at the Dallas Museum of Art* (Seattle, Washington 1996).

(Dilly 1997) G. Dilly and N. Mahéo: *Verreries antiques du Musée de Picardie* (Paris 1997).

(Dunbar 1929-30) D. Dunbar: 'Note on a Roman Glass Bottle from the Parish of Turriff, about 1857', in *PSAS* 64, 147-8 (1929-30).

(Duncan Jones 1995) J. Duncan Jones: 'Classical and Hellenistic Core-formed Vessels from Gordion', in *JGS* 37, 21-33 (1995).

(Dusenbery 1967) E. B. Dusenbery: 'Ancient Glass from the Cemeteries of Samothrace', in *JGS* 9, 34-49 (1967).

(Duval 1989) C. Duval: *Infinite Riches: Jewelry through the Centuries* (St Petersburg, Florida 1989).

(Empereur 1995) J.-Y. Empereur: *A Short Guide to the Graeco-Roman Museum Alexandria* (Alexandria 1995).

(Erim 1973) K. T. Erim and J. Reynolds: 'The Aphrodisias Copy of Diocletian's Edict on Maximum Prices', in *JRS* 63, 99-110 (1973).

(Evans, *et al.* 1997) H. C. Evans and W. D. Wixom (eds): *The Glory of Byzantium. Art and Culture of the Middle Byzantine Era, AD 843-1261* (New York 1997).

(Edison 2000) V. I. Edison: 'The Frankish Glass Vessels', in K. Reynolds Brown, D. Kidd and C. T. Little (eds), *From Attila to Charlemagne. Arts of the Early Medieval Period in The Metropolitan Museum of Art*, 268-81 (New York 2000).

(Ferrari 1998) G. Ferrari, C. M. Nielsen and K. Olsen (eds): *The Classical Collection. The David and Alfred Smart Museum of Art. The University of Chicago* (Chicago 1998).

(*Fitzwilliam* 1978) *Glass at the Fitzwilliam Museum* (Cambridge 1978).

(Fleming 1996a) S. J. Fleming (ed.): 'Glass in the Roman World', in *Expedition* 38/2 (1996).

(Fleming 1996b) S. J. Fleming: 'Early Imperial Roman Glass at the University of Pennsylvania Museum', in Fleming 1996a, 13-37 (1996).

(Fleming 1997a) S. J. Fleming: 'Late Roman Glass at the University of Pennsylvania Museum: A Photo Essay of the Roman World', in *Expedition* 39/2, 25-41 (1997).

(Fleming 1997b) S. J. Fleming: *Roman Glass: Reflections of Everyday Life* (Philadelphia 1997).

(Follmann-Schulz 1992) A.-B. Follmann-Schulz: *Die römischen Gläser im Rheinischen Landesmuseum Bonn* (Cologne/Bonn 1992).

(Forbes 1957) R. J. Forbes: *Studies in Ancient Technology* (Leiden 1957), vol 5.

(Fossing 1940) P. Fossing: *Glass Vessels before Glass-Blowing* (Copenhagen 1940).

(Foy, *et al.* 2001) D. Foy and M.-D. Nenna: *Tout feu tout sable. Mille ans de verre antique dans le Midi de la France* (Aix-en-Provence 2001).

(Foy, *et al.* 2003) D. Foy and M.-D. Nenna: 'Productions et importations de verre antique dans la vallée du Rhône et le Midi méditerranéen de la France (Ier-IIIe siècles)', in D. Foy and M.-D. Nenna (eds), *Échanges et commerce du verre dans le monde antique, Monographies instrumentum* 24, 227-96 (Montagnac 2003).

(Foy, *et al.* 2006) D. Foy and M.-D. Nenna (eds): *Corpus des signatures et marques sur verres antiques* (Aix-en-Provence 2006).

(Freestone 1999) I. C. Freestone and Y. Gorin-Rosen: 'The Great Glass Slab at Bet She'arim, Israel: An Early Islamic Glassmaking Experiment?', in *JGS* 41, 105-16 (1999).

(Fremersdorf 1959) F. Fremersdorf: *Römische Gläser mit Fadenauflage in Köln* (Cologne 1959).

(Gill 2002) M. A. V. Gill: *Amorium Reports, Finds I: The Glass (1987-1997)*, BAR International Series 1070, 253-5 (Oxford 2002).

(Gill, *et al.* 2002) M. A. V. Gill and C. S. Lightfoot: 'The Dichroic Fragments', in Gill 2002, 253-5 (2002).

(Goepper 1984) R. Goepper and R. Whitfield: *Treasures of Korea* (London 1984).

(Goldstein 1979) S. M. Goldstein: *Pre-Roman and Early Roman Glass in the Corning Museum of Glass* (Corning, New York 1979).

(Gorin-Rosen 1995) Y. Gorin-Rosen: 'Hadera, Bet Eli'ezer', in *Excavations and Surveys in Israel* 13, 42-3 (1995).

(Gorin-Rosen 2000) Y. Gorin-Rosen: 'The Ancient Glass Industry in Israel: Summary of the Finds and New Discoveries', in M.-D. Nenna (ed.), *La Route du verre: Ateliers primaires et secondaires du millénaire av. J.-C. au Moyen Âge*, Travaux de la Maison de l'Orient Méditerranéen 33, 49-63 (Lyon 2000).

(Goring 1988) E. Goring: *A Mischievous Pastime: Digging in Cyprus in the 19th Century* (Edinburgh 1988).

(Grose 1974) D. F. Grose: 'Roman Glass of the First Century AD: A Dated Deposit of Glassware from Cosa, Italy', *Annales du 6e Congrès de l'AIHV*, 31-52 (1974).

(Grose 1977) D. F. Grose: 'Early Blown Glass: The Western Evidence', in *JGS* 19, 9-29 (1977).

(Grose 1979) D. F. Grose: 'The Syro-Palestinian Glass Industry in the Later Hellenistic Period', in *MUSE* 13, 54-67 (1979).

(Grose 1984) D. F. Grose: 'Glass Forming Methods in Classical Antiquity: Some Considerations', in *JGS* 26, 25-34 (1984).

(Grose 1989) D. F. Grose: *The Toledo Museum of Art: Early Ancient Glass* (New York 1989).

(Grose 1991) D. F. Grose: 'Early Imperial Roman Cast Glass: The Translucent Coloured and Colourless Fine Wares', in Newby 1991, 1-18 (1991).

(Grossmann 2002) R. A. Grossman: *Ancient Glass: a Guide to the Yale Collection* (New Haven 2002).

(Hadjisavvas 1987) S. Hadjisavvas: 'A Roman Imperial Tomb on Troodos', in *RDAC*, 253-7 (1987).

(Hævernick 1978) Th. E. Hævernick: 'Modioli', in *Glastechnische Berichte* 51, 328-30 (1978).

(Hævernick 1981) Th. E. Hævernick: *Beiträge zur Glasforschung. Die wichtigsten Aufsätze von 1938 bis 1981* (Mainz 1981).

(Harden 1935) D. B. Harden: 'Romano-Syrian Glasses with Mould-blown Inscriptions', in *JRS* 25, 163-86 (1935).

(Harden 1936) D. B. Harden: *Roman Glass from Karanis*, University of Michigan Studies, Humanistic Series 41 (Ann Arbor 1936).

(Harden 1944-5) D. B. Harden: 'Two Tomb Groups of the First Century AD from Yahmour, Syria, and a Supplement to the List of Romano-Syrian Glasses with Mould-blown Inscriptions', in *Syria* 24, 81-95, 291-2 (1944-5).

(Harden 1949a) D. B. Harden: 'Tomb-groups of Glass of Roman Date from Syria and Palestine', in *Iraq* 11, 151-9 (1949).

(Harden 1949b) D. B. Harden and A. I. Loewental: 'Vasa Murrina', in *JRS* 39, 31-7 (1949).

(Harden 1958) D. B. Harden: 'Appendix I. – The Glass', in J. du Plat Taylor, 'Roman Tombs at «Kambi», Vasa', in *RDAC* 1940-1948, 46-60 (1958).

(Harden, *et al.* 1968) D. B. Harden, K. S. Painter, R. H. Pinder-Wilson and H. Tait: *Masterpieces of Glass* (London 1968).

(Harden 1970) D. B. Harden: 'Ancient Glass, II: Roman', in *ArchJ* 126 [1969], 44-77 (1970).

(Harden 1978) D. B. Harden: 'Roman and Frankish Glass from France in the British Museum', in *Centenaire de l'Abbé Cochet – 1975. Actes du Colloque International d'Archéologie*, 301-12 (Rouen 1978).

(Harden 1981) D. B. Harden: *Catalogue of Greek and Roman Glass in the British Museum. Vol. 1: Core- and Rod-formed Vessels and Pendants and Mycenaean Glass Objects* (London 1981).

(Harden 1987) D. B. Harden: *Glass of the Caesars* (Milan 1987).

(Harter 1999) G. Harter: *Römische Gläser des Landesmuseums Mainz* (Wiesbaden 1999).

(Hayes 1975) J. W. Hayes: *Roman and Pre-Roman Glass in the Royal Ontario Museum* (Toronto 1975).

(Heisserer 1986) A. J. Heisserer: *Classical Antiquities. The Collection of the Stovall Museum of Science and History. The University of Oklahoma* (Norman, Oklahoma 1986).

(Herbert 1964) K. Herbert: *Ancient Art in Bowdoin College* (Cambridge, Mass 1964).

(Higashi 1991) E. L. Higashi (ed.): *Glass from the Ancient World: So Diverse a Unity* (Dearborn, Michigan 1991).

(Hill 1972) D. K. Hill: 'Precious Metal and Glass. An Alabastron at the Walters Art Gallery', in *JGS* 14, 23-5 (1972).

(Hill, *et al.* 2003) D. Hill and M. Taylor: 'Mosaic Glass and Ribbed Bowls', in *Current Archaeology* 186, 249 (2003).

(*Holy Land* 1998) *Ancient Glass from the Holy Land* (Brisbane, California 1998), exhibition catalogue.

(Höricht 1986) L. A. Scatozza Höricht: *I vetri romani di Ercolano* (Rome 1986).

(Höricht 1991) L. A. Scatozza Höricht: 'Syrian Elements among the Glass from Pompeii and Herculaneum', in Newby 1991, 56-85 (1991).

(Hunter 2006) F. Hunter: 'Scotland before Scotland: New Discoveries', in *Minerva* 17/4, 26-8 (2006).

(Isings 1957) C. Isings: *Roman Glass from Dated Finds* (Groningen/Djakarta 1957).

(Isings 1964) C. Isings: 'A Fourth Century Glass Jar with Applied Masks', in *JGS* 6, 59-63 (1964).

(Israeli 1991) Y. Israeli: 'The Invention of Blowing', in Newby 1991, 46-55 (1991).

(Israeli 2003) Y. Israeli: *Ancient Glass in the Israel Museum: the Eliahu Dobkin Collection and Other Gifts* (Jerusalem 2003).

(Israeli 2005) Y. Israeli: 'What did Jerusalem's First-Century BCE Glass Workshop produce?' *Annales du 16e Congrès de l'AIHV*, 54-7 (Nottingham 2005).

(Jackson, *et al.* 1998) C. M. Jackson, H. E. M. Cool and E. C. W. Wager: 'The Manufacture of Glass in Roman York', in *JGS* 40, 55-61 (1998).

(Jacobson 1992) G. L. Jacobson: 'Greek Names on Prismatic Jugs', in *JGS* 34, 35-43 (1992).

(Joukowsky 1985) T. Hackens and R. Winkes (eds): *Love for Antiquity: Selections from the Joukowsky Collection* (Leuven 1985).

(Kent, *et al.* 1977) J. P. C. Kent and K. S. Painter: *Wealth of the Roman World AD 300-700* (London 1977).

(Keppie 1986) L. Keppie: *Scotland's Roman Remains: An Introduction and Handbook* (Edinburgh 1986).

(Kisa 1908) A. Kisa: *Das Glas im Altertume* (Leipzig 1908), vol. 2.

(*Kofler* 1985) *Ancient Glass. Formerly the Kofler-Truniger Collection* (London 5-6 March 1985), Christie, Mason & Woods sale catalogue.

(Kunina 1997) N. Kunina: *Ancient Glass in the Hermitage Museum* (St Petersburg 1997).

(La Baume 1964) P. La Baume: *Römisches Kunstgewerbe zwischen Christi Geburt und 400* (Brunswick 1964).

(La Baume, *et al.* 1977) P. La Baume and J. W. Salomonson: *Römische Kleinkunst, Sammlung Karl Löffler*, Wissenschaftliche Kataloge des Römisch-Germanischen Museums Köln, 3 (Cologne 1977).

(*La fragilitat* 2005) *La fragilitat en el temps. El vidre a l'antiguitat* (Barcelona 2005), exhibition catalogue.

(Lang 1978) D. M. Lang: *Armenia: Cradle of Civilization*, 2nd ed. (London 1978).

(Lierke 2002) R. Lierke: 'With 'trial and error' through Ancient Glass Technology', in G. Kordas (ed.), *Hyalos, Vitrum, Glass: History, Technology and Conservation of Glass and Vitreous Materials in the Hellenic World*, 181-6 (Athens 2002).

(Lightfoot 1988) C. S. Lightfoot: 'A Fragment of Roman Cameo Glass', in P. Hinton (ed.), *Excavations in Southwark 1973-76, Lambeth 1973-79* (LAMAS/SAS Joint Publication 3), 374-8 (London 1988).

(Lightfoot 1989) C. S. Lightfoot: *A Catalogue of Glass Vessels in Afyon Museum/Afyon Müzesindeki Cam Eserler Kataloğu*, BAR International Series 530 (Oxford 1989).

(Lightfoot 1990) C. S. Lightfoot: 'Some Types of Roman Cut-glass Vessels found in Turkey', in *I. Uluslararası Anadolu Cam Sanatı Sempozyumu, 26-27 Nisan 1988 / 1st*

International Anatolian Glass Symposium, April 26th-27th 1988, 7-15 (İstanbul 1990).

(Lightfoot 1991) C. S. Lightfoot: 'A Group of Roman Perfume Bottles from Asia Minor', in *Erol Atalay Memorial* (Ege Üniversitesi Edebiyat Fakültesi, Arkeoloji Dergisi 1), 107-12 (İzmir 1991).

(Lightfoot 1992) C. S. Lightfoot and M. Arslan: *Ancient Glass of Asia Minor: The Yüksel Erimtan Collection* (Ankara 1992).

(Lightfoot 1993) C. S. Lightfoot: 'Some Examples of Ancient Cast and Ribbed Bowls in Turkey', in *JGS* 35, 22-38 (1993).

(Lightfoot 2003a) C. S. Lightfoot: 'From East to West: The Early Roman Glass Industry', in D. Foy and M.-D. Nenna (eds), *Échanges et commerce du verre dans le monde antique*, Monographies instrumentum 24, 341-47 (Montagnac 2003).

(Lightfoot 2003b) C. S. Lightfoot: 'Ancient 'Nails' (Curator's Choice)', in *Archaeology Odyssey* 6/6, 15 (2003).

(Lightfoot 2005) C. S. Lightfoot: 'Anomalies amongst Early Roman Mould-Blown Glass Vessels', in *Annales du 16e Congrès de l'AIHV*, 85-8 (Nottingham 2005).

(Lombard 1989) P. Lombard and M. Kervran (eds): *Bahrain National Museum Archaeological Collections. Vol. 1: A Selection of Pre-Islamic Antiquities from Excavations 1954-1975* (Bahrain 1989).

(Lubsen-Admiraal 2004) S. M. Lubsen-Admiraal: *Ancient Cypriote Art. The Thanos N. Zintilis Collection* (Athens 2004).

(Luzern 1981) *3000 Jahre Glaskunst von der Antike bis zum Jugendstil* (Lucerne 1981).

(Maier, *et al.* 1994) F. G. Maier and V. Karageorghis: *Paphos: History and Archaeology* (Nicosia 1994).

(Matheson 1980) S. B. Matheson: *Ancient Glass in the Yale University Art Gallery* (New Haven 1980).

(McClellan 1983) M. C. McClellan: 'Recent Finds from Greece of First-Century AD: Mold-blown Glass', in *JGS* 25, 71-8 (1983).

(McFadden 1946) G. H. McFadden: 'A Tomb of the Necropolis of Ayios Ermoyenis at Kourion', in *AJA* 50, 449-89 (1946).

(*Merseyside* 1979) *Historic Glass from Collections in North West England* (Merseyside County Museums 1979).

(Naumann 1991) F. Naumann-Steckner: 'Depictions of Glass in Roman Wall Paintings', in Newby 1991, 56-85 (1991).

(*Napoli* 1986) *Le Collezioni del Museo Nazionale di Napoli* (Rome 1986).

(Nenna 1993a) M.-D. Nenna: 'La Verrerie d'époque hellenistique à Delos', in *JGS* 35, 11-21 (1993).

(Nenna 1993b) M.-D. Nenna: 'Eléments d'incrustation en verre des nécropoles alexandrines', *Annales du 12e Congrès de l'AIHV*, 45-52 (Amsterdam 1993).

(Nenna 2006) M.-D. Nenna: 'Marques conserves dans les musées français de provenance inconnue ou étrangère', in Foy and Nenna 2006, 201-13 (2006).

(Neuburg 1949) F. Neuburg: *Glass in Antiquity* (London 1949).

(Newby, *et al.* 1991) M. Newby and K. Painter (eds): *Roman Glass: Two Centuries of Art and Invention*. The Society of Antiquaries Occasional Papers 13 (London 1991).

(Newby, *et al.* 1999) M. Newby and D. Schut: *The Fascination of Ancient Glass: Dolf Schut Collection* (Lochem 1999).

(Nicolaou 1984) I. Nicolaou: 'A Hellenistic and Roman tomb at Eurychou-Phoenikas', in *RDAC*, 234-56 (1984).

(Nielsen 1992) A. M. Nielsen: *Catalogue. The Cypriote Collection. Ny Carlsberg Glyptotek* (Copenhagen 1992).

(Nolte 1968) B. Nolte: *Die Glasgefässe im alten Aegypten* (Berlin 1968).

(Oliver 1967) A. Oliver Jr: 'Late Hellenistic Glass in the Metropolitan Museum', in *JGS* 9, 13-33 (1967).

(Oliver 1968) A. Oliver Jr: 'Millefiori Glass in Classical Antiquity', in *JGS* 10, 48-70 (1968).

(Oliver 1970) A. Oliver Jr: 'Persian Export Glass', in *JGS* 12, 9-16 (1970).

(Oliver 1975) A. Oliver Jr: 'Tapestry in Glass', in *JGS* 17, 68-70 (1975).

(Oliver 1980) A. Oliver Jr: *Ancient Glass in the Carnegie Museum of Natural History, Pittsburgh* (Pittsburgh 1980).

(Oliver 1983) A. Oliver, Jr: 'Tomb 12 at Episkopi', in *RDAC* 1983, 245-56 (1983).

(Oliver 1992) A. Oliver, Jr: 'The Glass', in V. Karageorghis, O. Picard and Chr. Tytgat (eds), *La Nécropole d'Amathonte, Tombes 113-367. VI. Bijoux, Armes, Verre, Astragales et Coquillages, Squalettes*, 101-21 (Nicosia 1992).

(Oppenheim, *et al.* 1970) A. L. Oppenheim, R. H. Brill, D. Barag and A. von Saldern: *Glass and Glassmaking in Ancient Mesopotamia*, Corning Museum of Glass Monograph 3 (Corning, New York 1970).

(Özgen, *et al.* 1996) İ. Özgen and J. Öztürk: *Heritage Recovered: The Lydian Treasure* (İstanbul 1996).

(Özet 1987) A. Özet: 'Ankara Anadolu Medeniyetleri Müzesindeki cam örnekleri ile antik çağda cam yapımı', in *Belleten* LI/200, 587-609 (1987).

(Painter, *et al.* 1991) K. S. Painter and D. B. Whitehouse: 'The Portland Vase', in Newby 1991, 33-45 (1991).

(Perrot, *et al.* 1894) G. Perrot and R. de Lasteyrie: *Monuments et Mémoires* (Paris 1894), vol. 1.

(Philippe 1975) J. Philippe: 'Sur les plaquettes byzantines à décor crucifère doré', in *JGS* 17, 97-100 (1975).

(Pilosi, *et al.* 1998) L. Pilosi and M. T. Wypyski: 'Two Ancient Glass Vessels with Modern Decoration in the Metropolitan

Museum of Art', in A. B. Paterakis (ed.), *Glass, Ceramics and Related Materials*, 17-29 (Vantaa 1998).

(Pilosi, *et al.* 2002) L. Pilosi and M. T. Wypyski: 'The Weathering of Ancient Cold Worked Glass Surfaces', in G. Kordas (ed.), *Hyalos, Vitrum, Glass: History, Technology and Conservation of Glass and Vitreous Materials in the Hellenic World*, 101-7 (Athens 2002).

(Plantzos 1997) D. Plantzos: 'Crystals and Lenses in the Graeco-Roman World', in *AJA* 101, 451-64 (1997).

(Platz-Horster 1976) G. Platz-Horster: *Antike Gläser. Ausstellung im Antikenmuseum Berlin* (Berlin 1976).

(Price 1977) J. Price: 'Roman Unguent Bottles from Rio Tinto (Huelva) in Spain', in *JGS* 19, 30-49 (1977).

(Price 1978) J. Price: 'Trade in Glass', in J. du Plat Taylor and H. Cleere, *Roman Shipping and Trade: Britain and the Rhine Provinces*, 70-8 (London 1978).

(Price 1985a) J. Price: 'Early Roman Vessel Glass from Burials in Tripolitania: A Study of Finds from Forte della Vite and Other Sites now in the Collections of the National Museum of Antiquities in Tripoli', in D. J. Buck and D. J. Mattingly (eds), *Town and Country in Roman Tripolitania. Papers in Honour of Olwen Hackett*, BAR International Series 274, 67-106 (Oxford 1985).

(Price 1985b) J. Price: 'The Roman Glass', in L. F. Pitts and J. K. St. Joseph, *Inchtuthil, the Roman Legionary Fortress*, Britannia Monograph series 6, 303-12 (London 1985).

(Price 1992) J. Price: 'Hellenistic and Roman Glass', in L. H. Sackett (ed.), with K. Branigan *et al.*, *Knossos. From Greek City to Roman Colony*, 415-62 (Oxford 1992).

(Price, *et al.* 1998) J. Price and S. Cottam: *Romano-British Glass Vessels: A Handbook*, Practical Handbooks in Archaeology 14 (York 1998).

(Price 2006) J. Price: 'Mould-blown and impressed designs and names on vessels in Spain', in D. Foy and M.-D. Nenna (eds), *Corpus des signatures et marques sur verres antiques*, 283-324 (Aix-en-Provence/Lyon 2006), vol. 2.

(Roffia 1993) E. Roffia: *I vetri antichi delle civiche raccolte archeologiche di Milano* (Milan 1993).

(Rottloff 1999) A. Rottloff: 'Römische Vierkantkrüge', in M. J. Klein (ed.), *Römische Glaskunst und Wandmalerei*, 41-9 (Mainz 1999).

(Rudolph 1973) W. & E. Rudolph: *Ancient Jewelry from the Collection of Burton Y. Berry* (Bloomington, Indiana 1973).

(Saguì 1998) L. Saguì: *Storie al caleidoscopio: i vetri della collezione Gorga: un patrimonio ritrovato* (Rome 1998).

(*Sangiorgi* 1999) *Ancient Glass formerly in the G. Sangiorgi Collection* (New York 3 June 1999), Christie's sale catalogue.

(Salviati 1999) F. Salviati: 'Celebrating Ancient Glass in Italy', in *Minerva* 10/3, 17-19 (1999).

(Schlick-Nolte 2002a) B. Schlick-Nolte: 'Catalogue of Ancient Glass Vessels', in Bianchi, 47-109 (2002).

(Schlick-Nolte 2002b) B. Schlick-Nolte: 'Catalogue of Phoenician and Punic Head Pendants and Beads', in Bianchi 2002, 179-214 (2002).

(Scranton 1967) R. L. Scranton: 'Glass Pictures from the Sea', in *Archaeology* 20/3, 163-73 (1967).

(Seefried 1982) M. Seefried: *Les Pendentifs en Verre sur Noyau des Pays de la Méditerranée Antique* (Rome 1982).

(Seefried 1986) M. Seefried: 'Glass in Cyprus from the Late Bronze Age to Roman Times', in *RDAC*, 145-9 (1986).

(Seligman 1939) C. G. Seligman: 'The Roman Orient and the Far East', in *The Smithsonian Report for 1938*, 547-68 (1939).

(Sennequier 1985) G. Sennequier: *Verrerie d'époque romaine. Musée des Antiquités de Rouen* (Rouen 1985).

(Shindo 1993) Y. Shindo: 'Islamic Marvered Glass from al-Tur, South Sinai', in *Annales du 12e Congrès de l'AIHV*, 297-305 (Amsterdam 1993).

(*Shining Vessels* 1991) *Shining Vessels: Ancient Glass from Greek, Roman and Islamic Times* (New York 1991), sale catalogue.

(Smith 1957) R. W. Smith: *Glass from the Ancient World: The R. W. Smith Collection* (Corning, New York 1957).

(*Solid Liquid* 1999) *Solid Liquid: Greek, Roman, Byzantine and Islamic Glass* (New York 1999), sale catalogue.

(Sorokina 1987) N. P. Sorokina: 'Glass Aryballoi (First-Third Centuries AD) from the Northern Black Sea Region', in *JGS* 29, 40-6 (1987).

(Souyoudzoglou-Haywood 2004) C. Souyoudzoglou-Haywood: *Cypriot Antiquities in Dublin. The Collections of the National Museum of Ireland and University College Dublin* (Nicosia 2004).

(Spaer 1988) M. Spaer: 'The Pre-Islamic Glass Bracelets of Palestine', in *JGS* 30, 51-61 (1988).

(Spaer 1992) M. Spaer: 'Islamic Glass Bracelets of Palestine: Preliminary Findings', in *JGS* 34, 44-62 (1992).

(Spartz 1967) E. Spartz: *Antike Gläser*, Kataloge der Staatlichen Kunstsammlungen Kassel 1, (Kassel 1967).

(Stern 1991) E. M. Stern: 'Early Exports Beyond the Empire', in Newby 1991, 141-54 (1991).

(Stern 1995) E. M. Stern: *The Toledo Museum of Art. Roman Mold-blown Glass. The First through Sixth Centuries* (Rome 1995).

(Stern 1999a) E. M. Stern: 'Roman Glassblowing in a Cultural Context', in *AJA* 103, 441-84 (1999).

(Stern 1999b) E. M. Stern: 'Ancient Glass in Athenian Temple Treasures', in *JGS* 41, 19-50 (1999).

(Stern 2000) E. M. Stern: 'Three Notes on Early Roman Mold-Blown Glass', in *JGS* 42, 165-7 (2000).

(Sternini 1998) M. Sternini: *La Collezione di Antichità di Alessandro Palma di Cesnola* (Bari 1998).

(Tait 1991) H. Tait (ed.): *Five Thousand Years of Glass* (London 1991).

(Tal, *et al.* 2004) O. Tal, R. E. Jackson-Tal, and I. C. Freestone: 'New Evidence of the Production of Raw Glass at Late Byzantine Apollonia-Arsuf, Israel', in *JGS* 46, 51-66 (2004).

(Taniichi 1983) T. Taniichi: 'Pre-Roman and Roman Glass Recently Excavated in China', in *Bulletin of the Okoyama Orient Museum* 3, 83-105 (1983).

(Taniichi 1990) T. Taniichi: 'Early Roman Faceted Beaker Recently Excavated at Loulan in China', in *Collected Papers for the Thirty-fifth Anniversary of the Establishment of the Society for Near Eastern Studies in Japan*, 315-30 (1990), in Japanese.

(Tartari 2005) F. Tartari: *Prodhime qelqi lë shekujve I-IV të erës sonë nëShqipëri* (Durrës 2005).

(Tatton-Brown 1981) V. Tatton-Brown: 'Rod-formed Glass Pendants and Beads of the First Millennium BC', in Harden 1981, 143-55 (1981).

(Tek 2003) A. T. Tek: 'Prismatic glass bottles with Greek inscriptions from Arycanda in Lycia', in *Annales du 15e Congrès de l'AIHV, New York-Corning 2001*, 82-7 (Nottingham 2003).

(Thirion-Merle 2005) V. Thirion-Merle: 'Les Verres de Beyrouth et les verres du Haut Empire dans le monde occidental: Etude archéométrique', in *JGS* 47, 37-53 (2005).

(Thomas 1976) N. Thomas: *Ancient Glass: The Bomford Collection of Pre-Roman and Roman Glass on loan to the City of Bristol Museum and Art Gallery* (Bristol 1976).

(Thorpe 1933-4) W. A. Thorpe: 'A Glass Jug of Roman Date from Turriff', in *PSAS* 68, 439-44 (1933-4).

(Trowbridge 1930) M. L. Trowbridge: *Philological Studies in Ancient Glass* (University of Illinois 1930).

(Tytgat 1990) C. Tytgat: 'Chronologie des Tombes', in Chavane 1990, xiii-xvii (1990).

(Uberti 1993) M. L. Uberti: *I Vetri Preromani del Museo Archeologico Nazionale di Cagliari* (Rome 1993).

(Vanderhoeven 1958) M. Vanderhoeven: *Verres Romains tardifs et Mérovingiens du Musée Curtius* (Liège 1958).

(Venclová 1983) N. Venclová: 'Prehistoric Eye Beads in Central Europe', in *JGS* 25, 11-14 (1983).

(Verres 1985) G. Loudmer and A.-M. Kevorkian: *Verres antiques et de l'Islam* (Paris 3-4 June 1985), sale catalogue.

(Vessberg 1953) O. Vessberg: 'Notes on the Chronology of the Roman Glass of Cyprus', in G. E. Mylonas and D. Raymond (eds), *Studies Presented to D. M. Robinson*, 163-7 (St. Louis, Missouri 1953).

(Vessberg 1956) O. Vessberg: 'Glass: Typology–Chronology', in O. Vessberg and A. Westholm (eds), *The Swedish Cyprus Expedition. Vol. IV, Part 3: The Hellenistic and Roman Periods in Cyprus*, 128-75 and 193-219 (Lund 1956).

(Vickers 1972) M. Vickers: 'An Achaemenid Glass Bowl in a Dated Context', in *JGS* 14, 15-16 (1972).

(Vickers 1996a) M. Vickers: 'Rock Crystal: the Key to Cut Glass and Diatreta in Persia and Rome', in *JRA* 9, 48-65 (1996).

(Vickers 1996b) M. Vickers: 'Antiquity, Utopias, Glass and Crystal', in Fleming 1996a (1996).

(von Saldern 1959) A. von Saldern: 'Glass Finds at Gordion', in *JGS* 1, 22-49 (1959).

(von Saldern 1968) A. von Saldern: *Ancient Glass in the Museum of Fine Arts Boston* (Meriden, Connecticut 1968).

(von Saldern, *et al.* 1974) A. von Saldern, B. Nolte, P. La Baume and T. E. Hævernick: *Gläser der Antike, Sammlung Erwin Oppenländer* (Hamburg/Cologne 1974).

(von Saldern 1980) A. von Saldern: *Glass 500 BC to AD 1900. The Hans Cohn Collection, Los Angeles* (Mainz 1980).

(von Saldern 1991) A. von Saldern: 'Roman glass with decoration cut in high-relief', in Newby 1991, 111-21 (1991).

(von Saldern 2004) A. von Saldern: *Antikes Glas* (Munich 2004).

(Walker, *et al.* 1997) S. Walker and M. Bierbrier: *Ancient Faces. Mummy Portraits from Roman Egypt* (London 1997).

(Walker 2004) S. Walker: *The Portland Vase* (London 2004).

(Watt 2004) J. C. Y. Watt: *China: Dawn of a Golden Age, 200-750 AD* (New York 2004), exhibition catalogue.

(Weinberg 1959) G. D. Weinberg: 'Glass Manufacture in Ancient Crete', in *JGS* 1, 10-21 (1959).

(Weinberg 1988) G. D. Weinberg (ed.): *Excavations at Jalame. Site of a Glass Factory in Late Roman Palestine* (Columbia, Missouri 1988).

(Weinberg 1992) G. D. Weinberg: *Glass Vessels in Ancient Greece*, Publications of the Archaeologikon Deltion 47 (Athens 1992).

(Welker 1987) E. Welker: *Antike Gläser aus dem Museum für Vor- und Frühgeschichte Frankfurt am Main*, Archäologische Reihe, Band 10 (Frankfurt am Main 1987).

(Whitcomb 1983) D. S. Whitcomb: 'Islamic Glass from al-Qadim, Egypt', in *JGS* 25, 101-108 (1983).

(Whitehouse 1989) D. Whitehouse: 'Begram, the Periplus and Gandaran Art', in *JRA* 2, 93-100 (1989).

(Whitehouse 1991) D. F. Grose: 'Early Imperial Roman Cast Glass: The Translucent Coloured and Colourless Fine Wares', in Newby 1991, 19-32 (1991).

(Whitehouse 1993) D. Whitehouse: *Glass: A Pocket Dictionary of Terms commonly used to describe Glass and Glassmaking* (Corning, New York 1993).

(Whitehouse 1996) D. Whitehouse: 'Glass, Gold, and Gold-Glasses', in Fleming 1996a, 4-12 (1996).

(Whitehouse 1997) D. Whitehouse: *Roman Glass in the Corning Museum of Glass* (Corning, New York 1997), vol. 1.

(Whitehouse 1999) D. Whitehouse: 'The Date of the Glass from Karanis', in *JGS* 41, 168-70 (1999).

(Whitehouse 2001a) D. Whitehouse: *Roman Glass in The Corning Museum of Glass* (Corning, New York 2001), vol. 2.

(Whitehouse 2001b) D. Whitehouse: 'Window Glass between the First and the Eighth Centuries', in F. Dell'Acqua and R. Silva (eds), *Il Colore nel Medioevo. Arte Sibolo Technica. La Vetrata in Occidente dal IV all'XI Secolo*, 31-43 (Lucca 2001).

(Whitehouse 2003) D. Whitehouse: *Roman Glass in The Corning Museum of Glass* (Corning, New York 2003), vol. 3.

(Wight 2000) K. Wight: 'Leaf Beakers and Roman Mold-Blown Glass Production in the First Century AD', in *JGS* 42, 61-79 (2000).

(Winfield Smith 1949) R. Winfield Smith: 'The Significance of Roman Glass', in *MMABulletin* 8/2 (1949), 49-60 (1949).

(Winfield Smith 1957) R. Winfield Smith: *Glass from the Ancient World: The Ray Winfield Smith Collection* (Corning, New York 1957).

(Witte-Orr 2003) J. Witte-Orr: 'Fresco and Mosaic Fragments from the Lower City Church', in C. S. Lightfoot, *Amorium Reports II: Research Papers and Technical Reports*, BAR International Series 1170, 139-56 (Oxford 2003).

(*Wolf* 1994) E. M. Stern and B. Schlick-Nolte: *Early Glass of the Ancient World. 1600 BC-AD 50: Ernesto Wolf Collection* (Ostfildern-Ruit 1994).

(Wolkenberg 1991) *The Alfred Wolkenberg Collection of Ancient Glass* (London 9 July 1991), Christie, Manson & Woods sale catalogue.

(Yağcı 1990) E. E. Yağcı: 'Hatay Müzesindeki bir Grup Cam Eser', 1., in *Uluslararası Anadolu Cam Sanatı Sempozyumu, 26-27 Nisan 1988 / 1st International Anatolian Glass Symposium, April 26th-27th 1988*, 30-36 (İstanbul 1990).

(Yalçın, *et al.* 2005) Ü. Yalçın, C. Pulak, and R. Slotta (eds): *Das Schiff von Uluburun: Welthandel vor 3000 Jahren* (Bochum 2005), exhibition catalogue.